God's Amazing Plan
BIBLE
The Price He Paid to Win Your Love

Amy Parker

God's Amazing Plan Bible
1st edition, 1st print
Copyright © Scandinavia Publishing House 2019
Drejervej 15, 3., DK-2400 Copenhagen NV, Denmark
info@sph.as | www.sph.as
Text and illustrations copyright © Scandinavia Publishing House
Illustrations by Jacqui Davis
Text by Amy Parker
Edited by Cecilie Fodor & Andrew Newton
Cover design & layout by Gao Hanyu

Printed in China
ISBN 9781788931106

Unless otherwise marked, all Bible references are taken from the Holy Bible, New International Version®, NIV® Copyright ©1973, 1978,1984, 2011 by Biblica, Inc.® Used by permission. All rights reserved worldwide.

All Bible verses marked CEV are taken from the Contemporary English Version (CEV) Copyright © 1995 by American Bible Society.

All rights reserved. No part of this book may be reproduced or utilized in any form or by any means, electronic or mechanical, including photocopying, recording, or by any information storage and retrieval system, without permission in writing from the publisher.

God's Amazing Plan
BIBLE

The price He paid to win your love

This book belongs to:

_____

It was given to me by:

_____

On:

_____

scandinavia

CONTENTS

The Old Testament

In the Beginning	8
The Perfect Garden	14
The Great Flood	21
A Promise to Abraham	29
Rebekah Trusts God's Plan	35
God Blesses Jacob, the Trickster	42
Joseph, the Dreamer	50
The Baby in a Basket	64
Out of Slavery	71
The Ten Commandments	80
Joshua's Impossible Victory	84
An Unlikely Hero	88
Samson's Supernatural Strength	94
Where You Go I'll Go	105
The Boy Who Heard God's Voice	112
Israel's First King	118
Facing Goliath	122
A True Friend	130
The Rule of King David	134
The Wisest King Ever	143
Fire from Heaven	147
The Sulking Prophet	155
A Mighty King's Nightmare	163
The Fiery Furnace	167
In the Lions' Den	172
An Orphan Saves Her People	177

The New Testament

Preparing for a Savior	190
An Unexpected Gift	195
An Unlikely King	200
"My Father's House"	209
The Lamb of God	213
The Devil Tempts Jesus	217
Fishing for People	222
Jesus, the Miracle Worker	226
The Most Important Thing	238
The Wind and Waves Obey	242
The Good Samaritan	245
The Small and the Lost	248
The Prodigal Son	253
The First Stone	260
"Lazarus, Come out!"	266
The Last Supper	272
Jesus is Betrayed	281
The Savior Dies	287
He Lives!	296
The Great Commission	303
The Helper is Here	306
Trouble for the First Church	312
Praising God in Prison	318
What Is to Come	324

THE OLD TESTAMENT

IN THE BEGINNING

Genesis 1-2

Along, long time ago, in the very beginning, God created the heavens and the earth. The earth was empty and shapeless, there was darkness all around, and God's Spirit moved over the waters.

Into the darkness, God said, "Let there be light!" and light flooded the earth. God saw that it was good. He separated the light from the darkness. He called the light "day" and He called the darkness "night." This was the first day of our world.

The next day, God created a space for air around the earth. He called the space "sky," and He placed some of the earth's water above the sky. The sky separated the water on the earth from the water above the earth. That was the second day.

On the third day, God gathered up the waters into one place so that dry land would appear. He called the dry land "earth," and He called the water "seas." He looked out over the land and seas, and He saw that they were good.

Then He said, "Let the earth produce plants." The land grew

IN THE BEGINNING

green with grasses, golden with grains, and lush with tall trees filled with leaves and fruit. God looked out at the beautiful earth and saw that it was good. This was the third day.

The next morning, God said, "Let there be lights to divide the day from the night, to make different seasons, and to measure days and years." With those words, God created a large, bright light for the daytime and a smaller light for the night. He set each and every star in place, and they began to shine their radiant light throughout the vast night sky. That was the fourth day.

The next day, God filled the sea and the sky with living things. Crabs and clownfish, porpoises and pufferfish, swordfish and sea turtles swirled and splashed in the water. Bursts of color filled the air as cardinals and toucans took flight. The very first songs of canaries and cockatiels were carried on an afternoon breeze. Eagles and ospreys built their nests high above as God said, "Multiply and fill the earth." That was the fifth day.

Finally, God said, "Let there be creatures to fill the earth." Just like that, animals large and small creeped and crawled over the land. Antelope leapt, and armadillos waddled. Mice scurried, and monkeys swung from tree to tree.

Kangaroos jumped, and cows chewed the grasses of their lush, new home. God looked around and saw that it was all good. He had created a vibrant new world, brimming with colorful plants and playful creatures—but day six wasn't over yet!

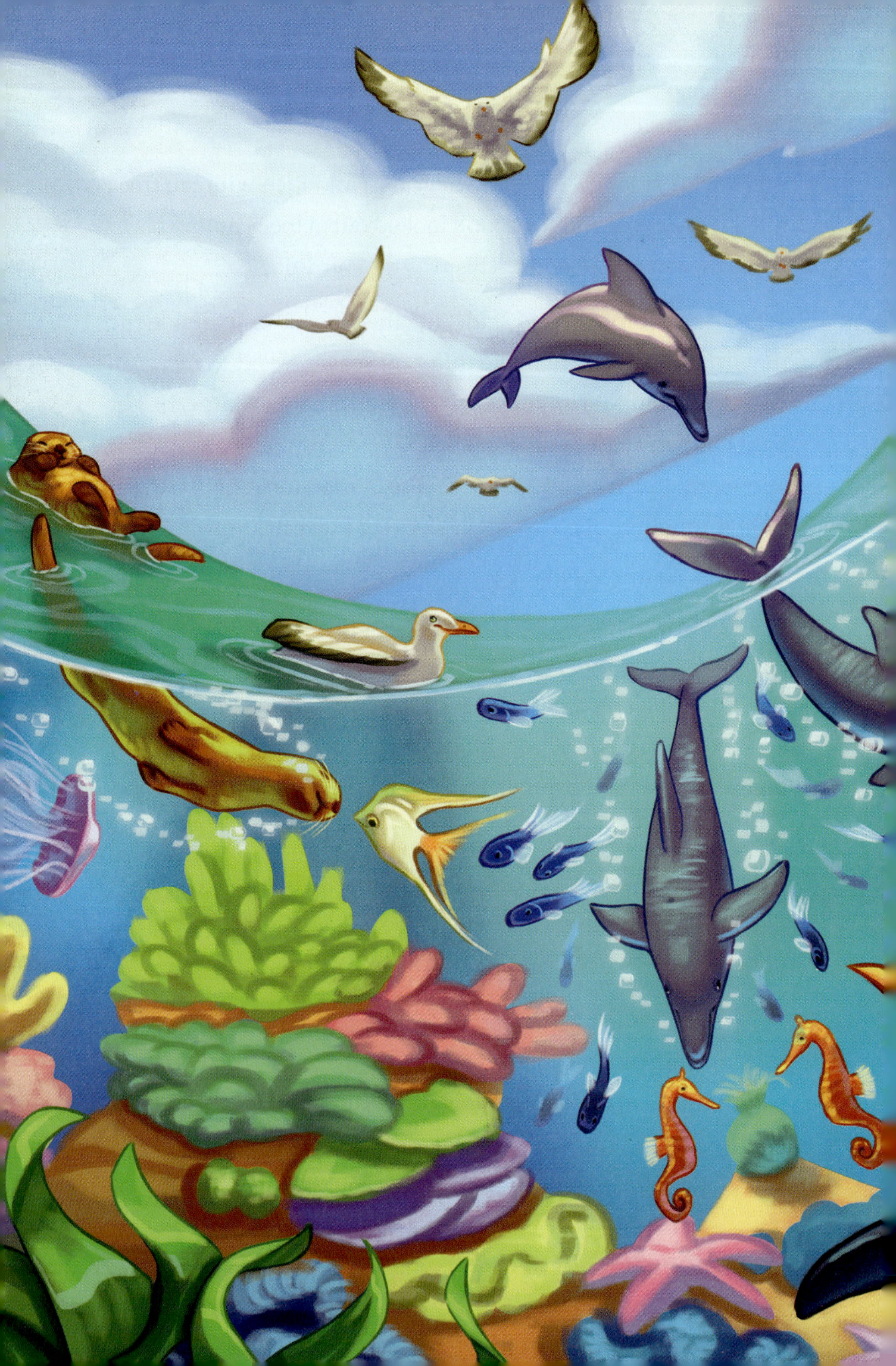

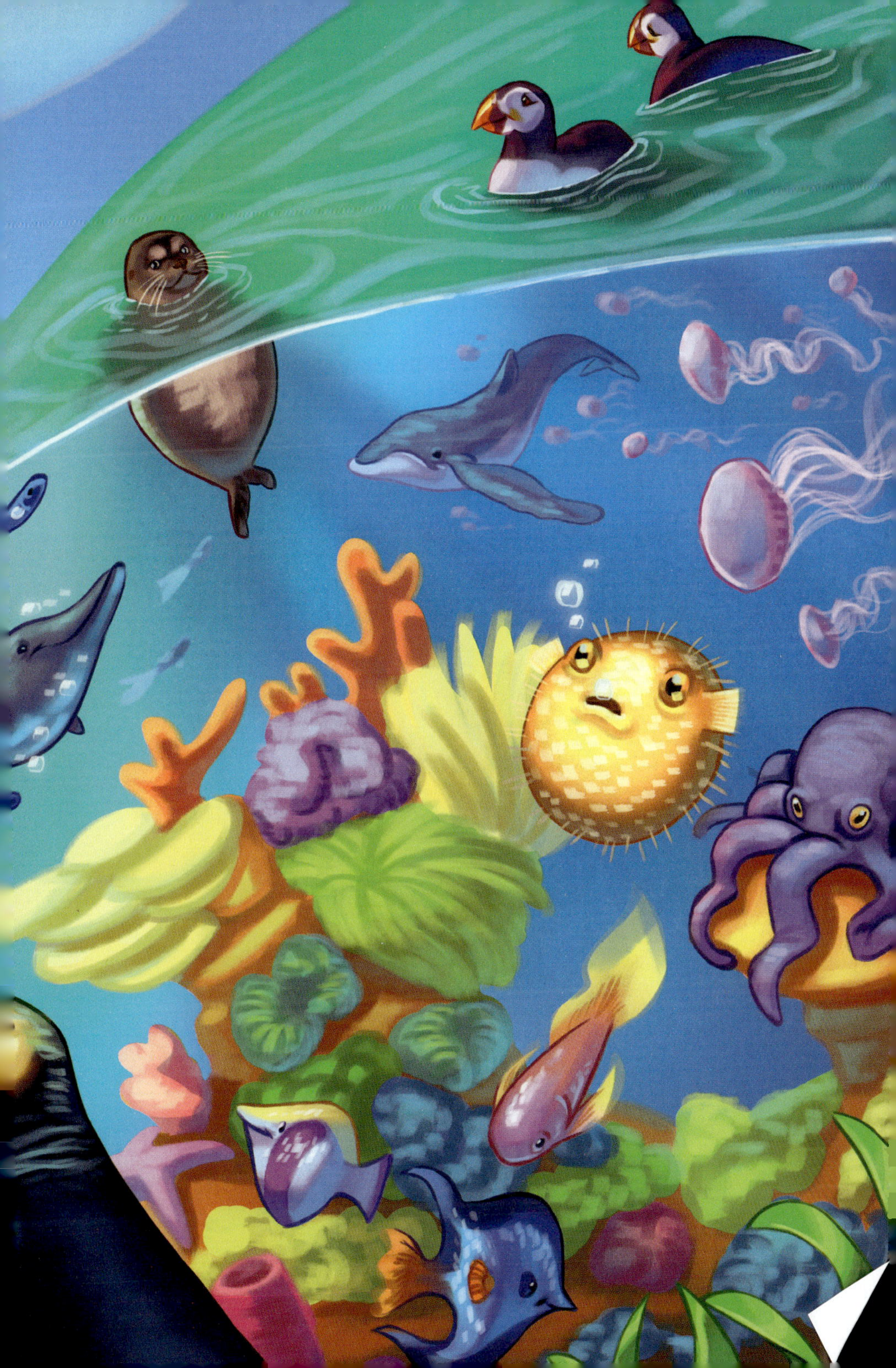

God then said, "Let's make people, to look like us and to be in charge of the creatures of the land, air, and sea." With those words, God created a man out of dust. He breathed His own breath into the man, and the man came to life.

God placed the man, Adam, in the Garden of Eden and taught him to care for it. God then brought all of the animals of the land and the birds of the air to Adam, so he could give them names. Whatever Adam called each creature became its name.

God looked at Adam and said, "It isn't good for him to be by himself. I will make a helper who is like him." Then God caused

Adam to fall into a deep, deep sleep. While he was sleeping, God took one of Adam's ribs, and from that rib, God created a woman and brought her to Adam.

When Adam woke up and saw the woman, he said, "She is like me, of my bones and of my flesh." So the man called her "woman," because she was taken from the body of the man. Together, they lived in the garden, in the wonderful abundance that God had created for them.

At last, God's work was complete. He rested on the seventh day and blessed it, making it a holy day: the day that He rested from His work of creating the world.

God always was, always is, and always will be. He was here before anything else, and He will be here forever, watching over the beautiful world He created and providing for His people.

> So God created mankind in his own image,
> in the image of God he created them;
> male and female he created them.
> *Genesis 1:27*

> God saw all that he had made, and it was very good. And there was evening, and there was morning—the sixth day.
> *Genesis 1:31*

THE PERFECT GARDEN

Genesis 2–3

Bliss. Beauty. Abundance. Perfection. That was the Garden of Eden.

God handcrafted the perfect home—a home that could only be dreamed of—for His pride and joy: His beloved children, Adam and Eve.

The land was filled with every color of the rainbow. Budding trees and blooming flowers unfolded before the new residents, and beautiful blossoms burst forth from the tree branches, filling the air with their sweet perfume. Strong trees grew branches full of luscious, nourishing fruits, and through it all, a river watered every tree and every plant, so that the land would never thirst. The garden continually yielded the life-giving fruit God had placed within it.

"Adam," God said, "this is all yours. Take good care of it. You'll have everything you could ever need, and I'll be right here with you."

Adam hugged Eve close as they looked out at the abundance all around them. They wore no clothes, yet they were not ashamed. They were living in paradise, and they were filled with the presence of God.

In the middle of the garden, God placed two unique trees: the tree of life and the tree of the knowledge of good and evil. "I only ask one thing," God continued. "You may eat the peaches and pears, the apples and avocados, the kiwis and coconuts—everything in this garden! However, do not eat from the tree of the knowledge of good and evil. If you eat from that tree, you will die."

It seemed like a simple request. With all of the other trees and fruit that God had provided, why would they ever need to eat from the one tree that he warned them not to eat?

One day while Eve was out in the garden alone, a voice called to her. "*Ssso*, let me get this *ssstraight*," the voice whispered. "God told you not to eat from *any* tree in the garden?"

Eve stepped back and looked toward where the voice was coming from; she saw a serpent camouflaged in the trees. "Oh, no," Eve answered, "we may eat from any tree at all, just not the one in the middle of the garden. God told us that if we eat from that tree, or even touch it, we would die."

"*Nonssssensssse*!" the serpent replied. "You will not die! God just knows that if you *do* eat from it, you will know good and evil. You will be as smart as God is."

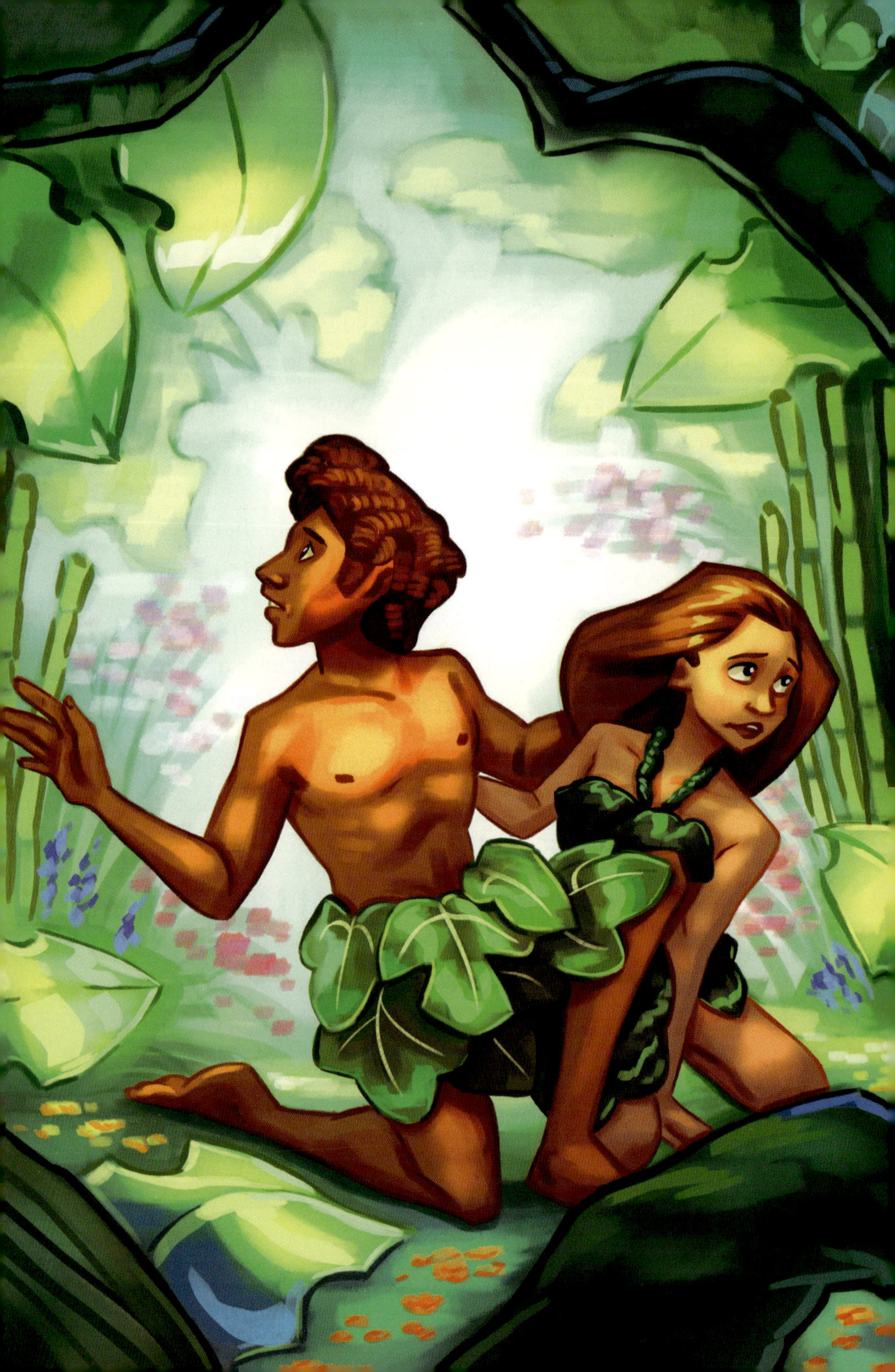

Eve considered the words of the serpent. She stepped a little closer to the tree in the middle of the garden. She ignored the words of God as she hid within its branches. *Oh, just look at this fruit!* she thought. It seemed so smooth, so shiny. *I bet it tastes delicious and it will make me wise. As wise as God? Why wouldn't I try it? One little bite won't hurt!*

Eve pulled the fruit from the tree, snapping the stem from the branches. She sank her teeth into the fruit and committed the world's first sin.

Eve's sin didn't stop there, though. She took the fruit to her husband, Adam. "Here, just try it," she insisted, repeating the words of the serpent. He ate some of the fruit, and in doing so he disobeyed God too, committing a sin that would change the earth for all eternity.

Suddenly, everything looked different. They had never disobeyed God before. They had never felt ashamed of being naked, but now they wanted to cover themselves and hide.

"Here!" Adam said in a frenzy. "Take these fig leaves. We'll sew them together to make clothes."

"What's that sound?" Eve asked, looking around fearfully.

"It's God! Hide!" Adam answered, pulling his wife behind a tree, shielding her from the presence of their loving God.

With one bite, Adam and Eve's world had become completely confusing, stressful, and so unlike the perfection that God had created for them.

"Where are you?" called the soothing voice of God. Of course, He already knew.

"I heard you coming," Adam called from behind the tree. "I hid because I was naked."

"Yes," God continued. "And how did you know you were naked? Did you eat fruit from the one tree that I told you not to eat from?"

Adam's eyes widened. "Well, the woman that You gave me, she handed me this fruit, and she said to eat it. So I ate it."

God looked at Eve. "What have you done?" He asked.

Eve looked to Adam, then back to where she had first heard the voice of the serpent. "He tricked me!" she said, pointing. "The serpent is the reason I ate from the tree!"

The serpent looked out from where he had been hiding, and God spoke to him first. "You will be cursed for what you have done—cursed more than any other animal. You will crawl on your belly and eat dust every single day of your life. I will make Eve's descendants and yours hate each other. One of her descendants will crush your head, but you will strike His heel."

Then God turned to Eve. "From now on," He said, "you will endure great pain when you have children. Also, you will have conflict in your relationship with your husband."

"And you, Adam," God said to the man, "you ignored my commands and ate from the one tree that I told you to leave alone. Because of you, the ground will be cursed. It will grow thorns and thistles for you. Only through sweat and hard work will you be able to grow food from the land. You will work the soil for the rest of your days, until you return to the dust from which you were made."

"Because you have both eaten from this tree," God explained, "you must now leave the garden I created for you. You enjoyed the bounty of the garden, but now you will have to work the ground to grow food and build everything you need with hard labor."

God placed angels with flaming swords at the entrance to the garden to guard the other tree, the tree of life, so that man may not ever eat from it and live forever in his sin.

"One more thing," God said to Adam and Eve. "I've made you some clothes to wear. They're made from animal skins and are thicker than those fig leaves you're wearing. They should last you a long time."

Adam and Eve bowed their heads in shame. How could they have ruined this perfection? How could they have disobeyed the one rule God had asked them to follow? And how could God still love them after they betrayed His trust, bringing the ugly blemish of sin into the perfect garden?

How would they ever make it right again?

Of course, they wouldn't. They couldn't. Only God could, and He would. He had a plan that would rescue His people from the sin and serpents of this world. He had a plan that would bridge the gap between the perfect and imperfect, allowing the unholy man to walk in the holy presence of God.

Would His people be ready for such a plan? How would they respond to His grace? Would they understand the gift of His sacrifice?

Only time would tell.

> So the Lord God said to the serpent, "Because you have done this, cursed are you above all livestock and all wild animals! You will crawl on your belly and you will eat dust all the days of your life. And I will put enmity between you and the woman, and between your offspring and hers; he will crush your head, and you will strike his heel."
>
> *Genesis 3:14-15*

THE GREAT FLOOD

Genesis 6–9

Adam and Eve now had knowledge of right and wrong, but it didn't do them any good at all. Adam and Eve's spirit of rebellion gradually spread throughout the earth. Generations later, when God looked out on the world, He saw nothing but wickedness, evil, and chaos. The very sight of it made God's heart ache. This was not what He had created for His beloved children, yet this is what they had chosen. God was sorry that He had created the world and decided to get rid of all that He had made.

Noah was the exception. He wasn't perfect, but he loved God wholeheartedly. It seemed that he was the only one who did. No matter what the world around him did or said, no matter how they made fun of him, Noah focused on obeying God. God saw Noah's faithfulness and was pleased with his obedience.

"Look around you," God said to Noah. "This world has become so evil, so violent, that I am going to destroy it all—the earth and everything in it."

Destroy the earth? What about me? What about my family? Before Noah could even voice his questions, God answered them, saying, "As for you, Noah, you will need to build an ark—a big boat with many rooms. Cover both the inside and the outside with tar to make the wood waterproof. Make it 450 feet long, 75 feet wide, and 45 feet tall. Give it a window and a door, along with lower, middle, and upper decks."

A three-story boat? For what?

"I will send a flood to wash the earth clean from all of the evil in it," God continued. "Every living thing will die. But not you, Noah. With you, I will make a promise. This promise will be for you and your wife, and your sons and their wives. Your family will all come with you into the ark. You will also take a pair of every kind of animal, bird, and creeping, crawling thing to care for on the ark. Take plenty of food for your family and the animals."

Destroy the world? 450 feet long? My whole family and every kind of animal on a boat?

It seemed unbelievable, impossible; yet Noah believed. Noah obeyed.

For months and months, Noah stacked up the wood and consulted his plans—God's plans. For months and months, people stopped, people stared, and peopled laughed. Who on earth would build a boat? In the middle of the desert? Where you couldn't even see water? Still, Noah just kept on working, building the boat that would carry him and his family into whatever future God had planned for them.

After one hundred and twenty years, the ark was complete. Noah stood in the shadow of its three stories, in awe of God's plans, now built into a reality. This was just the beginning.

"Noah," God said, "it is time to enter the ark. In seven days, I will send rain on the earth. For forty days and forty nights, the rain will fall, and the flood will rise, washing away all of the evil from the face of the earth."

Again, Noah obeyed. He and his wife rounded up their three sons: Shem, Ham and Japheth. Each one took his wife by the hand and joined their parents. One by one, they carried bags and baskets of food and supplies up the ramp and into the largest boat any of them had ever seen.

It was time.

Noah ushered camels and goats, rodents and wrens—every kind of animal and bird and creeping, crawling thing—in through the big wooden door of the ark. Shem spread fresh bedding while Ham poured the animals some water and Japheth secured them in their pens. "You will be safe here," Noah said. "Of that, I am sure."

Seven days later, just as God had said, water burst up from the ground and began to fall from the sky. Big, fat drops of rain fell on the people who had laughed at, mocked, and doubted Noah

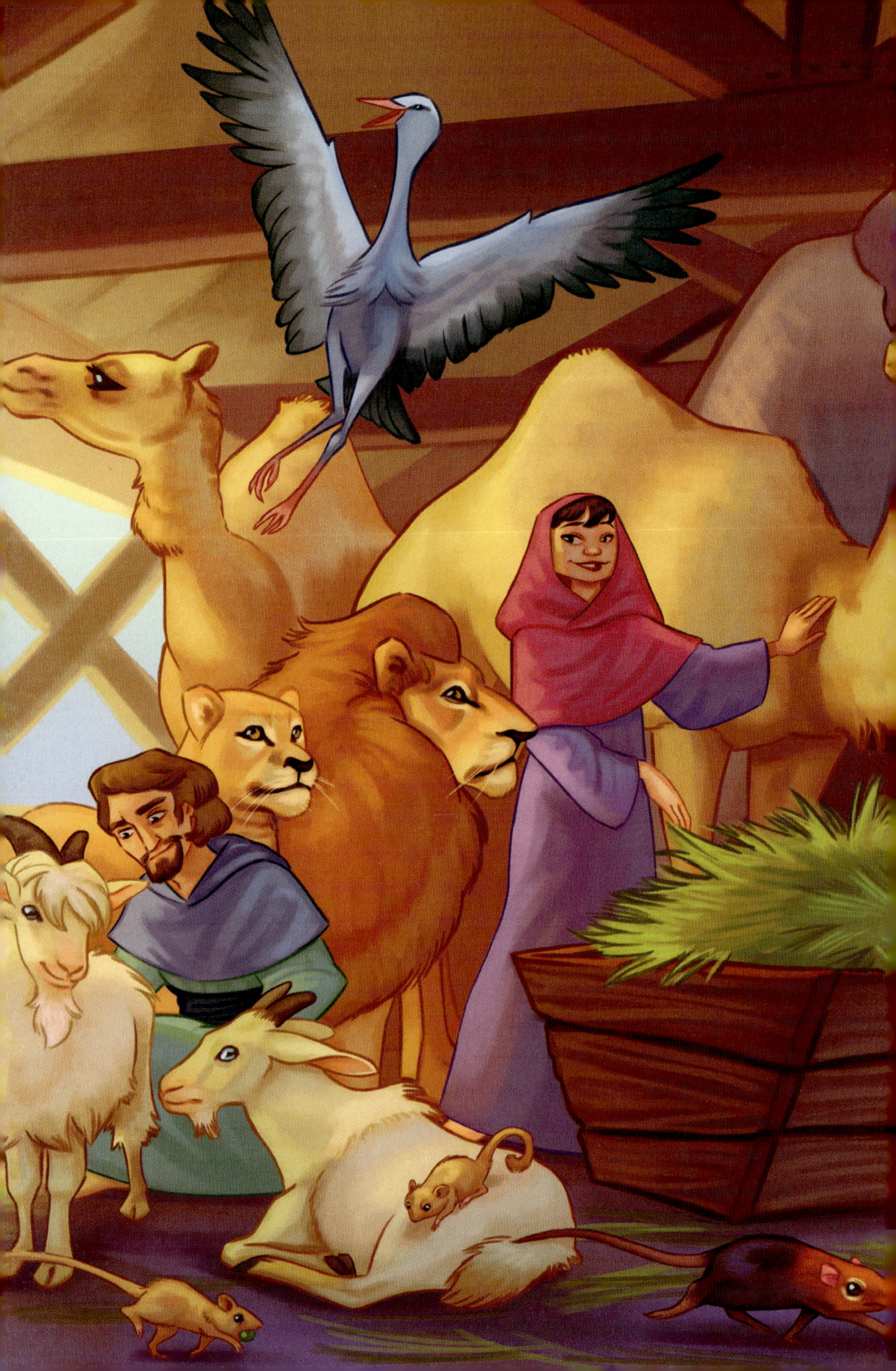

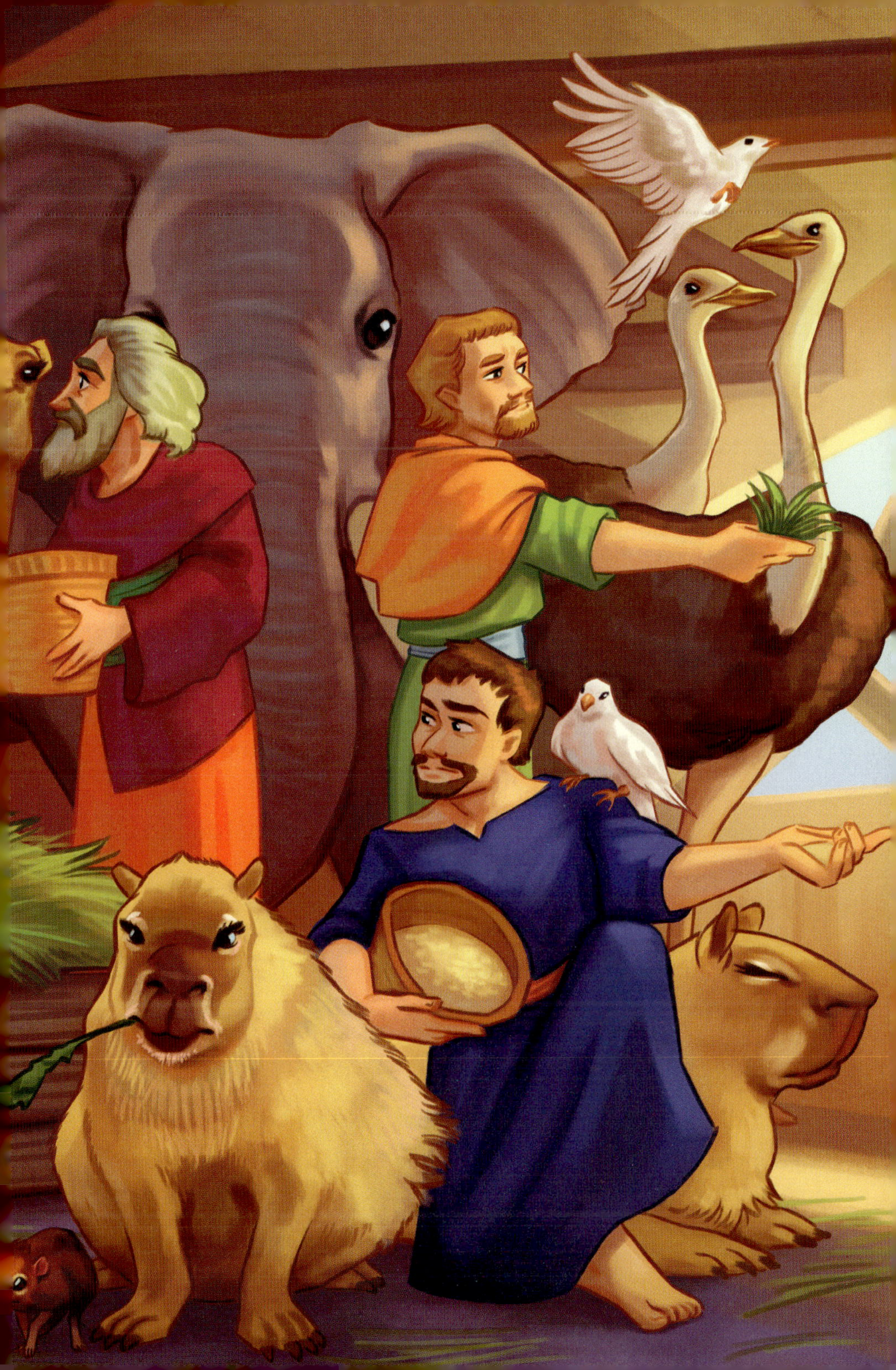

and the giant ark that he had built. Where trees and homes once stood, a great, rushing flood swirled and crashed, destroying everything in its path. However, God Himself had closed the door of the ark, keeping Noah, his family, and every kind of animal safely inside.

For forty days, the rain came pouring down, and the ark began to float as the water continued to rise. Soon, water covered even the highest mountains. For forty nights, the ark rocked peacefully above mountains and valleys, forests and deserts, and over the remains of what humanity had built. Everyone but the inhabitants of the ark had been swept away into the deep darkness of the waters.

For months, Noah and his family tended to the animals on the ark, passing the days thinking about the unknown—what their future would be in the empty world that the waters left behind. Through it all, they trusted God's plan. It had carried them this far.

After what must have seemed like an eternity aboard the ark, a slow and steady wind began to blow across the earth, and the water began to recede.

"Did you feel that?" Noah asked. "We've stopped moving."

Indeed they had. Their three-story boat had come to rest on a mountain as the waters continued to disappear. Noah could see the tops of the mountains around him, and he had an idea.

He took a smooth, black raven and sent it out of the window of the ark. The raven flew back and forth over the earth until the water had disappeared.

A week later, Noah sent out a dove. The dove quickly returned after finding nowhere to land. Seven days later, Noah sent out the dove again, and it returned with an olive leaf. The third time, after another seven days, Noah sent out the dove, and it never returned. Noah knew that the bird had found a home on the fresh, new earth.

"Come out!" God called. "Bring your wife, your sons, their wives, and all of the animals, birds, and creeping, crawling things, and step out into this new world. Multiply and fill the earth again."

It was time.

Noah and his family stepped out onto the lush, green grass and breathed in the freshness of the world. They worshipped God for His good, good plan, for His faithfulness, and for keeping them safe. They watched as a rainbow burst forth from the light between the clouds.

God said, "This rainbow is a sign of My promise to you, Noah, to you and to all mankind. I promise that never again will I destroy the earth with a flood. Every time you see the rainbow, remember My promise."

THE GREAT FLOOD

And Noah did.

Sadly, the obedience displayed by Noah's family didn't last. Sin spread across the earth once again. Despite this, God would stay true to His promise. He had another plan to wash away the sins of the world.

The smell of the burning offering pleased God, and he said:
Never again will I punish the earth for the sinful things its people do. All of them have evil thoughts from the time they are young, but I will never destroy everything that breathes, as I did this time.

Genesis 8:21 CEV

A PROMISE TO ABRAHAM

Genesis 12–22

Ten generations after Noah, a man named Abram and his wife, Sarai, lived in Haran, along with Abram's father, Terah, and nephew, Lot.

One day, after Terah had died, God spoke to Abram. "Leave your country, your home, and your father's house, and go where I will show you. I will bless your family and make you a great nation. I will make your name great. I will bless those who bless you and curse those who curse you. Through you, all of the families of the world will be blessed."

That was a big request, with an even bigger promise. Abram had heard stories about God, about how He had created the world and everything in it and how He had kept Noah's family and every kind of animal safe on a big, wooden boat in order to give the world a brand-new start. Abram didn't even need to question whether God's promises were true—he believed. He, Sarai, and Lot packed up their belongings and set out to follow God's plan—to see God's promise fulfilled.

They had journeyed for some time—through Canaan and

Egypt to a desert called the Negev—and had gathered so much wealth and livestock along the way that Abram and Lot needed to move away from each other to give their livestock enough room to graze. Lot decided to move toward the city of Sodom, and Abram stayed in the land of Canaan.

While Abram was settling in Canaan, God spoke to him, saying, "Look around you, Abram. See this land? I will give it all to your family, to your descendants. You will have as many descendants as the dust of the earth and I will give them this land forever. Go walk this land. Walk the entire width. Walk the entire length. Go see this land that I am giving you!"

As Abram did what the Lord told him to do, he tried to imagine what God's promises meant for his family. *My family will be a great nation? With more descendants than the dust of the earth? How could this be?* After all, Abram didn't even have a child yet. Could Sarai even have children?

As always, God heard Abram's concerns. A little while later, God answered those concerns. He said, "Don't be afraid, Abram. I will protect you and greatly reward you. You will have a child, and he will be your heir." Then God led Abram outside, saying, "Look at the sky. Can you even count the stars? Your descendants will be just like that—too many to even count!"

Abram trusted God's promise. Even after Abram grew to be an old man of ninety-nine years, and even though he could have been a great-grandfather by then and didn't have any children, he continued to believe that, one day, he would eventually become a father as God had promised.

After a while, God appeared to Abram. He said, "I am the Almighty God and My promise is with you." Abram bowed to the ground before God, who continued, "Your name will now be Abraham, because I have made you the father of many nations. Sarai, your wife, will now be called Sarah. I will bless you and she will give you a son in the next year. You will name him Isaac."

The next day, Abraham looked out from his tent and saw three men standing by some tall trees. He knew that God was appearing to him again. He ran to the men and bowed low, saying, "Please let me wash your feet while you rest under this tree. We'll prepare you something to eat so that you may be refreshed before continuing on."

They agreed, so Abraham ran to Sarah. "Please," he told her, "get the finest flour and bake some bread—quick!" Then he hurried out and asked his helper to prepare a calf. He served the men curds, milk, meat, and bread.

"Where is Sarah?" the men asked.

"She's in the tent," Abraham answered.

"This time next year, I will return to you, and she will have a son," one of the men said.

Sarah was listening to the men speak from inside the tent. When she heard this, she laughed and said, "Will I, an old woman with an old man for a husband, really be able to have the joy of a child?"

The Lord heard Sarah and asked Abraham, "Why did Sarah laugh? Is anything too difficult for Me to do? You will both see; I will return to you this time next year, and you will have a son."

Just as God had promised, Sarah gave birth to a son. Abraham named him Isaac, meaning "laughter." Sarah said, "God has given me laughter; everyone who hears about Isaac will laugh with me."

Abraham adored his son, and he watched and guided him as he grew. He was content, but God had one more test for

Abraham's faithfulness. One day God told him, "Take your son Isaac to the land of Moriah. Offer him as a sacrifice on one of the mountains there."

Was God going to take away the son that He had promised? What about his descendants being as numerous as the stars? Abraham wasn't sure, but as always, he trusted God.

Early the next morning, Abraham loaded his donkey and split wood to prepare the burnt offering. He and Isaac set out for the place God had told them to go. When they arrived in Moriah, Abraham gave his son the wood, and he carried the fire. Together they ascended the mountain.

On the way, Isaac said, "Father, I have the wood, but where is the sacrifice for our offering?"

Abraham, trusting God every step of the way, said, "God will provide the sacrifice, son."

When they arrived, Abraham built the altar, arranged the wood, and performed the heartbreaking task of tying up his son to be placed on the altar. As he slowly raised the knife above Isaac, Abraham heard a loud voice calling his name.

Abraham looked toward heaven and heard an angel say, "Don't hurt the boy. You have shown God that you will keep nothing, from Him, not even your son."

At that very moment, there was a rustling in the bushes nearby. Abraham looked up to see a ram caught in the brush by its horns. Abraham thanked God for providing the sacrifice, and he named that very place "The Lord Will Provide."

God did, and does, provide. Again, and again, through the very land that He had promised to Abraham's descendants, God provided rescue and safety, food and water, and a plan for His people to live in His presence. Then, when God's people had disregarded all that He had given them, God would provide yet another sacrifice. He would do what He had asked Abraham to do—give up His Son. God's Son would save the world from its sin.

> The LORD had said to Abram, "Go from your country, your people and your father's household to the land I will show you.
> "I will make you into a great nation, and I will bless you;
> I will make your name great, and you will be a blessing."
>
> *Genesis 12:1-2*

REBEKAH TRUSTS GOD'S PLAN

Genesis 24–25

By the time Isaac became a young man, Sarah had died and Abraham had become a very old man. Abraham wanted to see his son happily married, so he called his head servant, the manager of his entire household. "Swear to me," Abraham said to him, "by the God of heaven and earth, that you will find a wife for Isaac back in my home country, not here in Canaan."

The man answered, "Okay, but what if she doesn't want to leave her home? Should I take your son to live there, with her?"

"No, they must return here to live," Abraham answered. "God has given this land to us, to my descendants, beginning with Isaac. If she will not move here, then you are free from your promise."

So, the servant promised. He gathered some camels and other gifts from his master's home and set out to find a wife for Isaac. After many days of traveling through the desert and plains, he arrived outside the city of Nahor. There, he led the camels to rest by a well. He prayed, "Oh God, help this mission for my master Abraham to be successful. Help me to find a wife for his son Isaac so that Abraham may be at peace, knowing that his son will have a wife as he has hoped." The servant looked up at the people around him, then continued to pray, "See this spring and the people coming to it? I'm going to say to a woman, 'Please, may I have a drink from your jar?' When I do, please let the right woman answer, 'Yes, and I will water your camels too.' Then I will know that she is the one whom you have chosen for Isaac." Before the servant could even finish his prayer, a beautiful young woman named Rebekah approached with a jar on her shoulder.

As Rebekah got closer to the well, the servant took a deep breath. He asked her, "Please, may I have a little water from your jar?"

"Drink, my lord," she said, quickly lowering her jar to give him a drink. "I will water your camels until they've had enough water, too." She poured the rest of the jar into the trough for the camels and went back to the well to get more.

The servant watched Rebekah caring for the camels and was amazed at God's answer to his prayers. *Is it really her? Could this really be the woman that God had chosen to marry Isaac?*

When she was finished, the servant said, "Please, take these," and gave the young woman some of the gifts that he had brought along: a beautiful gold ring and two bracelets. "Would there be room for us to stay at your father's home for the night?" he asked.

"Yes, we have plenty of room!" Rebekah answered, and she ran home to tell her family about the guest who was coming.

Rebekah told her brother Laban about the man and showed him the precious jewelry he had given to her. Laban ran to meet him, saying, "Come on! We've prepared a place for you and your camels." Laban helped the man unload the camels, then gave them food and water.

Rebekah's family also prepared dinner for the man. When they placed his food in front of him, however, he said, "I can't eat anything until I tell you why I have come."

"Tell us," Laban answered.

The man continued, "I am Abraham's servant, and God has blessed him greatly. He has cattle and sheep, silver and gold, servants and maids, camels and donkeys. He has left all of this

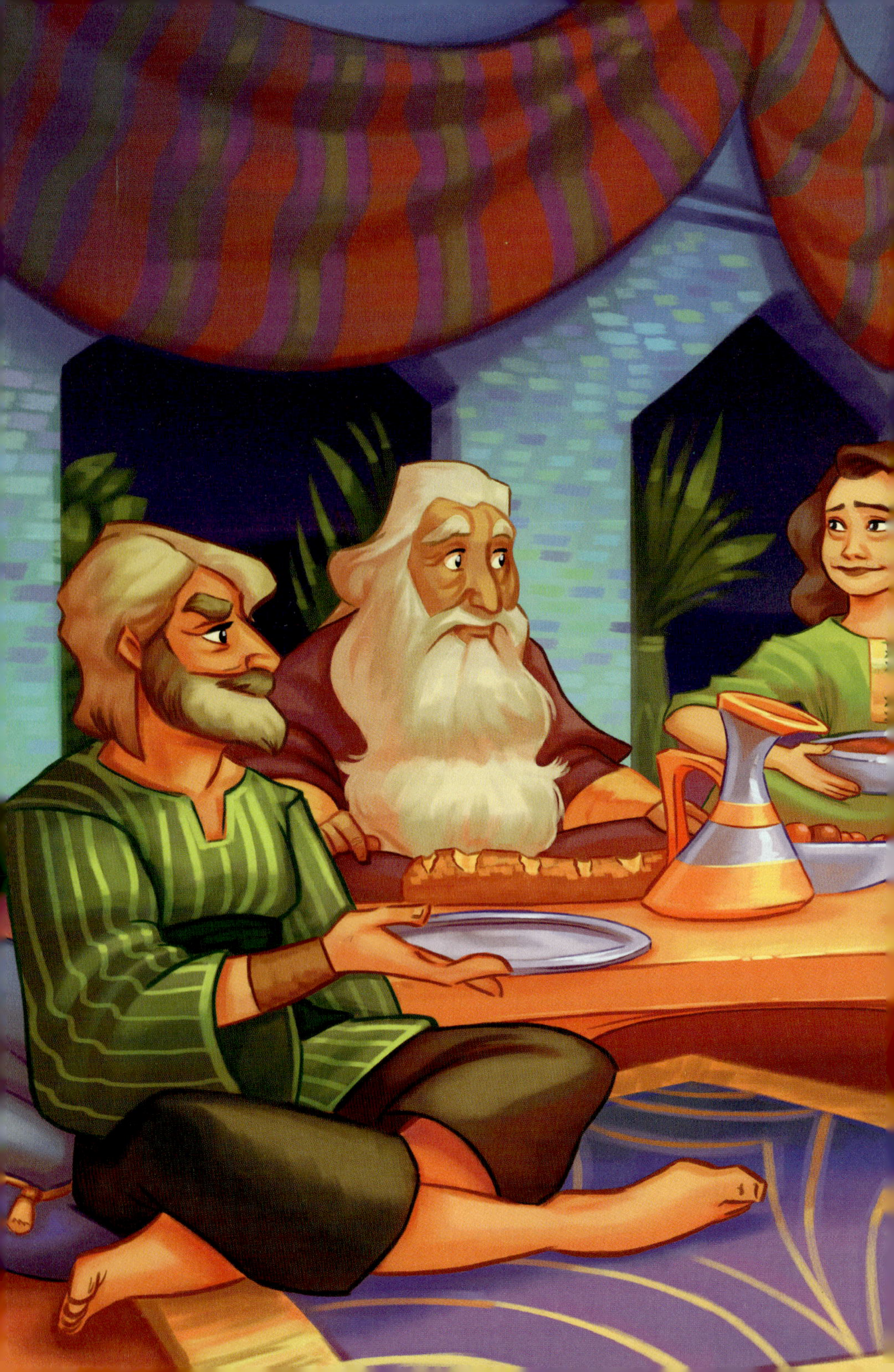

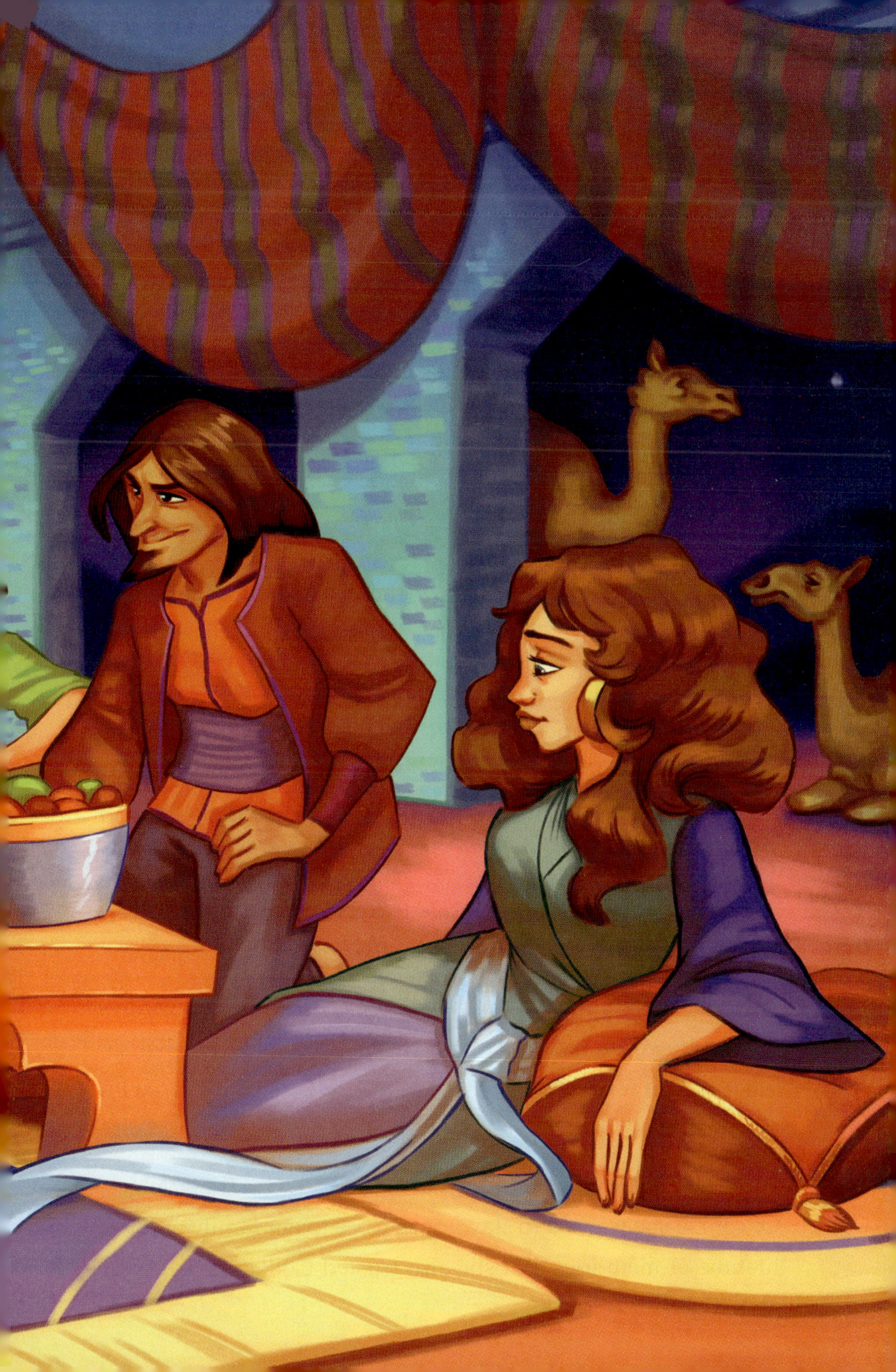

to his son Isaac. My master made me promise not to find a Canaanite wife for Isaac, but a wife from here, from his home, from his people."

Then the man told Rebekah's family of how he had prayed for God to show him the right woman, and how Rebekah had appeared, saying the very words that he had whispered to God.

"So, I must know right now whether or not this can be true, whether or not Rebekah will return to be the wife of my master's son."

Rebekah's father and brother looked at each other, nodding in agreement. They said, "If this is how God wants it, how can we be against it?"

The servant clapped his hands together and bowed to the ground, thanking God. He ran to his bags and pulled out gifts for everyone, showering them with the blessings that God had given to Abraham.

The next morning, the man said to Rebekah's family, "Please, let us return now, so that I can share the news with my master."

Rebekah's mother and brother wanted her to stay a few days longer, however, so they called Rebekah to them. "Rebekah, what do you want to do?" they asked. "Do you want to go with this man now?"

Rebekah looked at her family, then she looked at the stranger. Of course she wanted to stay home, close to her family and her lifetime of memories, but she also trusted God's plans for her life. "I will go with him," she said.

Rebekah's mother, father, and brother blessed her, kissed her, and sent her to become Isaac's wife, not knowing what the future held, but knowing Who held her future.

One evening, several days later, Isaac was out in the fields. When he looked up, he saw some camels riding toward him. As Rebekah came closer, she looked into the fields and saw Isaac.

"Who is that man?" Rebekah asked the servant.

"That is my master's son, Isaac," he replied.

Rebekah and Isaac were soon married, and Isaac loved Rebekah.

God's promise to Abraham—to His people for generations to come—was only getting started.

> *"Make sure that you do not take my son back there," Abraham said. "The LORD, the God of heaven, who brought me out of my father's household and my native land and who spoke to me and promised me on oath, saying, 'To your offspring I will give this land'—he will send his angel before you so that you can get a wife for my son from there.*
>
> *Genesis 24:6-7*

GOD BLESSES JACOB, THE TRICKSTER

Genesis 25–27

As Rebekah and Isaac were preparing for the birth of their first baby, she could feel something wrestling inside her belly. She asked God, "Why is this happening?"

The Lord answered her, "You are carrying two nations; one of them is stronger than the other. The older one will serve the younger one."

When it was time for the babies to come, Rebekah did indeed give birth to twins. The first baby boy was covered with thick, red hair. Isaac and Rebekah named him Esau, meaning "hairy." The second son was born gripping the heel of his brother. They named him Jacob, meaning "he holds the heel."

As the boys got older, Esau spent much of his time out in the fields hunting, but Jacob was quiet and stayed around the house. One day, Esau was returning home after a long hunt. He was tired, he was dirty, and he was starving. As he got closer to home, an irresistible smell enticed him to hurry. When he arrived, he saw his brother, Jacob, standing over a pot of red stew.

GOD BLESSES JACOB, THE TRICKSTER

"Give me some of that!" Esau demanded. "I'm starving!"

"Okay," Jacob answered, raising an eyebrow. "But only if you give me your birthright."

It was quite a demand for a bowl of stew. According to tradition, Esau was in line to inherit all of his father's possessions, simply because he was the firstborn. Jacob, born only a few minutes after Esau, didn't have the same right—unless, of course, he could convince his older brother to give it to him.

"I'm about to die anyway!" Esau said, collapsing in a heap. "So what good is my inheritance going to do me?"

"Do you promise?" Jacob asked.

"Yes!" Esau answered. "Just give me the stew!"

Jacob grinned as he ladled the lentils into a bowl for his brother. Esau scarfed the whole thing down and left. For a little bowl of soup, to relieve a temporary hunger, he had carelessly given up his lifelong right to his father's legacy—his right as the firstborn son.

Despite this carelessness, life carried on. Esau got married, and his father grew older, eventually losing his sight due to old age. One day Isaac called for Esau.

"I don't know how much longer I'll be with you," Isaac said, holding his son's hairy arm. "Go hunting, and bring back my favorite meal. Then, I will bless you before I die."

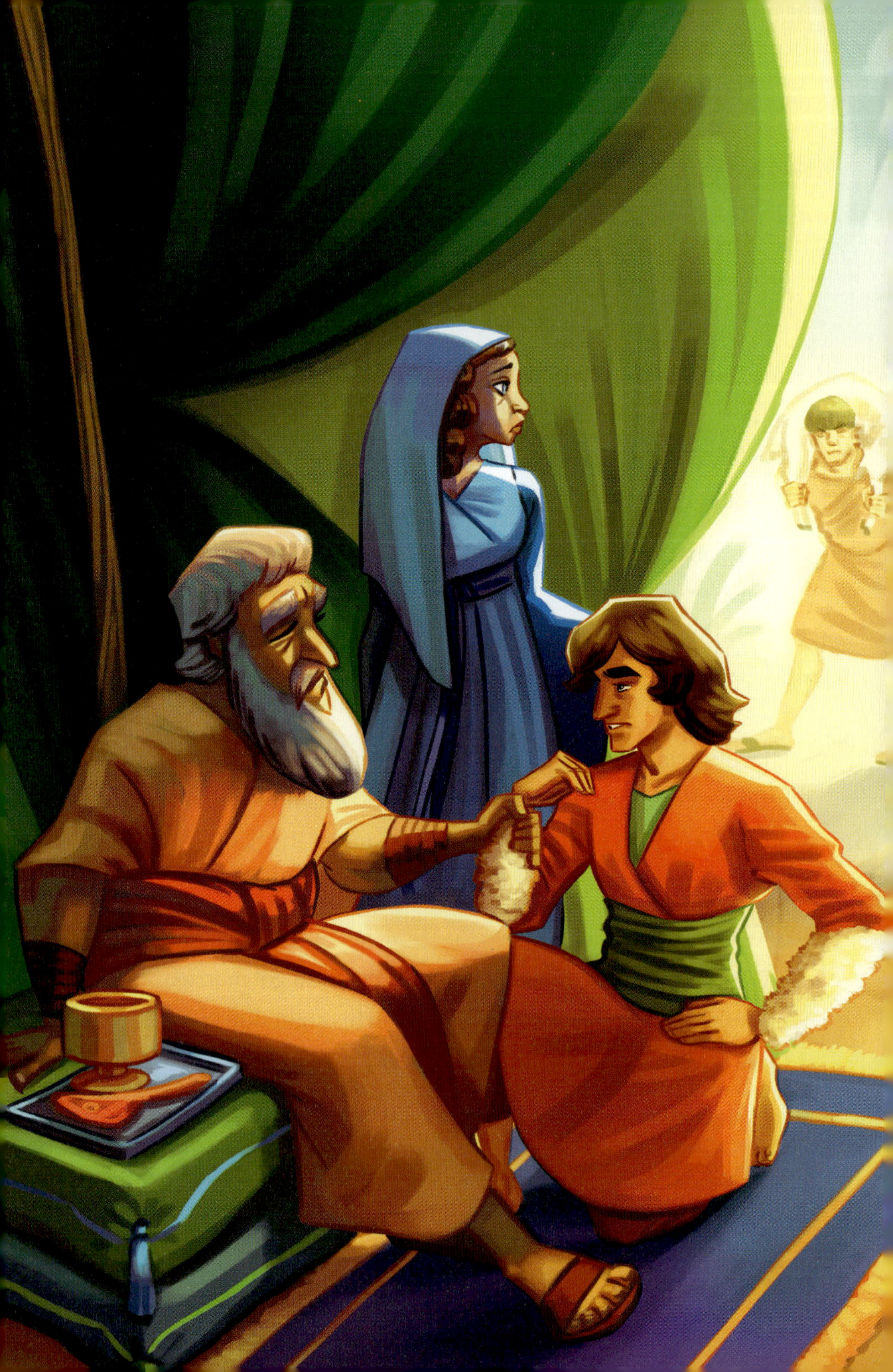

GOD BLESSES JACOB, THE TRICKSTER

Rebekah had been listening and called Jacob to her, telling him what his father had said. "Now," she said, "bring me the best young goats you can find in our flock, and I'll make your father's favorite meal. Then you can take it to him, and he will bless you."

"But won't he realize that I'm not Esau?" Jacob asked. "Just one touch of my skin and he'll know. Then I'll get a curse instead of a blessing!"

"Let me worry about that," his mother assured him.

Jacob obeyed and brought the best goats to her. As the food simmered, Rebekah gathered Esau's nicest clothes and gave them to Jacob. She took the skins of the young goats and placed them on his hands and neck. Then she smiled and handed Jacob his father's favorite meal.

"Ahem, Father?" Jacob said, carefully approaching Isaac.

"Yes, son, which one are you?" Isaac asked.

"Esau, your firstborn," Jacob answered. "Sit up and eat some of this delicious food. Then you can bless me as you said."

"But, son," Isaac's brow furrowed, "how did you get this game so quickly?"

"The Lord helped me," Jacob answered.

Isaac ran his withered hand over his son's and muttered, "The voice is Jacob's, but the hands are Esau's." Isaac turned toward his son. "You're really Esau?"

Jacob swallowed hard. "I am," he replied.

"Well, then," Isaac answered, "give me some of this delicious food, and I will bless you." Jacob sighed in relief and quickly offered the food to his father.

Isaac breathed in the smell of Esau's clothes. "Mmm, this is the scent of a field, blessed by the Lord. May God bless you, son, with an abundance from the land and from the fresh morning dew. May nations serve you and bow down to you. Lead your own brother as he, too, bows to you. Anyone who curses you will be cursed. Anyone who blesses you will also be blessed, my son."

Before long, Esau came home and prepared the game he had brought back for his father. "Father, sit up and eat," Esau said. "Then you can bless me."

"Wait!" Isaac exclaimed, sitting up. "Who are you?"

"Father, it's me, Esau," Esau replied.

Isaac began trembling as he realized what had happened. "Who was here before you then?" he asked. "Because it is that person who will be blessed!"

"Jaaaaacob!" Esau shouted and began to cry. "No, Father, no! You can bless me, too, can't you? Bless me, too, Father!"

"I'm sorry," Isaac answered. "I have made him your master, given him all of his relatives as servants, and I've asked for him to have an abundance of food. What else do I have to give?"

"I don't know, Father!" Esau sobbed at his father's side. "But bless me! Please, just bless me!"

"Okay," Isaac answered, searching for the words. "You will live far from the abundance that the fields have to offer, far from the sweet morning dew. You will depend on your sword. You will serve your younger brother, but you will eventually turn against him and no longer be under his control."

Esau bowed his head and left the room. "It doesn't matter what Jacob has done. It doesn't matter what Father has said," Esau muttered. "When my father is gone, I will kill Jacob and take all that has been given to him."

When Rebekah heard about Esau's plan, she immediately called for Jacob. "Listen to me, son," she said. "Esau is planning to kill you, so you have to leave. Run away to your Uncle Laban's house until your brother cools down. When he does, I will send for you. I can't lose both of you in one day."

So Jacob ran. After days of traveling, he stopped to rest for the night. He had a vivid dream of a stairway that reached all the way to heaven, with angels going up and down the stairs. God spoke to him, saying, "I am the God of Abraham and Isaac. To you, I will give the land that you are sleeping on. Your descendants will be like the dust of the earth. I will watch over you always, wherever you go."

Jacob woke up and rubbed his eyes in disbelief. "God is here!"

he said. "This is the gate of heaven itself!" Jacob placed a stone there as a marker, anointed it with oil, and named it Bethel.

As Jacob set out on the rest of his journey, he didn't know that it would be decades before he returned this way again. When he returned, he would be surrounded by family and livestock: goats and cows and donkeys too numerous to count. At long last, he and his brother would throw their arms around each other in an act of forgiveness and brotherly love.

Jacob didn't know those things yet, but he did know that no matter what lay ahead, God had made a promise to be with him, to be watching over him wherever he would go. For Jacob, God's promise was enough.

"I am with you and will watch over you wherever you go, and I will bring you back to this land. I will not leave you until I have done what I have promised you."

Genesis 28:15

JOSEPH, THE DREAMER

Genesis 37, 39–49

As the years went by, Jacob married and had twelve sons. The second to the youngest, his eleventh son, was named Joseph.

All of Joseph's brothers knew he was Jacob's favorite.

Because of this, Joseph's brothers didn't like him—at all. Joseph would go back and report to his father all of the bad things that his brothers were doing while they were out tending the sheep. To make matters worse, their father made a beautiful, colorful robe, just for his favorite son. It also didn't help that Joseph had dreams about his older brothers bowing down to him—and that he chose to tell his brothers all about it.

"Listen to this dream I had!" Joseph announced to his brothers.

No one responded. Some of them exchanged glances. Some of them rolled their eyes. But none of them wanted to hear about their teenage brother's latest dream.

"We were all gathering grain," Joseph continued excitedly, "when suddenly, my bundle of grain stood up straight, and all

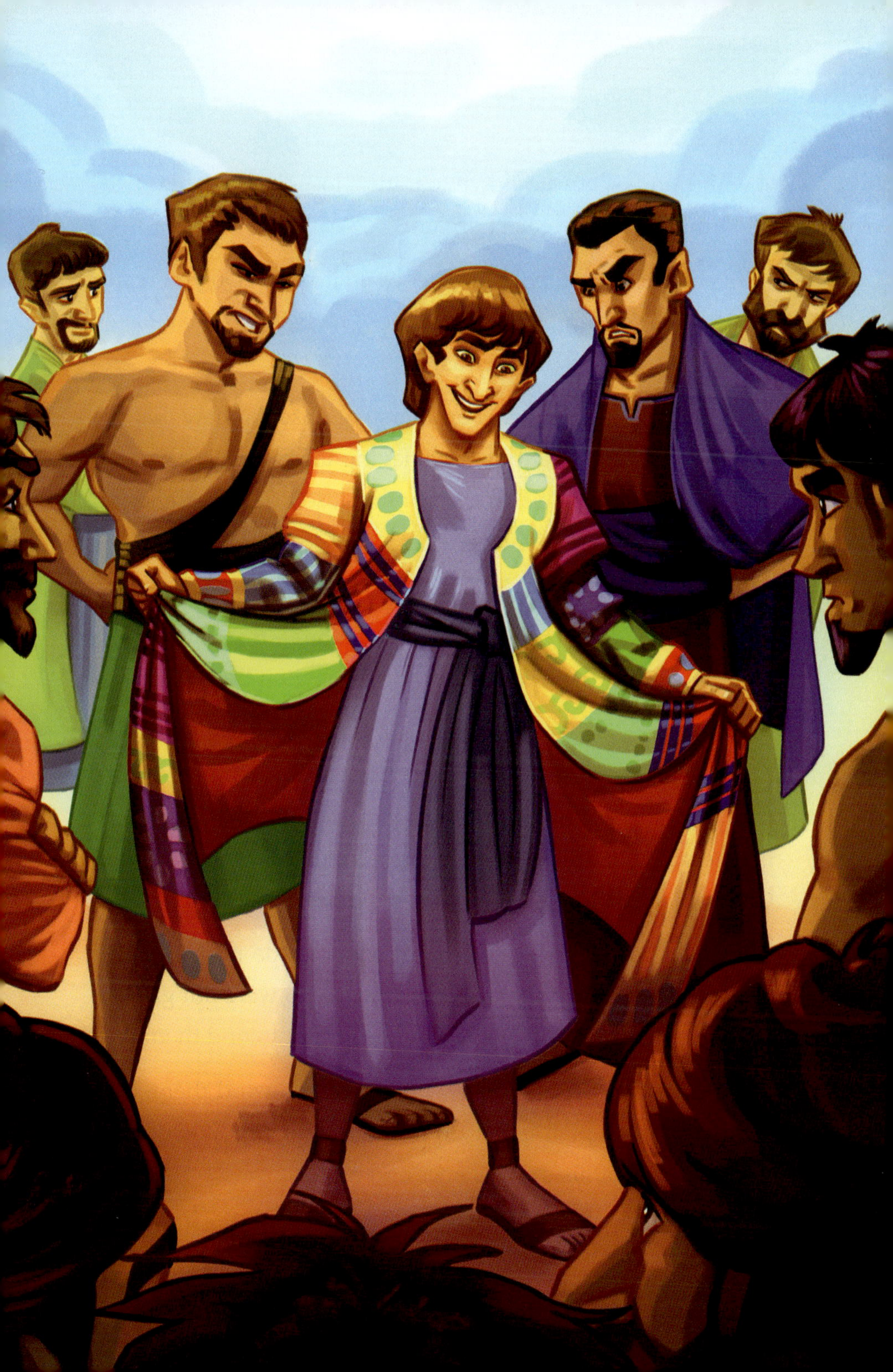

of your bundles bowed down to mine." Joseph shook his head. "Isn't that just the greatest dream?"

One brother could hold his silence no longer. "Do you really think this is actually going to happen?" he asked. "What makes you think you can rule over us?"

No matter how angry his brothers got, Joseph knew that his dreams were important; he was having them for a reason. So, even though it made his brothers angry, Joseph just kept sharing the dreams with his family.

"Hey, guess what? I had another dream!" Joseph announced a few days later. "This time—are you listening?—this time the sun and the moon and eleven stars were all bowing down to me!"

Even Joseph's father was a little annoyed by this latest dream. "What do you mean?" Jacob asked. "You think your mother and I will actually be bowing down to you, along with your eleven brothers?" Unlike the brothers, Jacob actually wondered what God was trying to tell Joseph through these dreams.

One day, as he had done many times in the past, Joseph's father sent him to check on his brothers who were out grazing the sheep. Joseph was obedient, so he set out to find them.

When Joseph's brothers saw him headed toward them, they came up with a plan to get rid of their annoying little brother and take care of his dreams once and for all.

As soon as Joseph arrived, they grabbed him and ripped off

the beautiful robe that his father had made for him. They threw him into a nearby well. There was no water in it, but Joseph could not climb out. He was stuck.

While the brothers were eating nearby, a caravan of traders came through. "Where are you headed with that load of goods?" one of the brothers asked.

"To Egypt," came the reply.

The brothers huddled for a moment, then called to the passing traders, "Hey, we've got a great deal for you! How about a slave for only twenty shekels of silver?"

For that low price, the brothers sold their little brother Joseph as a slave. They watched as the caravan moved further away, carrying their father's favorite son to Egypt.

Reuben, the oldest brother, had stepped away from his brothers for a moment, but he had already decided to let Joseph out as soon as he got back to the well. As annoying as Joseph could be, their father would be devastated if anything ever happened to him. When Reuben returned, he discovered that Joseph was gone, sold to traveling traders. Reuben ripped his clothes in despair. "What will we do now?" he wailed. "What will we tell our father?"

The brothers came up with a plan. They dipped Joseph's robe in goat blood and presented it to their father.

"Look what we found," they said. One of the brothers handed the robe to their father, saying, "Isn't this Joseph's?"

The color drained from Jacob's face. "It is!" he cried. "And is this blood? He's been torn apart by a wild animal!" Jacob mourned his son for many days. His family tried to comfort him, but he said, "I will mourn him until I join him again in the grave."

Over in Egypt, Potiphar, the captain of Pharaoh's guard, had just bought a new slave. This young man proved to be worth every shekel Potiphar had paid. Even as a slave, God gave Joseph great success.

Before long, Joseph was in charge of Potiphar's entire household, in charge of everything Potiphar owned. The whole time Joseph was in charge, Potiphar's household was blessed.

After a while, Potiphar's wife caused trouble for Joseph. She lied and told her husband that Joseph had tried to attack her, so Potiphar threw Joseph into prison without even asking Joseph what really happened.

Even in prison, God took care of Joseph and gave him success. Just like in Potiphar's house, Joseph was given more and more responsibility in the prison. Before long, Joseph was in charge of all of the prisoners!

One morning, Joseph noticed that two of the prisoners seemed really sad. One of the men had been in charge of carrying Pharaoh's cup, and the other had been Pharaoh's baker. When Joseph asked them what was wrong, he learned that they had both had strange, horrible dreams, but no one could interpret them.

"God can," Joseph answered. "Let's ask him."

Joseph listened to their dreams, and with God's help, he was able to interpret the dreams for the men. The cupbearer's dream meant that he would get to go back to serving Pharaoh. Joseph pleaded with him, saying, "When you go back to Pharaoh, please tell him about me so that I can get out of this prison."

Two long years passed before the cupbearer remembered Joseph. When Pharaoh had a dream that no one could explain, the cupbearer told him about Joseph's ability to interpret dreams.

Pharaoh sent for Joseph. He was pulled out of the prison, shaved, given new clothes, and brought in front of Pharaoh.

"I hear that you can interpret dreams," Pharaoh said to the prisoner before him.

"I can't," Joseph said. "But God can."

Pharaoh, intrigued by this prisoner's claims, began to recall his dreams. "I was standing by the Nile, when seven fat cows came up and started grazing," he said. "After them, seven skinny, ugly cows came up and ate the seven fat cows. However, the skinny cows were just as skinny, even after eating the fat cows. Then I woke up."

Joseph nodded as Pharaoh continued, "I then had another dream about seven large heads of grain. Then seven skinny heads ate the seven large heads of grain. No one can explain to me what these dreams mean."

"Your dreams both mean the same thing," Joseph answered. "God is telling you that there are going to be seven years of plenty followed by seven years of famine. The years of famine will be so bad that the seven years of plenty will be completely forgotten. Because God has told you this in two different dreams, it means that these things will happen soon."

Pharaoh leaned forward and listened. Who was this unknown prisoner with such wisdom?

"You will need to find a wise man to manage the seven years of abundance, storing up food for the seven years of famine," Joseph advised him.

Pharaoh looked around his court. His officials nodded agreement to Joseph's plan. Then Pharaoh turned back to Joseph and asked, "What about you?"

"Me?" Joseph asked.

"Yes," Pharaoh said. "Since God has revealed all of this to you, is there anyone better to oversee this plan? You'll be in charge of the palace, and the people will obey what you tell them to do. You'll be second only to me."

Joseph did just as he was told, and with God's wisdom and guidance, he continued to see success. He stored up grain in each of the cities of Egypt during the seven years of plenty. Eventually, there was so much grain that Joseph stopped counting it—there was too much to count!

When the years of plenty were over, the famine came. Because the Egyptians were prepared, there was no need to panic. "Just do whatever Joseph tells you to do," Pharaoh told his people.

Soon, people from all over the region were traveling to Egypt to buy grain.

Back in Canaan, Jacob told his sons, "Don't just stay here and starve. Go to Egypt and buy grain so that we may all live."

As soon as his brothers arrived in Egypt, Joseph recognized them. Not knowing who he actually was, they all bowed to him, the man in charge of all the food in Egypt.

"Who are you?" Joseph asked, pretending not to know them. "Why are you here?"

"We're from Canaan. We just need to buy some food for our family," the brothers said.

"You are spies!" Joseph shouted.

"No! Really! We're all brothers," Joseph's brothers insisted. "There were twelve of us, but the youngest is with our father back home, and one died."

"Prove it!" Joseph demanded. "Bring your youngest brother back to me! Until you do, I will keep one of your brothers here in prison."

One brother whispered to the others, "See! We are being punished for what we did to Joseph. He pleaded with us and we would not listen; the same is happening to us now."

Joseph heard their whispers and understood every word they said. It touched him so much that he turned around to hide the fact that he was crying. He pulled himself together, turned to his men and gave orders to fill the brothers' bags with grain and to give them back the silver they had brought to purchase the grain. He also ordered for the brothers to be given everything they would need for their journey back home.

When the brothers stopped to rest, one of them opened his sack and froze in shock. "Oh no!" he said. "Look! My silver is still here in my sack."

"Oh, we are surely being punished by God," one of the brothers answered. "They are going to think we stole all of this grain!"

Not knowing what else to do, the brothers returned home and told their father all that had happened in Egypt.

Jacob shook his head sadly as he listened to the story. He answered, "Joseph is gone. You left Simeon in prison in Egypt, and now you want to take Benjamin? Absolutely not."

Eventually, the family ran out of food again, and they had no choice but to return to Egypt with their youngest brother, Benjamin. They loaded up the best gifts from their land and doubled the amount of silver they had taken before, hoping to make peace with this stern leader of Egypt. Bowing before him again, they presented their gifts.

The ruler simply asked, "How is your aged father you told me about? Is he still living?"

"Yes, he is well," they answered.

"And this is your youngest brother?" he asked.

JOSEPH, THE DREAMER

The sight of Benjamin was too much for Joseph to take. He ran out of the room and cried uncontrollably. After a while, Joseph composed himself and returned to have dinner with his brothers.

Still not knowing the true identity of this Egyptian leader, the brothers again took their grain and headed for home. They didn't realize that Joseph had told his guard to hide a cup in Benjamin's bag.

"Stop!" a voice shouted.

The brothers turned around and saw the royal guards. "Our master was good to you and you repaid it with evil!" the guards said.

The brothers looked at each other. "Why would you say that?" they asked. "We've done nothing wrong!"

The guards began to search their things and found Joseph's silver cup in Benjamin's bag. "The owner of this bag will now be our slave," the guards said. "The rest of you can go."

The brothers knew they could not return home without Benjamin. They tore their clothes in sorrow and returned once again to Joseph. "Please," they begged, "our father is old and this is his youngest son. It would kill him to lose Benjamin. Please don't send us back without him."

"Leave us!" Joseph ordered his guards and servants. "Everyone out!" He began to cry so loudly that everyone in the house could hear him. Once he was alone with his brothers, he told them, "I am Joseph!"

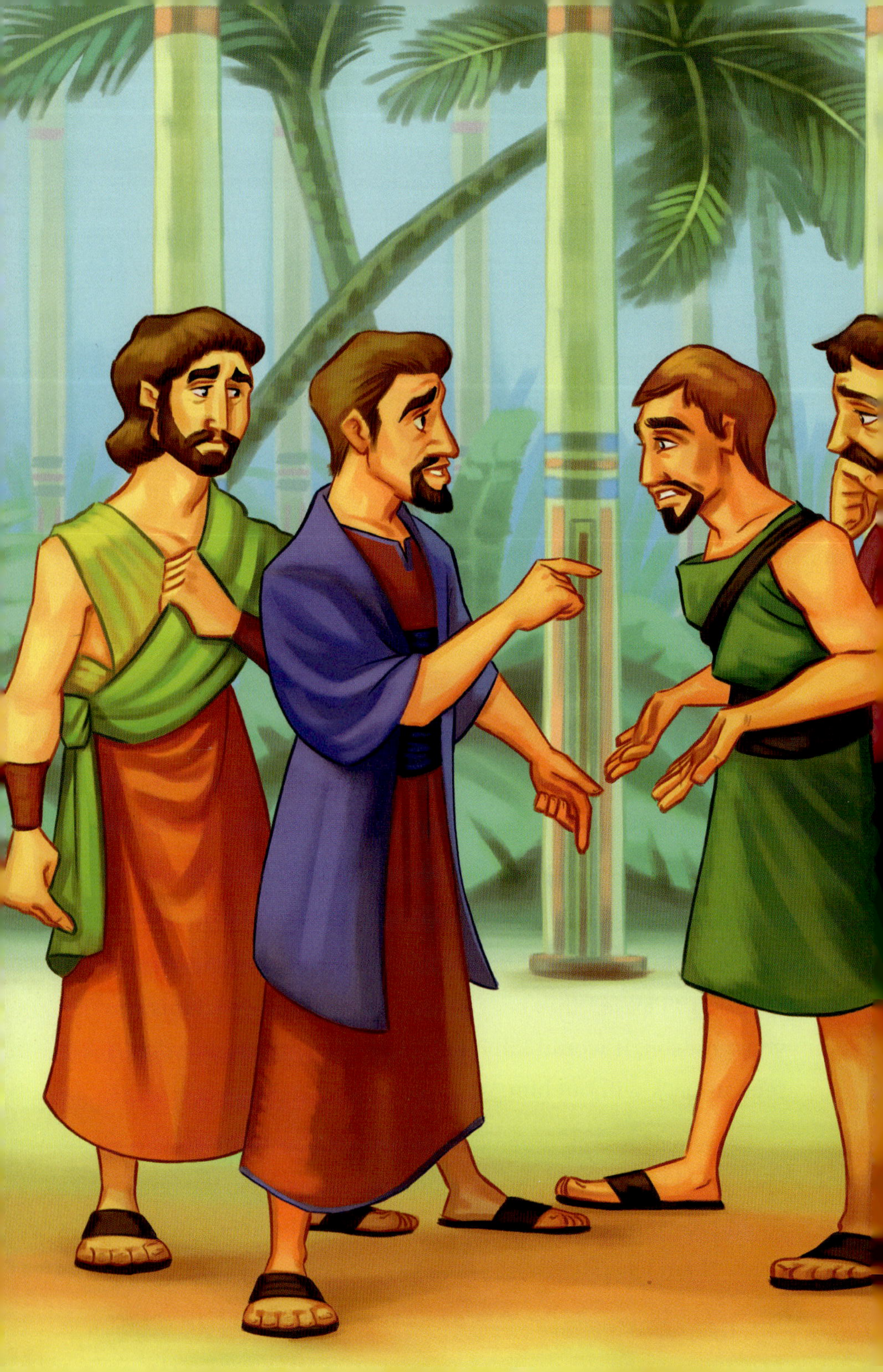

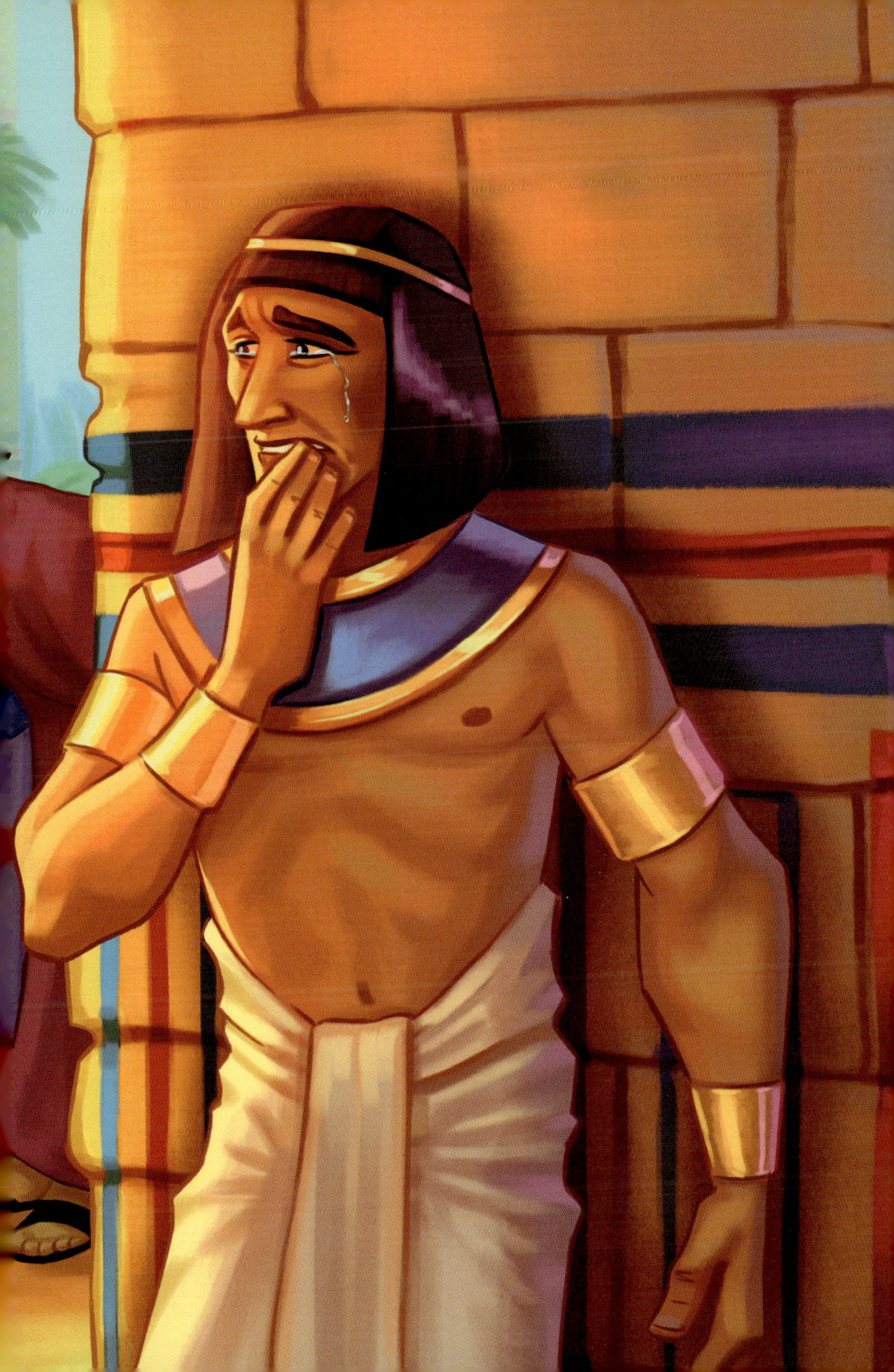

JOSEPH, THE DREAMER

The brothers froze, terrified.

"I am your brother," Joseph continued, "the one you sold as a slave! But don't be afraid—God sent me here. What you meant to hurt me, God used for good."

Joseph ran to Benjamin and threw his arms around him. He cried and hugged and kissed all of his brothers—forgiving them for the harm they did to him so long ago.

"Now, go; get your wives, your children, and our father and come live here in Egypt with me," Joseph said, smiling at his brothers. "The best Egypt can offer will be yours."

JOSEPH, THE DREAMER

This time—after all these years—they listened to their little brother Joseph, the dreamer.

As their father Jacob saw his life coming to an end, he also saw the restoration of God's perfect plan. Not only had God restored his favorite son Joseph to him, but God had given him the gift of seeing his sons' sons as well. Jacob blessed them all and died knowing the full legacy that he had left behind—the legacy that God had promised him so many years ago.

> *"You intended to harm me, but God intended it for good to accomplish what is now being done, the saving of many lives."*
> *Genesis 50:20*

THE BABY IN A BASKET

Exodus 1–2

It had been hundreds of years since Joseph welcomed his family into Egypt. The Israelite family, the descendants of Jacob who were also known as Hebrews, had grown and spread throughout the land. By this time, there was a pharaoh who didn't care about the honorable Joseph and his brothers. In fact, this pharaoh was afraid that all of those Israelites might turn against the Egyptians and defeat them.

The pharaoh's fear led him to enslave the Israelites to try to keep them from prospering. He forced them to work in the fields and in the cities. He worked them from the wee hours of the morning, through the harsh Egyptian midday, and well into the night. No matter how he tried, though, it seemed that the pharaoh could not keep the Israelites from increasing in numbers and strength. In fact, it seemed that the more he tried to crush them, the more the Israelites grew.

He was running out of options, so the pharaoh gave a terrifying order to the midwives, the women who helped the Hebrew mothers when their babies were born. He told them, "When a

Hebrew baby is born, if it's a boy, kill it." The midwives feared God more than they feared the king of Egypt, however, and they let all of the baby boys live. Then the pharaoh ordered all of his own people, "When a Hebrew boy is born, you must throw him into the Nile River!"

One day, a Hebrew woman, married to a man from the tribe of Levi, one of the sons of Jacob, gave birth to a baby boy. She looked at his perfectly formed fingers, his tiny toes, his round, rosy cheeks, and she knew that she would do whatever it took to keep this baby alive.

Months passed, and that little baby grew. His cries got louder and he became harder and harder to hide. His mother knew that she could no longer keep him safely hidden. Tears fell down her face as she carefully brushed tar on a little basket—a basket that was just his size.

The baby's big sister Miriam followed her mother as they took him, swaddled snugly into the basket, down to the Nile riverbank. The mother placed the basket in the reeds, just off the bank.

A little way down the river, servants walked along the riverbank as Pharaoh's daughter waded into the water to bathe. As she bathed, she saw a floating basket. "Bring it to me," she called to her servants.

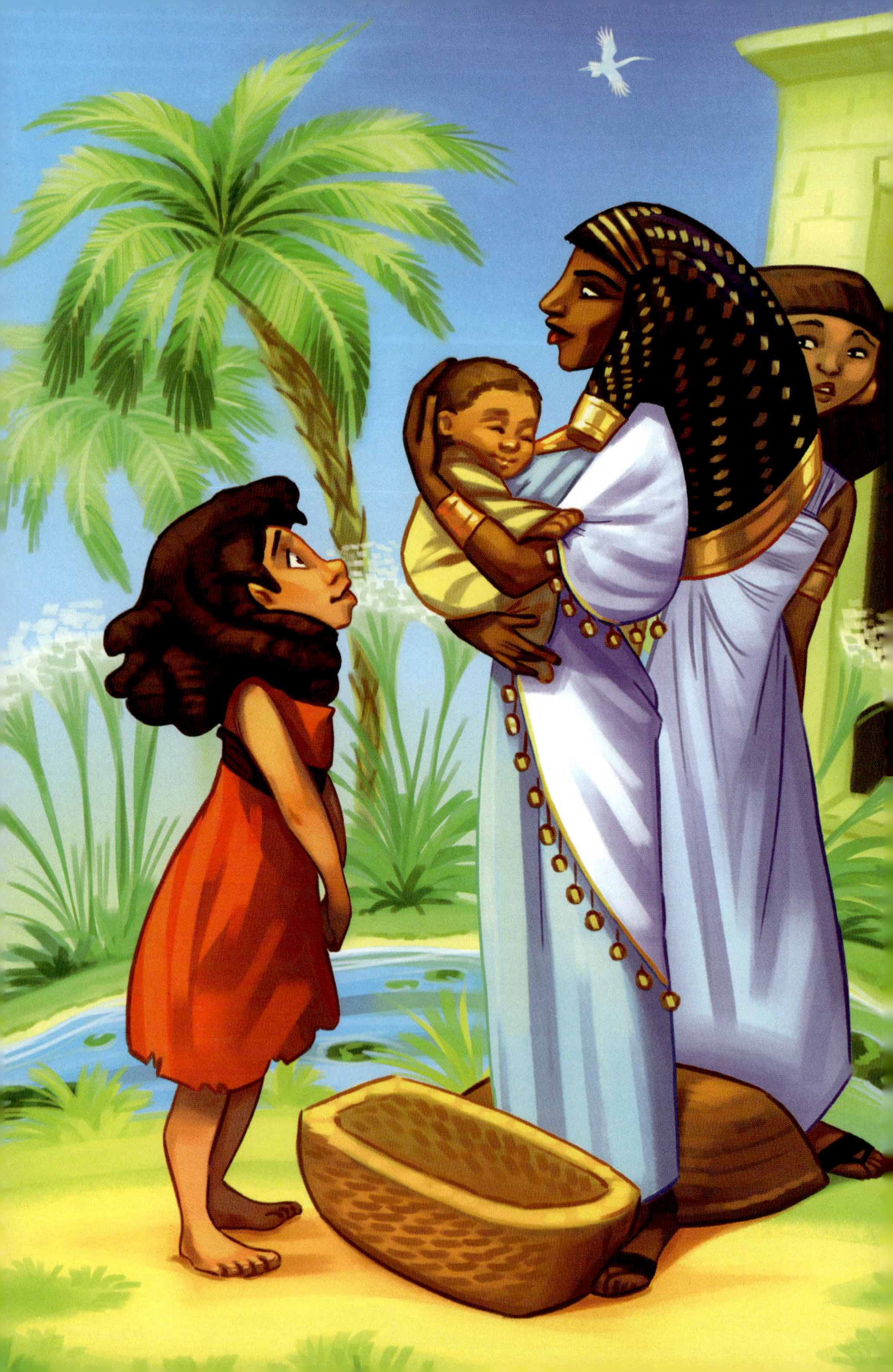

When the princess opened the basket, there was a precious, rosy-cheeked baby boy, crying. "Oh, look," she cooed. "It has to be a little Hebrew baby." She lifted him from the basket and held him close.

Just then, a little girl ran up to her. "Excuse me," she said, "but I know a Hebrew woman who can nurse him for you! Should I get her?"

The princess smiled. "Yes, please do."

Miriam ran to her mother and brought her back to the princess. The princess said to Miriam's mother, "Please, take this child and nurse him for me. I'll pay you for taking care of him."

It was more than the mother could have imagined! Not only did God save her son, but He allowed her to keep her baby boy a little longer before he moved to the palace to live as royalty.

After the baby had grown into a toddler, the mother knew it was time. She took the long walk back to the palace to leave her beloved son with the princess. The princess named him Moses, because she had pulled him from the water.

As difficult as it must have been to leave little Moses behind, his mother placed her faith in a mighty God, a God who cared for His people. One day, not too long after that, God would call Moses to lead the Israelites—God's people—to a land of promise,

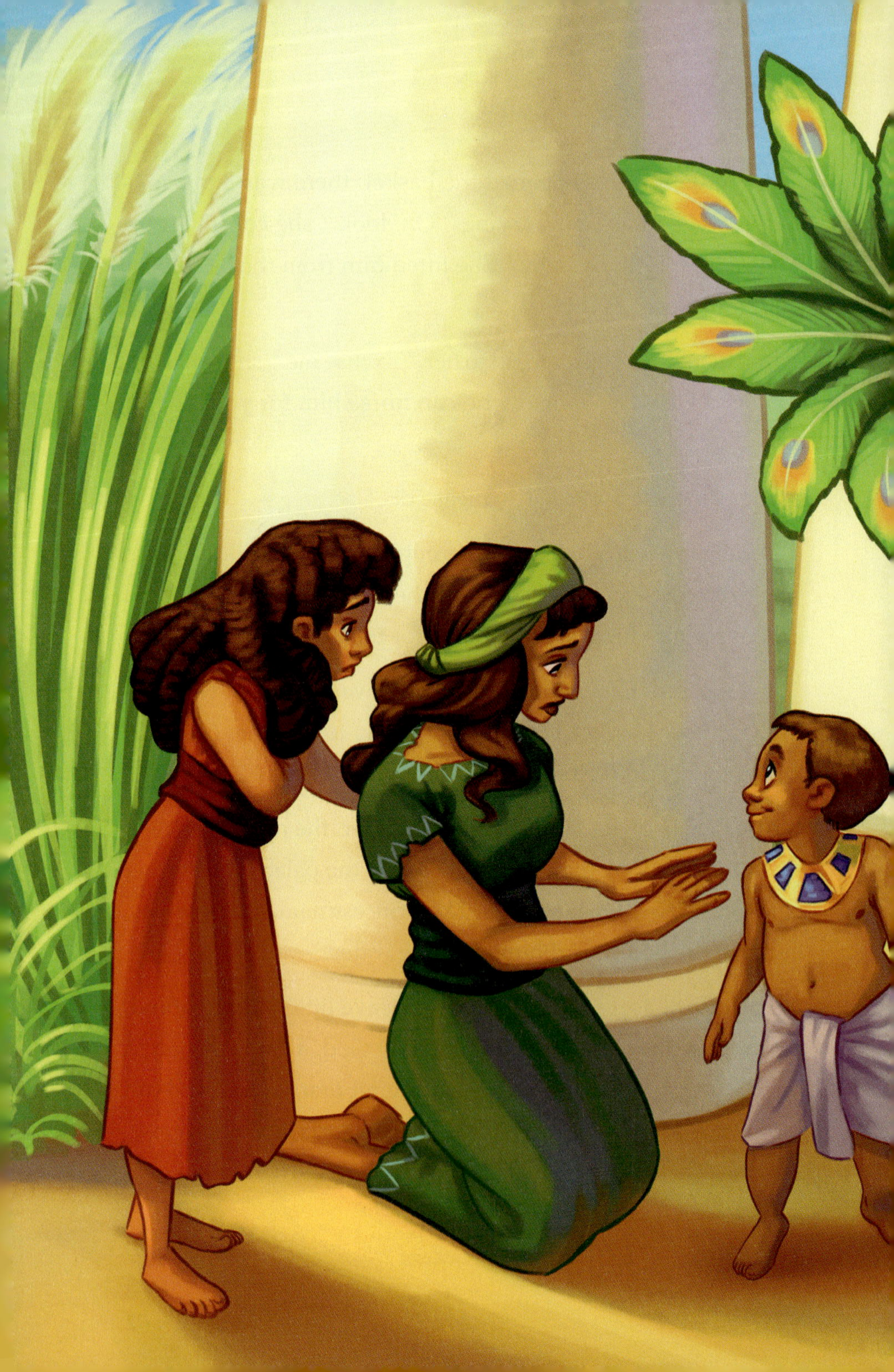

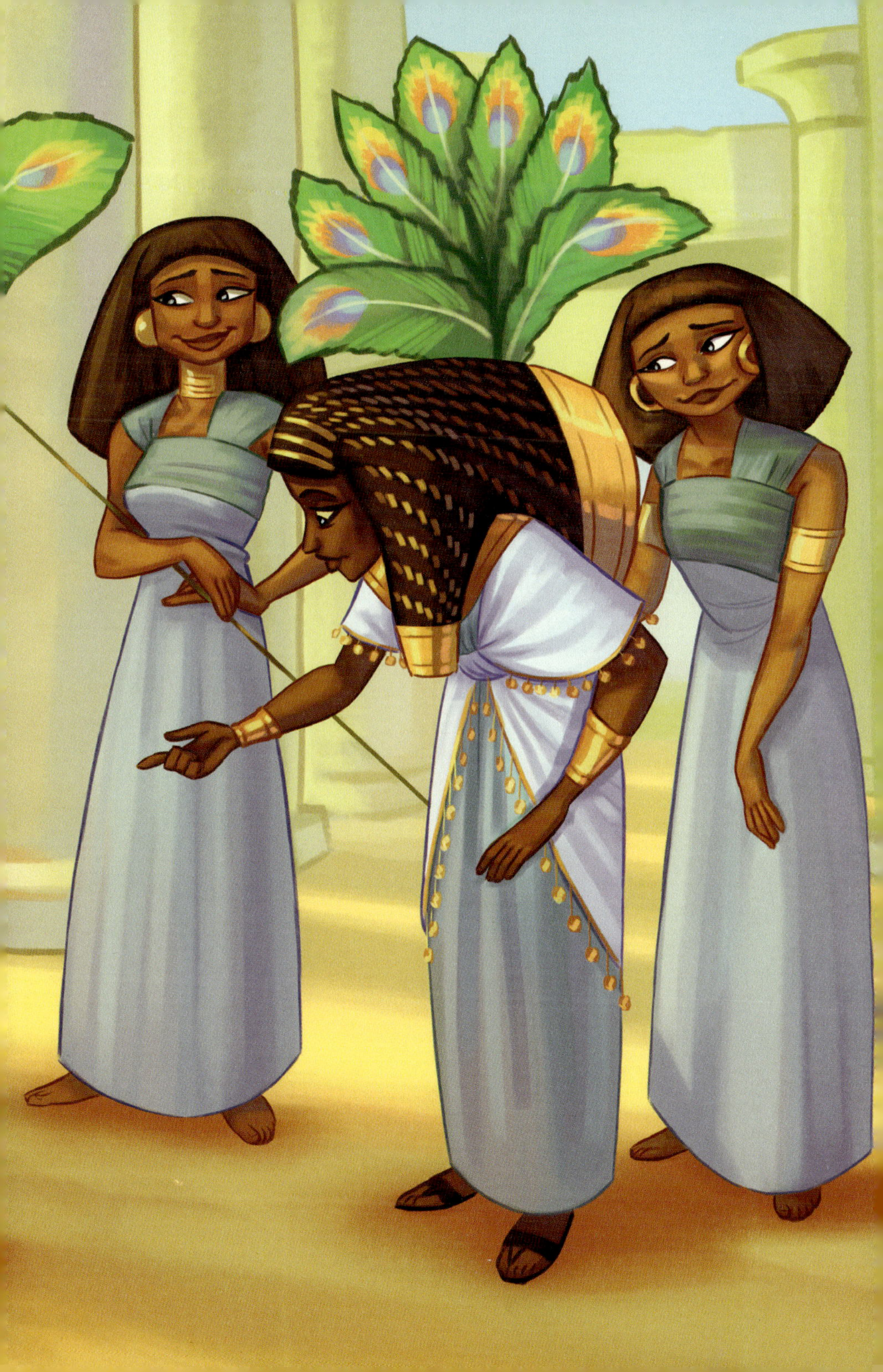

a land of freedom, a land where they could continue to serve and worship the God who would set them free.

> And the king's daughter told her, "Take care of this child, and I will pay you." The baby's mother carried him home and took care of him. And when he was old enough, she took him to the king's daughter, who adopted him. She named him Moses because she said, "I pulled him out of the water."
>
> *Exodus 2:9-10*

OUT OF SLAVERY

Exodus 2–15

One day, when Moses was a young man, he ventured away from the palace to where his own people, the Israelites, were. There he came upon an Egyptian soldier who was beating a Hebrew slave. When Moses thought that no one was around, he attacked the Egyptian and killed him. Moses buried the Egyptian in the sand, hoping no one would know.

The next day, however, Moses tried to break up a fight between two Hebrews. "Why are you fighting?" he shouted. "You are both from the same people!"

"Who made you the judge over us?" one of them shouted back. "Are you going to kill me like you killed that Egyptian?"

Oh no, Moses thought, *they know what I did*.

When Pharaoh heard about what Moses had done, he wanted to have him killed.

Moses didn't know what to do, so he ran. He ran and ran until he was hundreds of miles away from Egypt, from the pharaoh, from the palace, and from the only home he had ever known.

Eventually, he made a new home in a place called Midian. He met a woman named Zipporah, and they married and had two children.

By this time, back in Egypt, the pharaoh had died, but nothing had changed for God's people. They cried out to God, begging him to save them from their horrible life of slavery. Just as Moses was getting comfortable in his new life, God needed someone to lead His people out of their slavery in Egypt.

On an ordinary day when Moses was out with the flocks, he saw something strange up on the side of Mount Horeb, the mountain of God. First he noticed a flicker, then saw that a bush was on fire. After a while, he noticed that the fire wasn't actually burning up the bush.

He went a little closer, then he heard someone calling his name. It wasn't just anyone—it was God!

"Here I am," Moses answered.

"Stop and take off your sandals. You are standing on holy ground," God instructed. "I am the God of your father, the God of Abraham, Isaac, and Jacob."

Moses immediately bowed and hid his face.

The voice of God continued, "My people are suffering, and I have come to rescue them. I will bring them out of the land of Egypt and into the land of Canaan, a land with plenty of room and plenty of food. I am sending you to help them."

"Me?" Moses asked, confused. "How can I help them? Who am I to speak to Pharaoh and lead all of the Israelites out of Egypt?"

"I will be with you," God said simply. "As proof that I have sent you, when you bring the people out of Egypt, you will worship Me, with My people, on this very mountain."

Moses thought a moment, letting it all sink in. "Okay, let's say that I go and say to them, 'The God of your fathers has sent me.' When they ask me Your name, what do I tell them?"

"I AM. Tell them, 'I AM has sent me to you,'" God answered. "The leaders of the Israelites will listen to you, but the king of Egypt will not. After I perform wonders there, he will let my people go. You will walk out with the Israelites, and the Egyptians will even give you clothing and gold and silver as you go."

"But what if the Israelites don't believe me?" Moses asked, still unsure.

"Throw your staff on the ground," God directed him.

Moses did as God had said, and his staff turned into a snake. Moses ran from it, but God said, "Now pick it up by the tail." Moses did, and it turned back into a staff.

"That is how they will know that I sent you," God answered.

"But God," Moses began again, "I've never really been good at speaking."

"Who created the mouth?" God asked. "Who makes it speak?

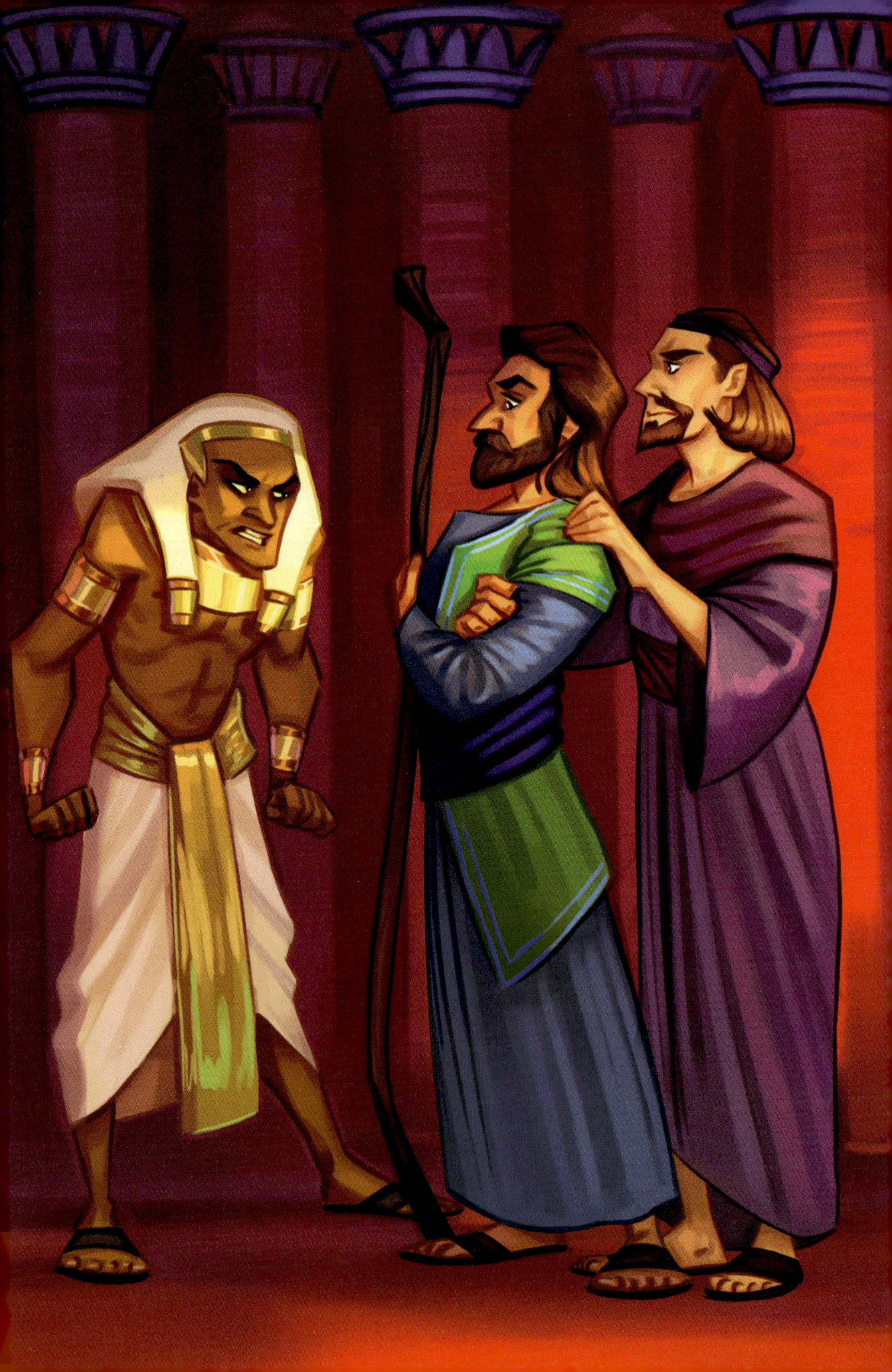

Who created the eyes and gives them sight? Was it not I? Now go. I will give you the words to say."

"Oh, Lord," Moses insisted, "send someone else."

God was angry with Moses, but still wanted to use him for this great mission. He said, "Your brother, Aaron, is already on his way to help you."

Together, Moses and Aaron made the journey to Egypt to tell the Israelites—and the pharaoh—that God was setting His people free. Just as God had said, the Israelites listened to Moses' plan, but Pharaoh did not.

"The Lord?" Pharaoh scoffed at Moses. "Who is that? I don't know your God, and I will not let the Israelites go anywhere." Just to be sure Moses and the Israelites wouldn't dare make another request like that, Pharaoh ordered his taskmasters to make the labor for the Israelite slaves twice as hard.

Moses and Aaron were not deterred, however. They went back to Pharaoh and said, "The God of the Israelites has sent us, and He says, 'If you do not let My people go, I will turn the Nile River to blood!'"

Pharaoh still refused, so God turned the Nile to blood.

Moses warned Pharaoh again. Again, Pharaoh refused. This time, millions of frogs swarmed up out of the river until there were frogs everywhere. There where frogs in ovens, frogs in dishes, frogs in people's sandals, and frogs on their heads. From the palace to the fields, from the highest officials to the lowest workers, no one could escape the swarm of frogs.

"Please! Beg your God to get rid of the frogs!" Pharaoh finally said.

"Okay," Moses replied. "Now let God's people go."

Once the frogs were gone, however, Pharaoh refused to let the Israelites go, and the cycle continued. God covered the land with gnats, sent flies, and wiped out the livestock with disease. He gave the Egyptians festering blisters and sent hail to devastate the trees and crops. He sent locusts to eat everything that was left, followed by a thick, murky darkness. All of Egypt was devastated—except, miraculously, the land of Goshen where the Israelites lived.

Stubbornly, Pharaoh still refused to let the Israelites go.

God said to Moses, "I will send one more plague on the Egyptians: I will kill every firstborn son of Egypt. This time, Pharaoh will beg you to leave and take my people with you."

God told Moses how to protect the Israelites from this final plague, and they obeyed. They painted their doorframes with the blood from the sacrifice of a lamb and waited for God to set them free.

They didn't have to wait very long. Just after midnight, the wails of the Egyptians began to ring out from their homes, from the fields, from the prisons, and from the palace itself. God had taken the firstborn of every family, from the greatest to the least—even the firstborn of the livestock and Pharaoh's own son. Not one family was spared, except for the Israelites, God's people, who had followed His instructions.

"Enough, enough! Go!" Pharaoh commanded Moses and Aaron. "Just leave us. Take the Israelites and take your flocks and go!"

As they went, the Israelites asked the Egyptians for supplies for their journey. Just as God had said, the Egyptians responded by giving them clothes and silver and gold—whatever the Israelites asked for, the Egyptians gave them.

The Israelites, God's people, were on their way—on their way to freedom!

God led them during the day with a tall pillar of cloud and at night with a pillar of fire so that they could see to travel, both day and night. As they reached the Red Sea, however, they heard a rumbling in the distance. They looked up to see a cloud of dust as Pharaoh, with his horses, chariots, and men, came chasing after them.

The Israelites were terrified, immediately forgetting God's great provision. "What have you done?" they shrieked at Moses. "Was there not enough room to bury us in Egypt? Is that why you brought us out into the desert to die?"

Moses answered, as calmly as possible, "Don't be afraid. God will fight for us."

God told Moses, "Why are you standing there crying to Me? Move! Reach out your staff over the sea!"

As Moses obeyed, a hush fell over the hundreds of thousands of Israelites. They watched as a great wind swept through the Red Sea and the waters began to part, to pile up, to stand on end, leaving a dry path for God's people to walk safely through. When the Egyptian soldiers arrived at the edge of the sea, they also followed the path through the middle of the Red Sea, gaining on the Israelites with every thundering step.

When the last Israelite foot stepped on to the other shore, God said, "Now, Moses, stretch out your hand again." Moses obeyed, and when he did, the mighty waves of the Red Sea returned to their rightful place, washing away the soldiers who were chasing after them.

The Israelites were safe. God's people were free.

While the tambourines rang out in celebration and the Israelites joined their voices in song, God looked down and knew that they would all too soon forget His provision and the miracles he had used to save them from slavery.

OUT OF SLAVERY

Moses answered the people, "Do not be afraid. Stand firm and you will see the deliverance the Lord will bring you today. The Egyptians you see today you will never see again. The Lord will fight for you; you need only to be still."

Exodus 14:13-14

THE TEN COMMANDMENTS

Exodus 19-20, 32-34

The journey out of Egypt was long and challenging. It seemed that everywhere Moses and the Israelites turned, there was another problem: no water, no food, then not the right kind of food, and finally, too much food. But everywhere they went, God was also there to provide. When they complained about being thirsty, water gushed out of a rock. When they complained about being hungry, bread fell from the sky. When they were bored with the heavenly food raining down on them, God sent a huge flock of quail so that they could have meat instead.

Still, no matter how much God provided for them, they wanted more. No matter how often He came to their rescue, they always seemed to forget His faithful love for them.

Two months after leaving Egypt—two months full of God's undeniable provision—the Israelites set up camp in the desert at the foot of Mount Sinai. There, Moses delivered another message from God to His people, saying, "You have seen the plagues of Egypt and how I brought you out of there to freedom. Now, if you will obey Me, you will be My people, and I will be your God."

THE TEN COMMANDMENTS

"We will do everything He says!" the people responded in unison.

God called Moses to the top of the mountain where He shared with him Ten Commandments for His people:

1. I am your God. You shall have no other gods besides Me.
2. You shall not have any idols.
3. You shall not misuse My name.
4. Keep the Sabbath holy by making it a day of rest.
5. Honor your father and mother.
6. Don't murder.
7. Don't commit adultery.
8. Don't steal.
9. Don't lie about your neighbor.
10. Don't be jealous of anything your neighbor has.

After Moses had received these rules, written on stone tablets, he stayed on the mountain with God for forty days and forty nights. After a while, the people started to wonder if he was ever coming back.

Giving up on Moses, the people told Aaron, "Make some new gods for us."

Rather than standing up for what was right, Aaron obeyed the people. He gathered their earrings, melted them down, and made an idol in the shape of a calf for the people to worship.

"Here it is!" the people said. "Here is the god who rescued us from slavery in Egypt!"

The people loved their idol so much that Aaron built an altar in front of it and said, "Tomorrow we'll have a celebration!"

That's exactly what they did. As they ate and drank and celebrated their new "god," God told Moses, "It's time for you to go back down. The people have already turned away from Me and are worshiping an idol!"

Moses went down the mountain with the two stone tablets. When he got closer to the camp, he saw the people dancing around the calf. This made him so angry that he threw the tablets on the ground and they shattered into pieces. He took the calf, melted it in the fire, ground it into dust, and put it into water.

As a punishment, Moses made the Israelites drink the water he had put the ground up idol in.

He turned to Aaron and said, "What were you thinking? Why did you lead them to this horrible sin?"

"They made me!" Aaron answered. "I just threw their gold into the fire, and out came a calf!"

"Lord," Moses prayed, "please forgive these people for this sin against You."

Although God punished their sin, He would still not abandon His people. After a few days, God called Moses again. "Moses," God said, "cut two tablets from stone and bring them up the

THE TEN COMMANDMENTS

mountain." Moses did just as God said, and as he climbed Mount Sinai early that morning, God came down in a cloud and said, "The Lord is compassionate, gracious, slow to anger, and full of love, faithfulness, and forgiveness."

Moses stayed in God's presence for forty days. He descended the mountain again, a new set of stone tablets in hand, and his face shone with the glory of God as Moses presented the tablets to the Israelites.

The Commandments that God had given to His people are much more than a list of rules. Engraved in stone by His own hand, they are instructions on how to live, given to humans by their Creator. They reveal God's nature and His values. They show what is needed in order to please Him, the perfect God.

God knew exactly what His people needed to live the most fruitful life possible. He told them Himself, using His own loving hand and two stone signs. He was pointing them down the right path to the best life ever.

And God spoke all these words:
"I am the Lord your God, who brought you out of Egypt, out of the land of slavery.
"You shall have no other gods before me."
Exodus 20:1-3

JOSHUA'S IMPOSSIBLE VICTORY

Joshua 1–6

Moses had faithfully led God's people all the way from Egypt to the edge of the Promised Land, the land of Canaan. But that, God told him, is where his duties would end.

Throughout the Exodus journey and all through the wilderness, a young man named Joshua had shown himself to be a strong leader of great faith, never doubting the promises God had in store for His people. Just before he died, Moses presented Joshua as the new leader of God's people. Moses encouraged Joshua to be strong and brave; he reminded him that God would always be with him.

Joshua wasted no time in leading God's people to their purpose, to the Promised Land. "Tell the people to get ready!" he said. "In three days, we will cross the Jordan into the land that God is giving us."

Joshua sent spies to check out the land, but the king of Jericho noticed the spies entering his city. "Find them!" the king demanded. The spies ran for their lives and hid in the house of a woman named Rahab. Rahab saw that the men were Israelites, but she agreed to hide them anyway. The king sent his men to Rahab's house. "Where are the men who came to your house?" they asked. "Give them to us!"

"Oh, those men?" Rahab asked, batting her eyelashes. "They've already left through the city gate. Hurry and you'll catch them!" The king's guards turned and ran in the direction of the city gate.

"They're gone now," Rahab whispered to the spies, who were hiding under some flax. She explained to the spies how the whole country had been talking about them, how they had heard that God was giving their land to the Israelites, and how they feared God's people and what was to come. Rahab's house was built into the city wall so that one window was an opening in the wall itself. She handed a rope to the spies and showed them the window. "Use this rope to lower yourselves down outside the city wall," she said. Before they left, she begged them, "Please, remember my family and the kindness I have shown to you."

"Of course," the men answered. "If you'll tie this red cord on your window, we will keep you and your family safe when we come back to take this land." The men reported to Joshua all that had happened.

Early the next morning, the Israelites packed up and left the camp. The priests hoisted the poles of the ark of the covenant—a large, holy chest carrying the Ten Commandments—onto their shoulders and walked toward the Jordan River. All the people followed.

The sound of rushing waters grew louder as they came closer. The Jordan was overflowing, as it usually did at harvest time. When the first priest's toe touched the water, however, the waters stopped. The raging river became a dry riverbed and the waters piled up near a town several miles upstream. The priests stood there, in the middle of the dry river, until every single one of God's precious people passed over to the other side.

Right there on the riverbank, the Israelites set up a monument of twelve stones, taken from the bed of the Jordan River, to remind them of God's power and provision—of how he had dried up a raging river for His people to pass into their Promised Land.

The Israelites had arrived! They had entered the land that the Lord their God had given them. It wasn't time to celebrate just yet though. There was still one huge problem: the wall that stretched around the entire city of Jericho. No one was coming out, and no one was getting in—especially not the Israelites. At least, that's what the people of Jericho thought.

The Israelites weren't discouraged, however. A freshly stacked pile of stones from the Jordan River reminded Joshua of God's faithfulness and power. Again, he looked to the Lord. "What do we do now?" he prayed.

While the troops on both sides of the wall braced for battle, God gave Joshua these simple instructions: "March around the city in silence, once a day, for six days. On the seventh day, march around seven times. When the priests give a long blast of the trumpets, have the whole army shout. The wall will fall, and everyone can walk in."

It had to be one of the strangest battle plans that Joshua had ever heard, but he also knew that seas split, water shot out of rocks, bread fell from the sky, and raging rivers went dry when God was in charge.

Joshua passed the commands along to the people. They did just as God instructed. On the seventh day, when the trumpet sounded, the men shouted, and that big wall fell to the ground! God's people walked right in to the now unprotected city of Jericho.

"Look! The red cord!" Joshua said. "Go bring out Rahab and her family." The men who had spied for Joshua nodded knowingly and ran to save the woman who had saved them.

A pile of stones, a scarlet cord, a freshly fallen wall, and the Promised Land beneath their feet—with all of these reminders of God's power and provision, would the Israelites finally come to trust in God's faithfulness?

"Have I not commanded you? Be strong and courageous. Do not be afraid; do not be discouraged, for the Lord your God will be with you wherever you go."

Joshua 1:9

AN UNLIKELY HERO

Judges 6–7

After many years in the Promised Land, the Israelites strayed far from their loyalty to God and His Commandments. God sent judges to lead and guide them, but time after time, His people turned to their own ways instead of seeking and following God. Eventually, God gave the Israelites over to be ruled by the Midianites. The Midianites were so harsh that the Israelites went into hiding, building their homes in mountains and caves and other hidden places. The Midianites were so destructive during their raids—ruining crops and taking livestock—that they left very little for the Israelites to live on. With nowhere to turn, the Israelites once again cried out to the Lord for help.

About that same time, a young man named Gideon was hiding down in a winepress, threshing wheat. Gideon knew that if the Midianites saw the cloud of dust from the chaff, if they saw him threshing wheat, they would come steal his family's food. While he was hiding down there, an angel appeared to him and said, "God is with you, mighty warrior."

Gideon looked around. Surely this angel wasn't talking to him, a young man hiding in a winepress. He replied, "If God is with us, then why is all of this happening to us?"

"I am sending you to save your people," the angel said.

"Who am I to save anyone, much less all of Israel?" Gideon asked. "My family is the weakest family in the tribe, and I'm the least in my family!"

The Lord answered Gideon, "I will be with you, and you will defeat the Midianites."

"Okay," Gideon answered. "If this is really true, give me a sign. I'll place this wool cloth on the floor. Tomorrow, if there is dew on the cloth, but the ground is dry, then I will know that you are sending me to save Israel, just as you said."

The next day, Gideon awoke to a dry floor and a dew-soaked cloth. He wrung out the dew, filling a whole bowl with water.

Even though he had received his sign, Gideon wasn't convinced. "Okay, God," he said, "don't be mad, but can You send me one more sign?" This time Gideon reversed his request, asking God to make the wool dry and the ground wet with dew. That night, God did just as Gideon asked, keeping the wool dry while covering the ground with dew.

Finally convinced, Gideon began to assemble his army. Before long, Gideon had gathered more than thirty thousand men. Then Gideon heard from God. "You have too many men. If you defeat Midian with that army, you'll think you were saved by your own strength," God explained. "Tell the men that if any of them are afraid, they may return home to their families."

Gideon did as God had said and watched as twenty-two thousand men left his camp.

God looked at the ten thousand men who were still there and said, "There are still too many. Take them to the water and watch them drink. If they drink out of their cupped hands, they can stay, but if they get on their knees to drink, send them home."

Only three hundred men drank from their hands. Gideon watched his army—once more than thirty-thousand strong—shrink down to only three hundred men.

"Now!" God said. "Now you're ready to attack the Midianites!"

The numbers made no sense to Gideon. Even though he trusted God's plan, he just couldn't see how three hundred men could defeat the entire Midianite army. To help Gideon understand, God told him, "Go down to the camp, and just listen to what those Midianites are saying."

Late that night, Gideon and his helper snuck into the Midianite camp. Wading through the masses of tents, people, and camels, they stopped when they heard a man talking nervously about a dream that he'd had.

"A loaf of bread just rolled into our camp, and it hit the tent so hard that the tent collapsed!" he exclaimed.

AN UNLIKELY HERO

"Then it's true!" his friend cried. "God has given the Midianites over to Gideon the Israelite!"

Hearing what the Midianites said, Gideon fell on his knees and thanked God. He ran back to camp. "Wake up, everyone!" he called. "Get up! God has given the Midianites to us!"

Gideon handed his men trumpets and empty jars, and they placed flaming torches inside the jars. "Now, follow me!" Gideon shouted.

Not only were they now a tiny army of three hundred men, but they were going to defeat a massive army using only clay jars, torches, and trumpets?

Gideon didn't hesitate. He followed God's instructions and marched forward confidently. When he and his men had encircled the camp, Gideon sent word, "Watch me and do as I do."

Gideon blew his trumpet, so all the men blew along with him. Gideon smashed his jar on the ground then held his torch high, and his men did the same. Together, they shouted, "For the Lord and for Gideon!"

Then they waited, and they watched.

Suddenly, the masses of Midianites began to scatter like mice, screaming and squealing as they ran. Confused by the powerful blast of three hundred trumpets, they began fighting each other, striking their own men with their swords. Gideon and his army watched their unlikely victory unfold just as God had promised.

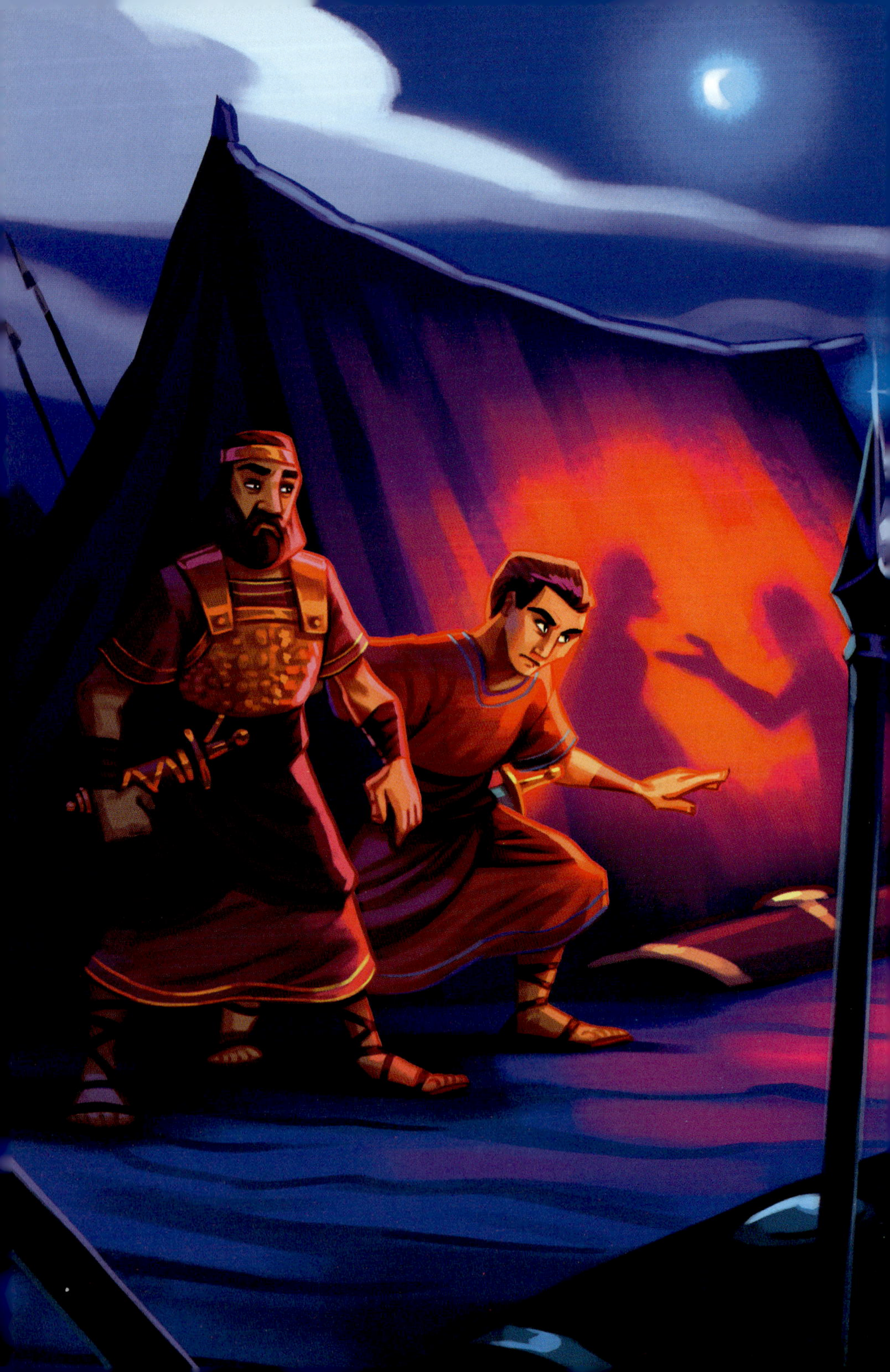

AN UNLIKELY HERO

The next morning, the sun rose on Gideon and his three hundred men, triumphant against the masses of Midianites.

God had sought out Gideon, the smallest man from the weakest clan, to lead an army to save His people. When Gideon placed his small, human hand in the mighty hand of God, he became a powerful warrior, defeating the intimidating forces that were oppressing his people. That same power, that same protection, that same Almighty God is right there waiting, available to us all, if we will only trust Him with the battles He leads us to fight.

> *Gideon replied, "But how can I rescue Israel? My clan is the weakest one in Manasseh, and everyone else in my family is more important than I am." "Gideon," the Lord answered, "you can rescue Israel because I am going to help you! Defeating the Midianites will be as easy as beating up one man."*
>
> Judges 6:15-16 CEV

SAMSON'S SUPERNATURAL STRENGTH

Judges 13–16

Many years had passed since God had led Gideon to save His people from the Midianites. Once again, the Israelites had turned away from obeying God. As a result, they found themselves under the harsh rule of the Philistines for forty years.

An angel of the Lord appeared to an Israelite woman. "I know you haven't been able to have children," he said, "but you are going to have a son." The woman listened, wide-eyed, as the angel spoke. "He will belong to God from the day he is born, so his hair must never be cut. Even before he is born you must not drink any wine or eat any foods forbidden by God's laws. Your son will begin to deliver Israel from the Philistines."

The woman couldn't believe what she had just heard. She ran to tell her husband the news, and together they prepared for the birth of their son. When he was born, they named him Samson.

God blessed Samson as he grew, and when he was ready to marry, he chose a Philistine woman. "Samson, couldn't you find someone from our people, another Israelite?" his parents asked, but Samson had made up his mind—he would marry a

SAMSON'S SUPERNATURAL STRENGTH

Philistine. In doing so, Samson was unknowingly setting in motion God's plan to defeat the Philistines and deliver His people.

Samson and his parents set out toward the town of Timnah to meet with his future bride. As Samson was walking alone, a lion suddenly jumped toward him with a fierce roar. With the incredible strength that God had given him, Samson fought and killed the lion using his bare hands.

Later, when Samson went back to Timnah for his wedding, he saw the dead lion lying on the ground. A swarm of bees had made a honeycomb inside the carcass, so Samson scooped out the honey and ate some as he walked. He shared it with his parents, too, but didn't tell them where the honey came from.

At the wedding feast, Samson told a riddle to the thirty other young men who were there: "Out of the eater, something to eat; out of the strong, something sweet. If you can answer this riddle within the seven days of the feast," Samson challenged them, "I will give you thirty sets of clothes! But if you can't answer it, *you* have to give *me* thirty sets of clothes."

For three days, the thirty men tried to figure out the answer, but they couldn't. On the fourth day, they went to Samson's wife, threatening her. "If you don't tell us the answer," they said, "we'll burn down your family's house with everyone in it!"

Samson's wife ran to him, crying, "Why did you do this to me? Do you hate me? Why would you give my friends a riddle and not tell me the answer? Tell me!"

But Samson refused. "I haven't even told my parents," he said. "Why would I tell you?"

For all of the remaining days of the feast, morning and night, Samson's wife cried, begging him to tell her the answer. Finally, on the seventh day, he gave in.

Soon after, the men of the town came to Samson, smiling

sneakily, and said, "What is sweeter than honey? What is stronger than a lion?"

Samson realized that he had been beaten, betrayed by his wife. In his anger, with his gift of strength, he went to a nearby town and stripped thirty men of their clothing. He marched back into Timnah and gave the clothes to the men who had answered the riddle. Furious and defeated, Samson returned home, leaving his wife behind with her family.

Several months later, Samson returned to visit his wife, taking a young goat as a gift. Her father wouldn't let Samson in, however. "I thought you hated her!" the father said. "I gave her to marry another man!"

Again, Samson was furious. *I'll show them*, he thought. He caught three hundred foxes, tied pairs of them together by their tails, and tied a flaming torch to each set of foxes. Then he turned the foxes loose to run through the grain fields of the Philistines, dragging the torches behind them. Flames lashed at the Philistines' crops—their grain, their grapes, their olives—everything was destroyed!

When the Philistines saw the devastation, they wanted to know who or what had caused their food to go up in flames and why. When they found out, they responded by burning Samson's wife and her father to death.

This only made Samson angrier. Then and there, he swore to never stop until he had defeated the Philistines.

The Philistines, meanwhile, had plans of their own to defeat Samson. After all, what was one man against an entire nation of people? What they didn't realize, however, was that this wasn't just any man. Even with all of his faults and failings, Samson was chosen and strengthened by an almighty God, who had sent him to deliver His people.

Samson hid out in a cave for a while, then one night he went into Gaza to visit a woman. When the Philistines found out he was in their town, they decided to kill him at sunrise. They lay in wait for him by the city gate, which was locked for the night. Their plans were foiled, however, when in the middle of the night, Samson got up and went to the gate. He ripped it loose from the city wall and walked out to a nearby hill, carrying the gate on his shoulders.

As time went by, Samson met a woman named Delilah and fell in love with her. When the Philistine leaders heard about it, they went to Delilah. "Oh, have we got a deal for you!" they tempted. "We will each give you a pile of silver if you will do a favor for us." Delilah listened more intently as the man leaned in to whisper, "If you can find out the secret of Samson's incredible strength, the silver is yours." Delilah smiled.

"Samson," Delilah cooed, combing her fingers through his hair, "how did you get so big and strong?"

"Well," Samson grinned, "I'm only strong until someone ties me up with seven fresh bowstrings."

Delilah told the Philistine leaders what Samson had said. They brought her the seven bowstrings and hid nearby, waiting. After Delilah had tied Samson up with the bowstrings, she yelled, "Samson, the Philistines are coming!" Samson sat up, snapping the strings like dry twigs.

"Oh, Samson," Delilah scolded, "you tricked me! Now tell me the truth."

"All right," Samson smiled. "The truth is, if you tie me with new ropes, I'll be as weak as any other guy."

Again, Delilah tied him up, using new ropes this time, while the Philistines waited. Again, when Delilah shouted, "The Philistines are coming!" Samson broke through the ropes with no problem at all.

Delilah pouted. "You're always lying to me, making me look stupid." She crossed her arms and turned her back to him. "Tell me the truth," she demanded.

"Okay, okay, if you weave my seven braids into the loom, I'll lose all my strength," Samson said.

Delilah smiled sweetly. As soon as she had the chance, she gently wove Samson's seven braids into the loom. Of course, as soon as she said, "The Philistines are here!" he awoke and pulled himself free.

Delilah refused to give up though. She whined and nagged and begged, day after day after day, until finally, Samson told her. He really told her the truth. "I am a Nazirite," Samson said. "My hair has never been cut. If it were, I would lose my power and have the strength of any other man."

Delilah's pout changed into a grin. She knew that this time, finally, Samson had told her the secret. The Philistines would capture him, and she would have her silver.

As soon as Samson fell asleep on her lap, Delilah called for the razor. She watched as one, two, three, and soon, all seven of his braids fell to the floor.

"Samson, the Philistines are here!" Delilah cried.

Samson sat up confidently, as he had done each time before, ready to overpower the Philistines. As they grabbed Samson he quickly flexed his shoulders, but nothing happened! He tried to push away their grip, but they wouldn't budge. The power of God had left him. His strength was gone.

The Philistines blinded Samson, bound him, and put him to work in a prison. There in that prison, Samson's hair began to grow again.

After a while, the Philistine leaders all gathered to congratulate themselves on their victory over Samson. They prepared sacrifices to thank their god Dagon for their success, for giving them Samson. After much celebration, someone cried, "Hey, where is Samson, anyway? Go get him so that he can entertain us!" The crowd laughed and cheered as Samson was presented and placed between the pillars of the temple.

The huge crowd stopped and stared. This legend of strength, propelled by the power of God, was now nothing but a prison slave. Thousands watched as he seemed to borrow the strength from a pillar to hold himself upright.

"What's he mumbling?" one of them asked, smirking at this great enemy who seemed to have been reduced to a babbling weakling.

Only those near Samson could hear the words he whispered. He turned his face to the sky and said, "Remember me, God. Just one more time, give me the strength to destroy the Philistines." Then he reached from one pillar to the other, holding within his grip the support of the entire temple. "Now, let me die with the Philistines!" he shouted. As the words left him, he pushed against the pillars.

Filled with the power of God once more, he brought the temple down on himself and everyone in it.

After his death, Samson would be remembered as one of Israel's most powerful leaders. For twenty years God had given Samson amazing strength. For twenty years Samson had used it to protect the Israelites from the Philistines.

With that one final act of God-given strength, Samson sacrificed his own life and secured the defeat of the Philistines—and the deliverance of God's people.

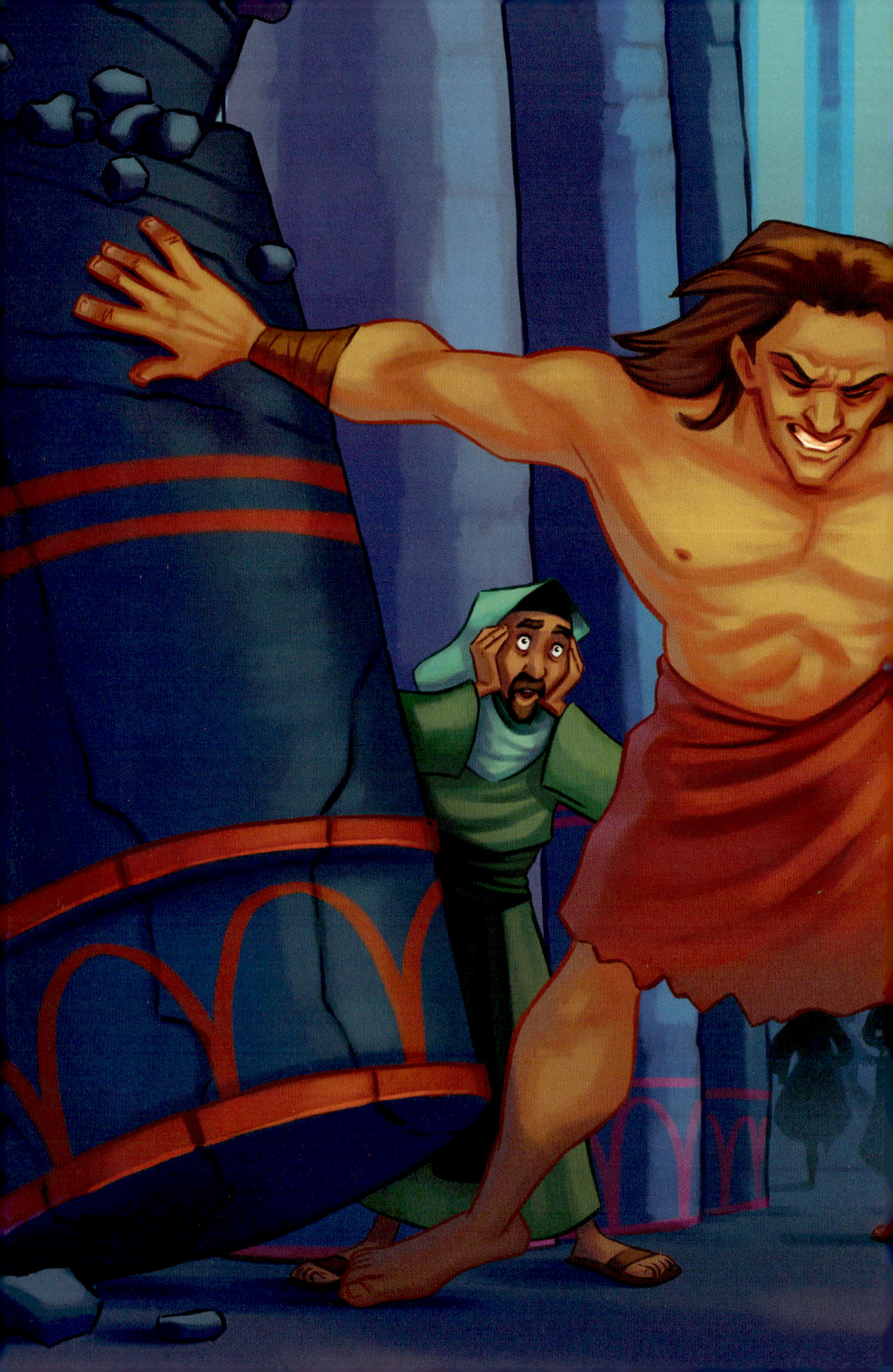

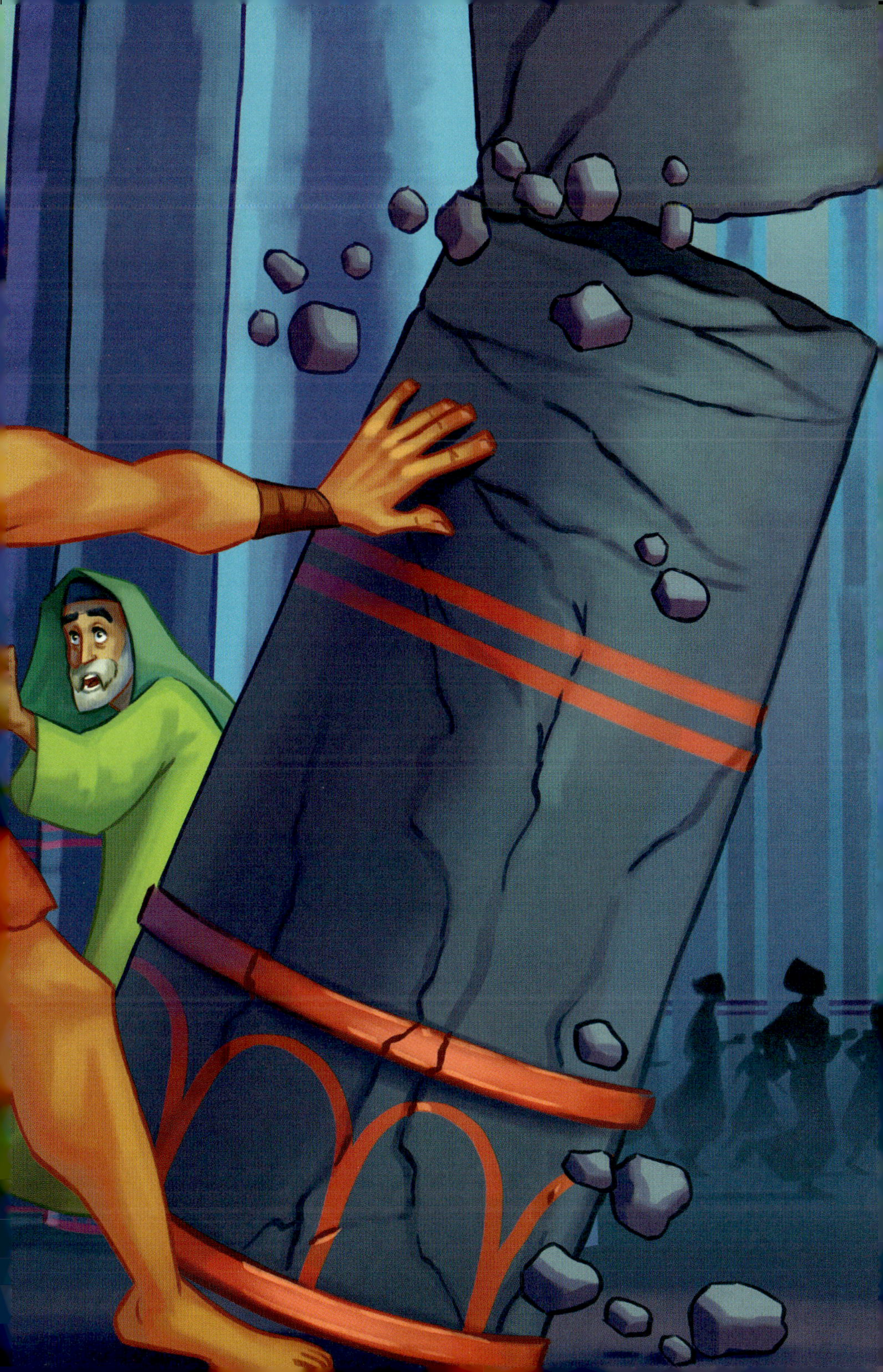

Of course, Samson was only human. His protection wasn't perfect, nor was it permanent. One day God would send another leader, another protector—all God and all man in one perfect package—to finally offer His people a perfect, permanent protection to see them through to eternity.

> *"You will become pregnant and have a son whose head is never to be touched by a razor because the boy is to be a Nazirite, dedicated to God from the womb. He will take the lead in delivering Israel from the hands of the Philistines."*
>
> Judges 13:5

WHERE YOU GO I'LL GO

The Book of Ruth

When a famine struck the land of Israel, a man named Elimelek moved his wife Naomi and his two sons to the neighboring country of Moab. While they were there Elimelek died, and his two sons married women from Moab. One son married a woman named Orpah and the other married a woman named Ruth. After living in Moab for about ten years, the two sons died as well, leaving Naomi heartbroken, bitter, and alone. She was far from her hometown with no sons and no husband to support her.

As soon as Naomi heard that the famine was over in Israel, she called her daughters-in-law to her.

"I am returning to Bethlehem, my home in Israel," she told them. "You must return to your homes. Because of the love you have shown to my family, I know that the Lord will bless you with the love and happiness of a new family."

"No!" they cried. "We will go with you!"

"Why?" Naomi responded. "I have nothing to offer you. I have no husband and no sons for you to marry. There is no more hope for me, but there is for you—you can still have a family. Now go! Go and find happiness again!"

The women cried and clung to one another. Finally, Orpah kissed her mother-in-law goodbye and set out to return home.

Ruth, however, still refused to leave Naomi.

"Ruth, go!" Naomi insisted. "Orpah is leaving. Go back with her!"

Through her tears, Ruth looked up at her mother-in-law. "Don't," Ruth whispered firmly. "Don't ask me to leave you. Wherever you go, I will go. Wherever you stay, I will stay. Your God will be my God. Wherever you die, I will die."

Naomi didn't know what to say. She knew that no matter what she said, she wouldn't convince Ruth to go back home and start a new life. Instead, the two women set out together for Bethlehem.

Ruth and Naomi arrived in Bethlehem just as the barley harvest was beginning. "We're going to need some food," Ruth said. "I'll go into the fields and see if someone will let me pick up their leftover grain." She walked until she saw a field being harvested and fell in behind the workers, picking up what they had missed.

The field Ruth had chosen just so happened to belong to a man named Boaz, a relative of Naomi's late husband, Elimelek. Boaz saw Ruth gathering grain behind his harvesters and asked, "Who is that woman?"

"She is the Moabite woman who just came back with Naomi,"

his workers said. "She asked if she could gather leftover grain, and now she has been out there since early this morning, only stopping for a short rest."

Boaz strode out into the fields, catching up with Ruth. "Listen, daughter," he said, "please stay here, working with the other women. Don't go to another field. When you're thirsty, please drink from the jars the men have filled."

Shocked by his generosity, Ruth bowed at his feet. "Why—why would you be so kind to me, a foreigner, a stranger?" she asked him.

"I've heard about you," he answered with a kind smile. "I heard that you left everything behind after the death of your own husband to care for your mother-in-law. I only pray that you are rewarded for all that you have done for her."

"I—I thank you, my lord," Ruth answered, still bowing.

At mealtime, Boaz called to Ruth. "Come, eat with us."

Ruth ate until she was full and left to continue gathering grain. After she had left, Boaz told his men, "Let her gather whatever she wants. You may even drop some on the ground for her to gather."

Ruth gathered until the evening. She threshed out the grain—piles and piles of it—and hurried back to her mother-in-law to show her what she had gotten.

"Where on earth did you get all of that grain?" Naomi asked.

Ruth grinned and told her all about Boaz and the kindness he had shown to her.

"Well, God bless him!" Naomi exclaimed. "God has not stopped showing kindness to us or our family. Boaz is actually our close relative and he is supposed to help us if we need it. He was a close relative of Elimelek."

"He asked me to come back," Ruth added. "He's asked me to stay until all of the barley and wheat are harvested!"

"Oh, that's wonderful, my daughter!" Naomi said. "Yes, stay there. You will be safe in Boaz's fields, and we will have plenty."

One day, Naomi looked at Ruth and smiled. She had an idea. "Now, daughter, you can't live here with me forever, taking care of your old mother-in-law alone, without a family of your own. We must find a home for you, a place where you will be happy and have everything you need."

Ruth listened as Naomi presented her plan. Naomi said, "Boaz, you know, is a relative. As our close relative, he is also the guardian of our family. That means he would take care of us—of you—if we asked. I know just where he'll be tonight after work."

"Okay," Ruth said, a little excited, a little nervous, and a little embarrassed. "I'll do as you say."

Ruth got dressed in her best clothes and dabbed on a little perfume, following the instructions of her mother-in-law. She found Boaz exactly where Naomi had said: on the threshing floor, asleep.

Quietly, she walked over to him and lay by his feet.

In the middle of the night, Boaz awoke suddenly to find Ruth lying at his feet. "Who, what—what are you doing here?" he asked.

"It's me, Ruth, your servant," she said quickly. "Naomi said that you are the guardian of her family, of our family. Since you are our closest living relative, will you help us?"

Boaz took a deep breath and smiled. He said, "Yes, yes. It is true. I am the guardian for the family, and I am honored that you asked. Everyone knows what a kind and generous woman you are." His smile faded as he continued, "Since there is a closer member of the family, I must check with him first. If he will not redeem you and your property, I would be happy to."

Ruth thanked Boaz and hurried back to tell Naomi everything.

"Just you wait," Naomi said, hugging Ruth close. "He won't rest until everything is settled."

Naomi was right: Boaz quickly returned and asked Ruth to become his wife. They were married and soon had a son, Obed, giving Ruth the new family that Naomi had wanted her to have ever since they left Moab. Ruth also stayed true to her promise to Naomi. She never left her, and what's more, she gave Naomi a new family to love and be a part of.

God had blessed Ruth's kindness and loyalty—not only in the present life of her new family, but also in the future of her family

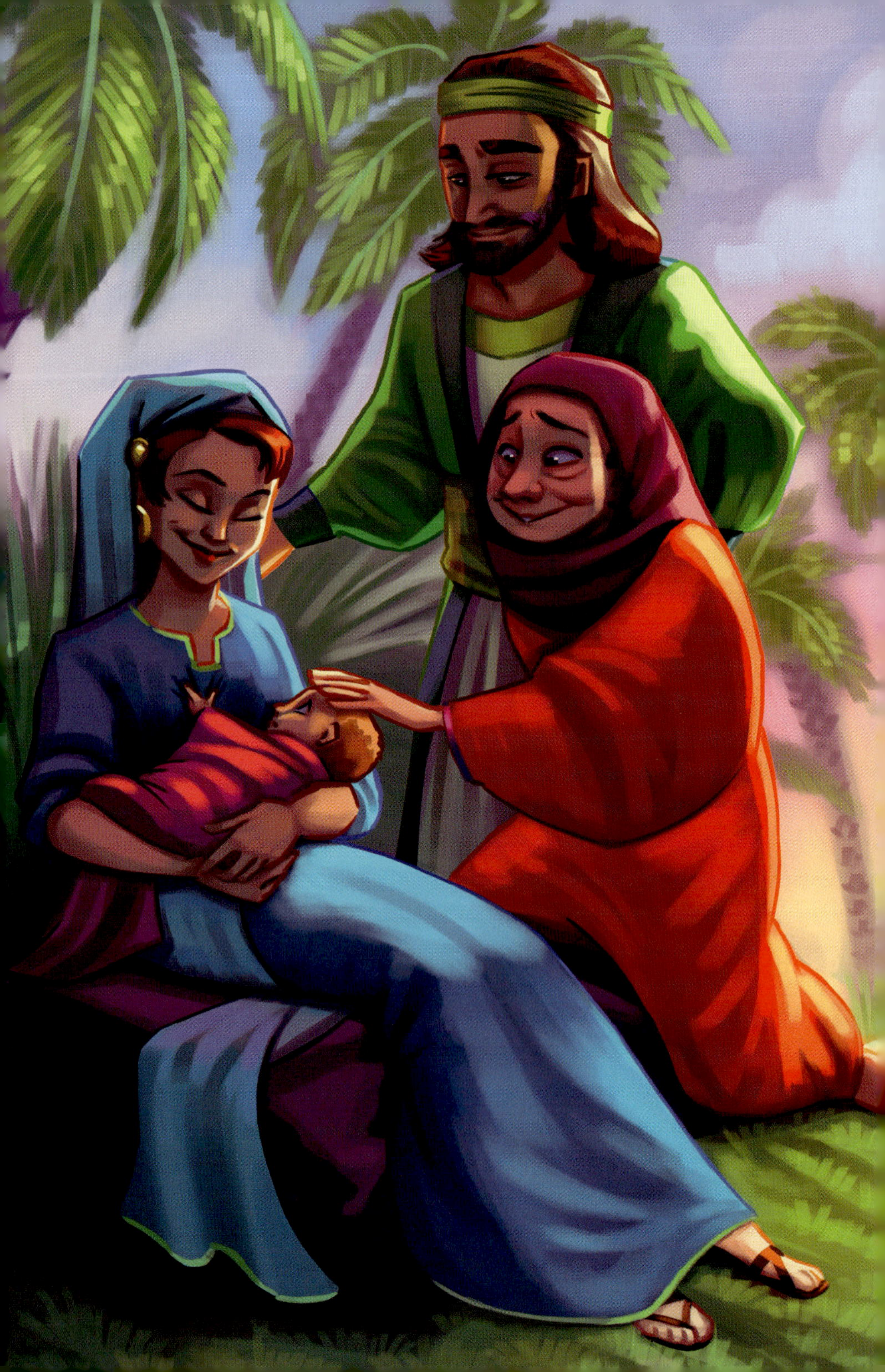

to come. You see, Obed would be the grandfather to Israel's most famous king: King David.

Ruth's family wouldn't stop there, however. Generations after King David, a new King, a descendant of David, would be born in Bethlehem. He would be the King of kings, unlike any king the world had ever seen. He would be laid in a lowly manger under a glorious, starry sky. The God of love and light would sleep peacefully on a bed of hay, waiting for the day that He, too, would be called on as a guardian-redeemer—the Redeemer of the world.

*Boaz replied, "I've been told all about what you have done for your mother-in-law since the death of your husband—how you left your father and mother and your homeland to come and live with a people you did not know before. May the L*ord *repay you for what you have done. May you be richly rewarded by the L*ord*, the God of Israel, under whose wings you have come to take refuge."*

Ruth 2:11-12

THE BOY WHO HEARD GOD'S VOICE

1 Samuel 1–3

There was a man who lived in Ramah, near Bethlehem, named Elkanah. Elkanah had two wives: Hannah and Peninnah. Every year, Elkanah and his family traveled to Shiloh to worship and make sacrifices to God. Elkanah would serve Peninnah and her children some meat from the sacrifice, but he would give Hannah twice as much. He did this because he loved Hannah and knew that she was sad because she couldn't have children.

Even though the trips to Shiloh were a time of worship and celebration, every year Peninnah would provoke and make fun of Hannah because she had no children. This always left Hannah crying, and she was so upset that she would not eat. Elkanah worried about Hannah and tried to comfort her, but it didn't help.

During one trip, at the end of the meal, Hannah stood up abruptly and went somewhere her crying would be heard by God alone. She stood in the shadows of the tabernacle, praying and weeping, pleading with God to remember her and to give her a son. "If you will only let me have one son," she said, "I will dedicate him to your service for the rest of his life."

Through the blur of her tears, Hannah hadn't seen Eli the priest sitting by the door of the tabernacle, but he had seen her. He watched her lips moving, but she made no sound that he could hear. "Woman," he scolded, startling Hannah from her depths of prayer, "you have drunk too much wine!"

"I haven't," Hannah said, shaking her head. "I just needed some time alone with God. He's the only One who knows my deep sadness, and He is the only One who can help."

Eli's voice softened. "Go, then," he said. "Go with peace, and may our God relieve your sadness, giving you what you ask."

Hannah looked up at Eli and nodded. Her sadness had lifted, and her appetite had returned. She rejoined the feast that night, and the next morning they traveled back home to Ramah.

Before long, Hannah began to feel a little funny, a feeling that she couldn't quite describe, that she had never felt before. That funny feeling quickly transformed into complete joy as Hannah realized that, finally, she was pregnant! God had heard her prayer!

Hannah would no longer have to live in shame; she wouldn't have to listen to Peninnah's insults any longer. She was going to have a baby!

A few months later, Hannah gave birth to a beautiful son.

She and Elkanah named him Samuel, which means "God has heard." As she stroked her son's hair, listening to his coos, she remembered her promise. She would soon give this precious little gift back to the Lord.

"Where are we going, Mama?" Samuel asked, watching his mother. She packed up flour and wine in a bag, then tied a harness on a young bull from Elkanah's herd.

"We're going to the tabernacle, Samuel," she answered, "to your new home."

Together, Hannah and Samuel made the journey to Shiloh, where the priest Eli greeted them. "Do you remember me?" Hannah asked him. "I stood here, praying to the Lord—praying for this child."

A smile of recognition grew across Eli's face. He nodded.

Hannah brushed a tear from her cheek and continued, "God gave me exactly what I asked of Him, and now, I give this child back to God."

Eli looked at the woman in disbelief and welcomed the young boy into the tabernacle.

Every year from then on, Elkanah's family continued to travel to Shiloh to bring their sacrifices and worship the Lord. During those trips, Hannah would visit Samuel, bringing him a new robe that she had made for him. Over the years, God honored

Hannah's great sacrifice by giving her three more sons and two daughters.

There in Shiloh, under Eli's guidance, Samuel grew into a strong young man who loved the Lord. Eli was also growing older, and his sight was failing him.

Samuel slept in the tabernacle, where the ark of the covenant was kept. One night, he heard someone call his name.

Samuel jumped out of bed and ran to Eli's side, saying, "Yes sir, here I am!"

Eli was confused. "Samuel, I didn't call you, son," he said. "Go back to bed."

A few minutes later, Samuel heard it again.

"Yes, Eli," he panted, "I'm here."

"Samuel, I didn't call you. Now go back to bed," Eli repeated.

Later, Samuel heard the voice a third time and returned to Eli's side. "Eli, you called me," he said. "I heard you. Here I am."

Then Eli realized that someone had been calling Samuel after all. "Samuel, son, go back to bed," he explained. "If you hear the voice again, answer, 'Speak to me, God. I am your servant and I am listening.'"

Still a little confused, Samuel returned to bed and waited. "Samuel! Samuel!" the voice called.

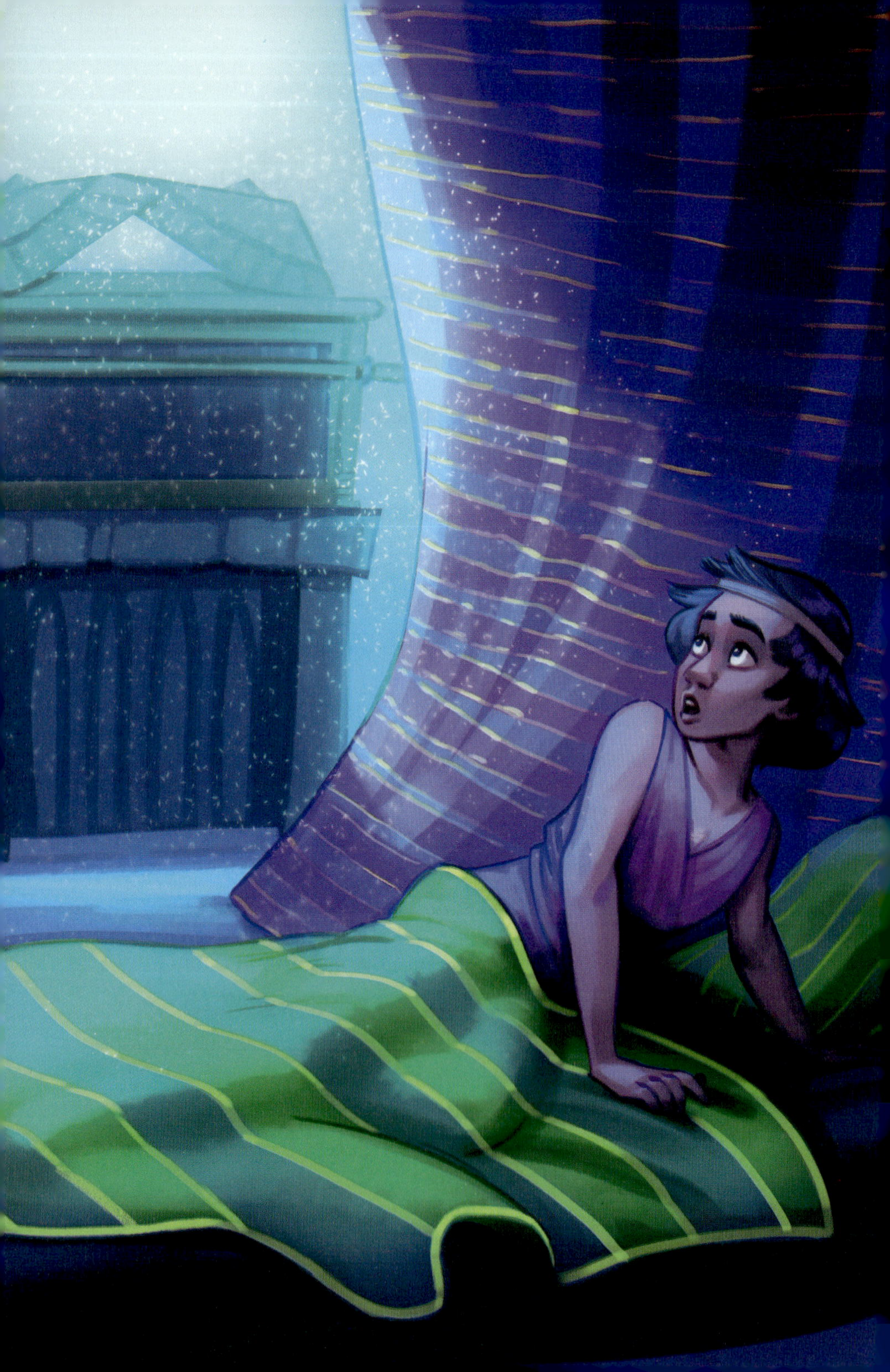

He sat straight up in bed. "Yes! Speak to me, Lord. I am listening!" he said.

From that moment on, God spoke to Samuel. Throughout Samuel's lifetime, God would reveal future happenings and great truths, trusting Samuel to carry His words to His people. Just as he had done as a young man in the tabernacle, Samuel obeyed, answering the Lord whenever He called.

> *The Lord was with Samuel as he grew up, and he let none of Samuel's words fall to the ground. And all Israel from Dan to Beersheba recognized that Samuel was attested as a prophet of the Lord. The Lord continued to appear at Shiloh, and there he revealed himself to Samuel through his word.*
>
> 1 Samuel 3:19-21

ISRAEL'S FIRST KING

1 Samuel 8–12

As Samuel grew old, he chose his two sons, Joel and Abijah, as judges after him. Joel and Abijah were not like their father, however. They misused their position to get whatever they wanted and took bribes from the people.

Israel's leaders agreed that something had to be done. They came to Samuel and said, "Your sons will not be good leaders like you have been. Find a king to lead us instead, just like the other nations have."

Samuel wasn't very happy about their suggestion: he wanted God to be Israel's king, not a man. Uncertain what to do, he asked for God's guidance.

God said, "Samuel, they aren't rejecting you as their leader; they are rejecting Me. Listen to them and give them what they ask for. Before you do, however, let them know exactly what their lives will be like under a king. He will take their rights, he will take their crops, and he will take their flocks. He will take their sons to fight in his armies or to plow his fields, and he will take their daughters to serve in his palace. When he does these things, they will cry out for help, and I will not answer."

Samuel told the people exactly what the Lord had said. Despite God's warning, the people were still determined to have a king. "We want a king! We want a king!" they declared.

"Okay," God said. "Samuel, give them what they want."

Soon after, God told Samuel, "Tomorrow, about this same time, I will send you the man that I have chosen to lead my people." The next day, Samuel saw a handsome young man who stood a head taller than everyone around him. This young man's name was Saul, and he was out looking for his father's donkeys, which were lost. When Samuel saw Saul, God said to Samuel, "That is the man I have chosen."

Samuel invited Saul to eat with him and stay at his home. The next morning, when Saul set out to leave, Samuel walked out with him.

"I have a message to give you from God," Samuel told him.

Samuel looked solemnly at Saul and anointed him with oil. As the oil dripped down Saul's head, Samuel said, "God has chosen you, Saul, to be ruler over His people."

Saul didn't know what to say.

Samuel went on to describe events that were to come, events that would help to show Saul that he had truly been chosen by God as the new king. "You will first meet two men who will tell you that your father's donkeys have been found and that your father is now worried about you," Samuel said. "Later, at the large tree at Tabor, you will meet three men who will give you two loaves of bread. Finally, you will meet a group of prophets playing music and prophesying. At this point, you will be filled with the Spirit of God and will begin to prophesy right along with the prophets. With this final sign, you will know that you are a new person. You will know that God is with you."

When Saul left Samuel, he felt a change growing inside of him. God had touched his heart, giving him the heart of a king. On his way home, Saul met the different groups of people just as Samuel had said. Finally, he met the group of prophets and Saul found himself joining in, prophesying right along with them. Everyone began to notice the change in Saul.

Soon, Samuel called all of God's people together and presented their new king, Saul, standing tall, handsome, and strong. "See this man?" Samuel said. "This is the man God has chosen! There is no one else like him."

Together, the Israelites cheered, "Long live the king!"

As the cheers settled down, Samuel made sure that the people understood the reality of having a king. He explained to Saul and God's people all of the rights and responsibilities that the king would have. Samuel then wrote it on a scroll, so that everyone would remember his words and warnings, and he presented the scroll before God.

Then Saul, Samuel, and the people went to Gilgal to confirm Saul as king. They made sacrifices and offerings to God. Together, they had a big party to celebrate their new king.

Samuel said to the people, "You asked for a king, and you chose one, although it was really the Lord who made him your king. If you and your king want to be followers of the Lord, you must do what He says. Don't be stubborn! If you're stubborn and refuse to obey the Lord, He will turn against you and your king.

"You must always follow the Lord and worship Him with all your heart. Do not follow idols that cannot help you. Know that I will not stop praying for you! I will always teach you how to live rightly. Remember to serve the Lord with all your heart. Remember all that He has done for you. Remember these things so that you and your king will do well in this land."

Instead of serving God directly, the people of Israel would now fall under the rule of a king.

And the Lord *told him: "Listen to all that the people are saying to you; it is not you they have rejected, but they have rejected me as their king."*

1 Samuel 8:7

FACING GOLIATH

1 Samuel 16-17

It didn't take long for God's people to realize that demanding a king wasn't the best decision. King Saul had become greedy, angry, and disobedient to God. Seeing this, God called on his faithful servant, Samuel.

"I have rejected Saul as king," God told Samuel. "Go to Jesse of Bethlehem. I have chosen one of Jesse's sons to be the future king of My people."

Upon Samuel's arrival, Jesse called all of his sons to be presented to Samuel. First Eliab, the oldest, stood before Samuel. Samuel looked at the young man and thought, *Surely, he is the one!* God told Samuel, "Do not consider their looks or their size, like people do. I don't look at those things—the Lord looks at the heart."

Next came the second oldest, Abinadab, but Samuel shook his head. "God has not chosen this one either," he said. One by one, seven sons of Jesse came forward, and each time, Samuel shook his head.

Samuel knew he had heard the Lord correctly, but God had

not chosen any of the young men standing before him. "Are these your only sons?" Samuel asked Jesse.

"Well, there's only the youngest one left," Jesse answered. "He's out watching the sheep."

"Please bring him to me," Samuel said. "We will stay right here until he comes."

Finally, the youngest son, David, stepped before Samuel, and God said, "Anoint him, Samuel. This is the one."

David may have been the future king in God's eyes, but to

everyone else, he was just a kid. Later on, when masses of Philistines stepped up to battle the Israelites, David was the last person anyone expected to save them.

Goliath was a huge bully of a man. He stood just over nine feet tall, and his armor alone weighed as much as a young man. Every day, he stepped out to taunt King Saul and the Israelites on the opposite side of the valley, and every day, the Israelites hid from him.

"Come on out!" Goliath would shout. "Just send one man out to fight me! If he wins, you all win! We'll become your servants!"

No one would answer the terrifying giant. This went on for forty days—Goliath threatened the Israelites and the Israelites ran and hid.

One morning, Jesse sent David out to check on his big brothers and bring them a fresh supply of food. When David arrived, he couldn't believe what he saw.

Goliath, huge and intimidating, stepped out into the valley and called to the Israelites, "Come on! Send out your best man so that we can settle this!" David watched as God's army continued to cower in fear.

"Who does this man, this Goliath, think he is?" David demanded. "How dare he speak out against the army of God!"

"Hey, what are you doing here?" David's brothers asked. "Aren't you supposed to be home with your sheep?"

"What?" said David. "What have I done wrong now?" Then David asked around the camp, wondering how the man who defeated Goliath would be rewarded.

When Saul heard what David was asking about, he sent for him.

"Don't worry, my king, I'll fight him!" David said.

"How can you fight this experienced warrior?" the king asked. "You're just a teenager, and Goliath has been fighting since he was a kid!"

"Maybe so," David answered, "but I've defended my father's sheep against lions and bears. I know that I can take down this Philistine the same way. He has spoken against God's own army!"

"Very well," King Saul answered. "May God be with you." The king presented David with his armor as protection against the Philistine, but when David tried it on he could barely even walk in it.

"I can't wear this," he told the king. Instead, he left for the valley armed with only a staff and a sling. On his way to meet the giant Philistine, David stopped by a stream and carefully chose five smooth stones, adding them to his pouch.

David looked up at the towering man. Goliath wore a bronze helmet on his head, his chest was covered in bronze scales, and his legs were protected by the same golden metal. He carried a

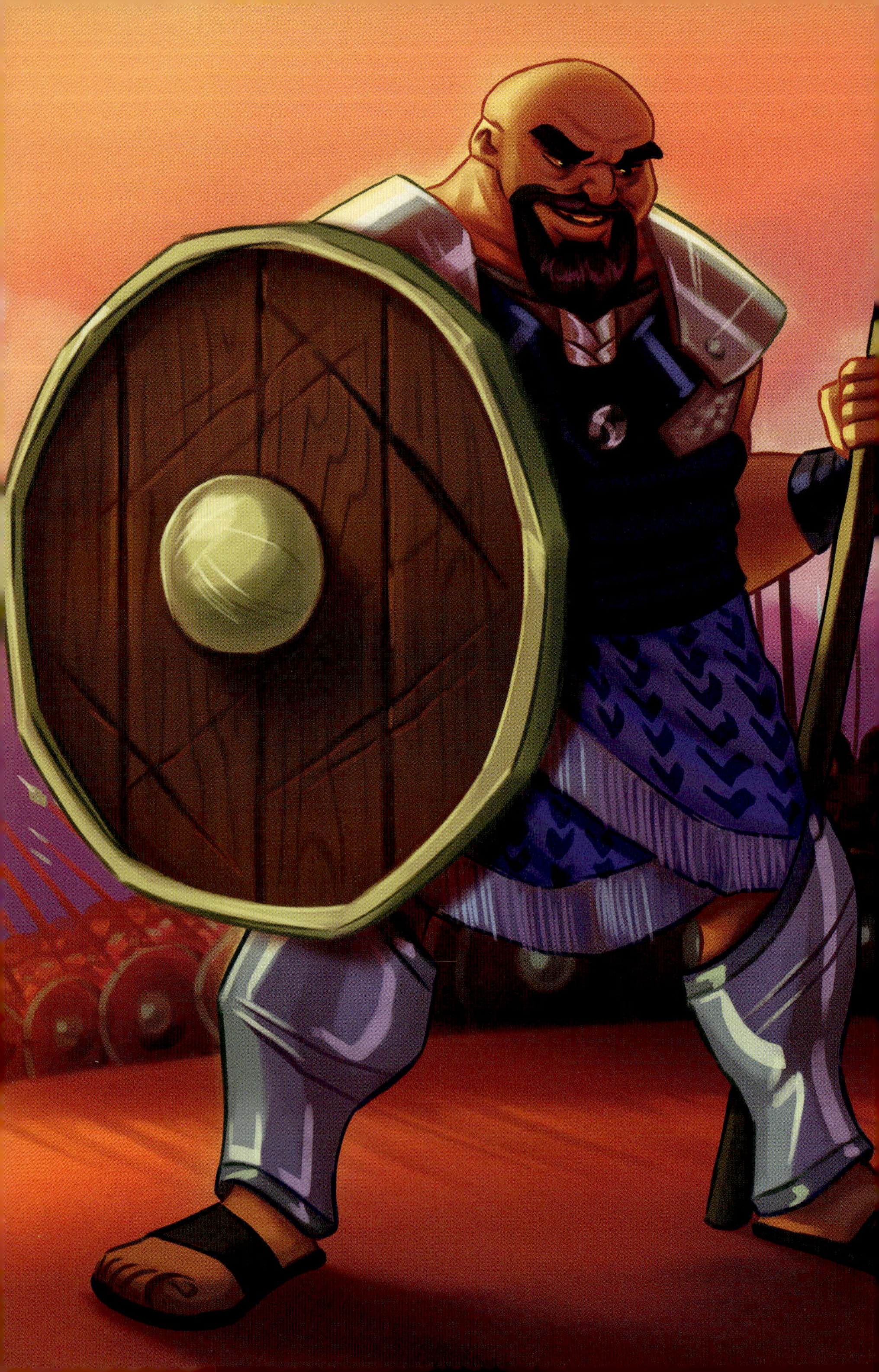

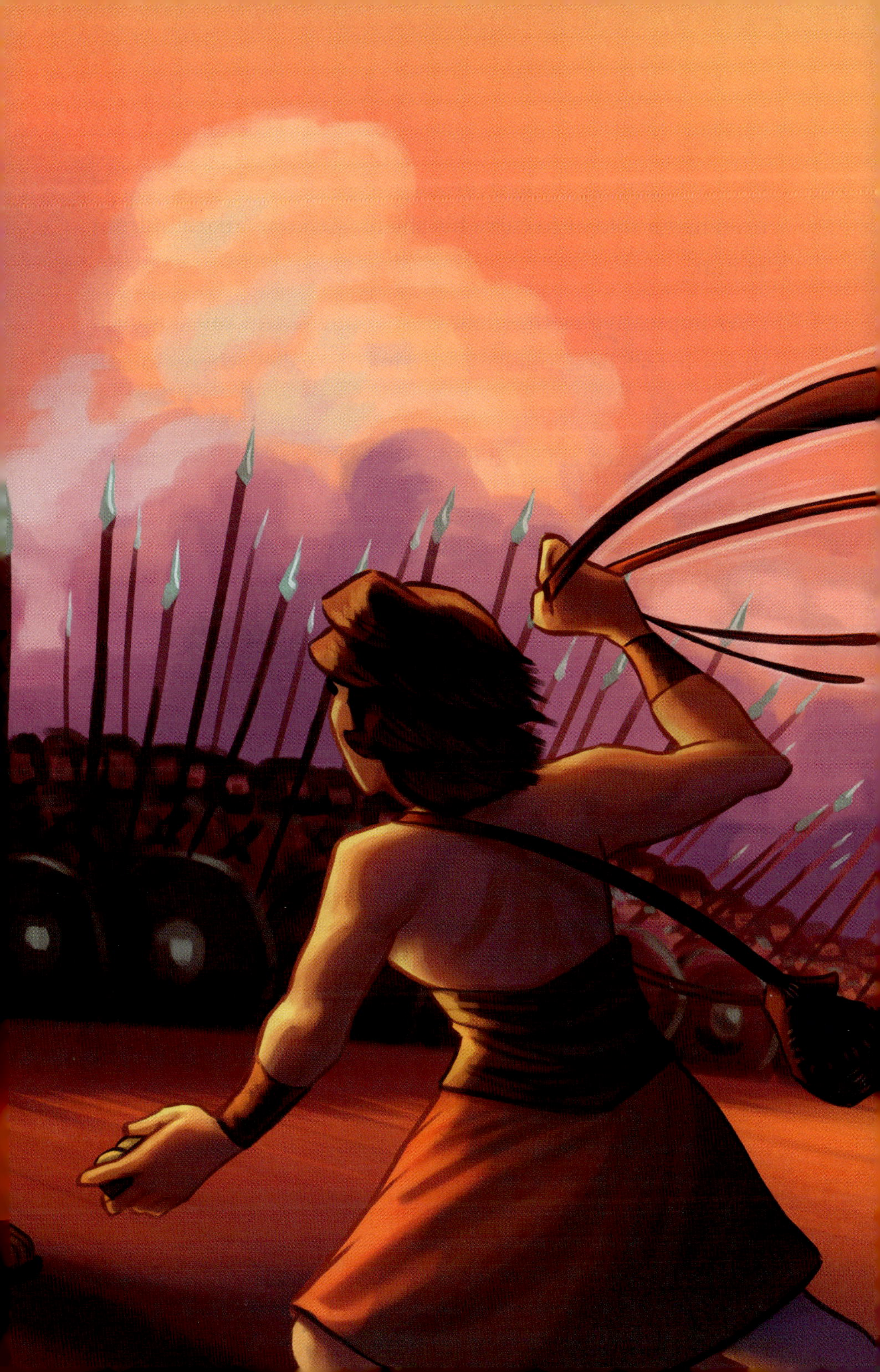

bronze javelin on his back and a heavy spear in his hands. He even had a soldier to carry his shield, standing guard in front of him.

As impressive as the giant was, young David did not back down. In fact, he stepped forward into the valley where Goliath stood.

Goliath looked at David with disgust. "You can't be serious," he said. "This is the best you've got? This is the mighty warrior that you're sending to fight me? Do you think this is a joke? Do you think that I'm a dog you can scare away with a stick?"

Again, all the Israelites were silent—all except for David, one of the youngest and least experienced among them. "You may have a sword, a spear, and a javelin," he shouted back at Goliath, "but I have God—the God of Israel, the God of the army that you are threatening. Today, I am going to take you down, and when I do, everyone here will know that God doesn't need swords, spears, and javelins to win His battles. This battle is the Lord's, and He alone will defeat you!"

When David didn't back down, Goliath took a giant step toward him, and David went running to meet the giant. With one swift movement, David took a stone in his hand, swung his sling in the air, and aimed for the Philistine.

Whoosh. Thwack. Thud.

All at once the tense silence erupted into a cry of victory as the Israelites realized what they had witnessed—the impossible. A teenage Israelite boy had defeated the giant Philistine warrior with only a sling and a stone. With renewed confidence in their army and their God, the Israelites stood tall, thrust their weapons into the air, and ran wildly after the fleeing Philistines.

Once again, God had shown His people that He was still with them—working among them, listening to their cries, and delivering them from the giant evils of this world.

> But the Lord said to Samuel, "Do not consider his appearance or his height, for I have rejected him. The Lord does not look at the things people look at. People look at the outward appearance, but the Lord looks at the heart."
>
> 1 Samuel 16:7

> David said to the Philistine, "You come against me with sword and spear and javelin, but I come against you in the name of the Lord Almighty, the God of the armies of Israel, whom you have defied."
>
> 1 Samuel 17:45

A TRUE FRIEND

1 Samuel 18–20

After David took on the giant Goliath, he served in King Saul's court. Whenever the king became anxious or angry, which was quite often, David would play the harp to sooth him.

During his time serving the king, David also became close friends with Saul's son Jonathan. Jonathan and David grew to love each other as much as brothers. To show his great love for David, Jonathan gave him the fine robe that he wore and even gave him his sword, bow, and belt.

As David grew older and became a successful warrior, however, King Saul grew more and more jealous, and even afraid, of him. Although Saul was God's chosen king, he had been disobedient to God, and the Spirit of God had left him. Now Saul saw that God was protecting David in battle and giving him great victories. All of this made Saul feel threatened by David, and he became obsessed with getting rid of David once and for all.

One day, Jonathan heard someone discussing the king's plans to kill David, so Jonathan went to warn his friend. He told David, "Be careful tomorrow. I think my father is looking for a way to

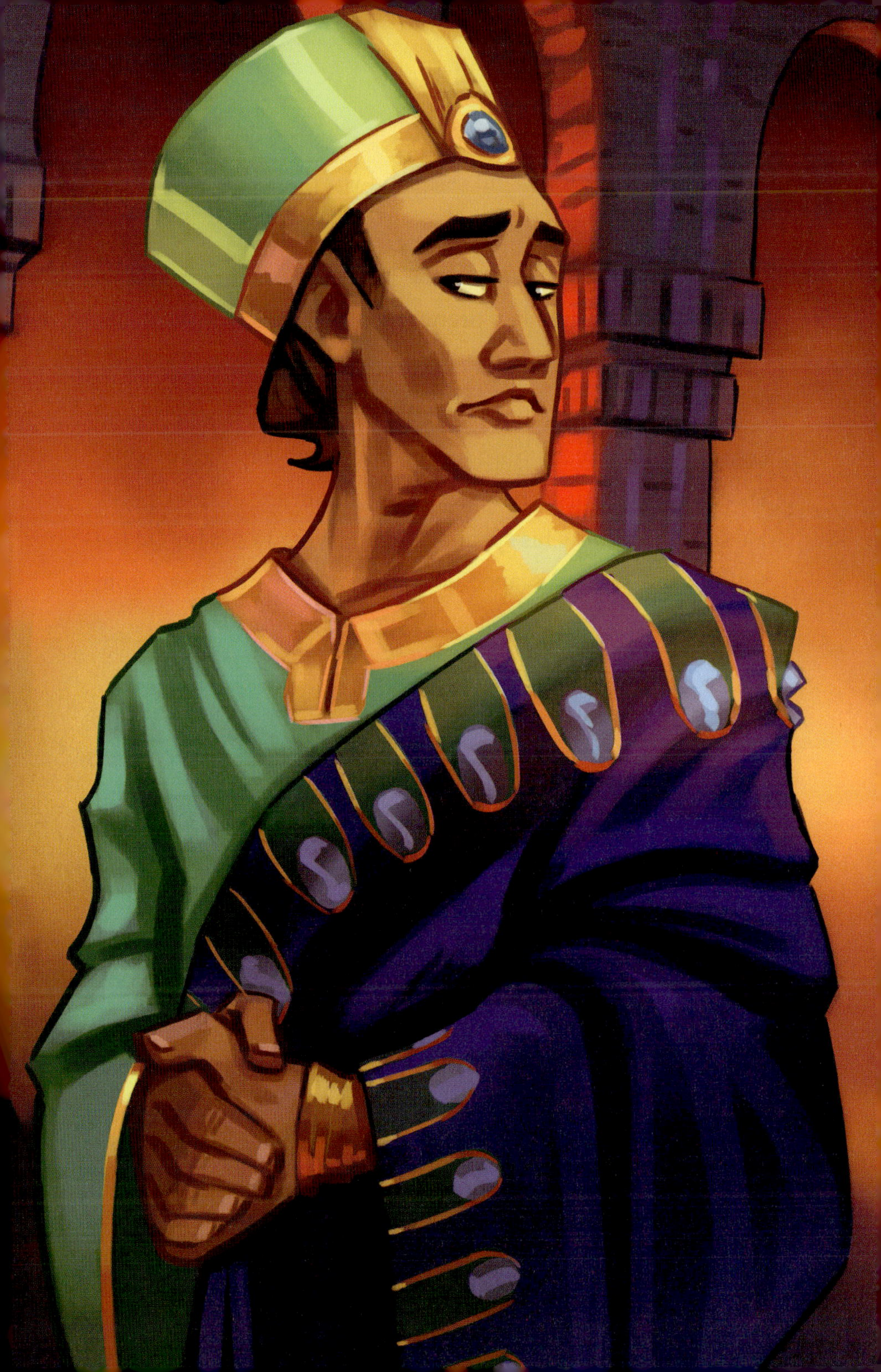

A TRUE FRIEND

get rid of you. I'll try to put in a good word for you, and I'll see what else I can find out."

Jonathan met with his father and pleaded with him not to hurt David. "Okay," King Saul promised. "As sure as there is a God, David will not be harmed."

Everything returned to normal for a little while, and David continued to play his harp for the king. One day, however, as David was playing his harp, King Saul was in a really bad mood. He suddenly threw his spear at David, trying to pin him to the wall! David barely escaped and ran home to stay away from the king.

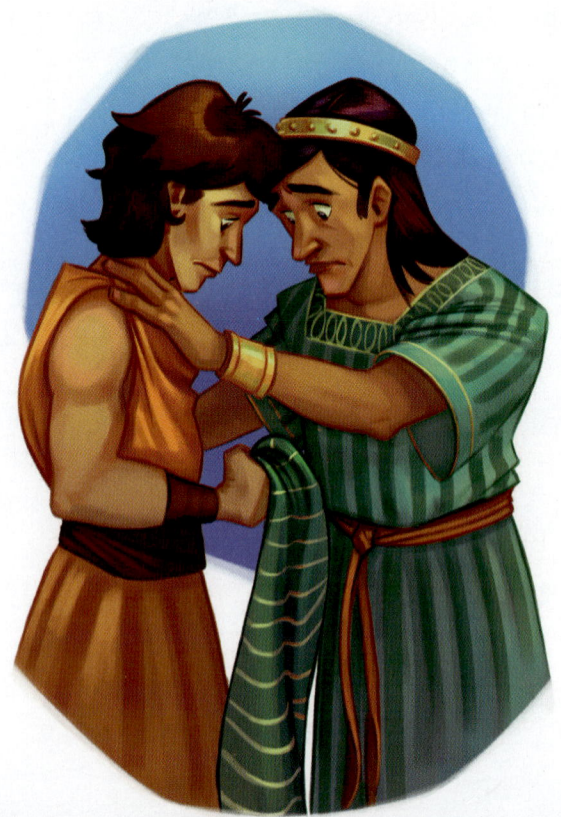

A TRUE FRIEND

After a while, David went back to Jonathan in secret to see if it was safe to return. Jonathan came up with a plan. He said, "I will mention you to my father at the feast tomorrow night to see if he still wants to get rid of you. The next day, we will return to this field, then I will shoot three arrows and send a boy to retrieve them. If I say, 'Bring the arrows here,' then it is safe to return, but, if I say, 'Go, the arrows are past you,' then it is not safe and you must leave."

After the feast, David hid in the field as planned, and Jonathan went out to shoot his bow, taking a young boy with him. Jonathan shot an arrow past the boy and said, "The arrow is past you! Go! And don't stop!" David rose from hiding and bowed before Jonathan. Knowing that David must leave, they both began to cry. They hugged and swore their friendship to one another one last time, saying, "May God be a witness to our promise of friendship, not only between you and me, but throughout all generations, forever."

With that, the two friends turned and walked in different directions, never to meet again, but bound forever by the same God.

David and Saul finished talking, and soon David and Jonathan became best friends. Jonathan thought as much of David as he did of himself.

1 Samuel 18:1 CEV

THE RULE OF KING DAVID

1 Samuel 21–2 Samuel 12

David remained on the run for many years after separating from his friend Jonathan. Although he had done nothing wrong, he had to hide in caves and out in the wilderness to avoid being captured by Saul's soldiers, who were searching near and far for him. More than once, while he was being hunted by King Saul, David had the chance to stop running and to end his fear and suffering by taking the king's life. But no matter how miserable he was, or how unfair it was that Saul was hunting him, David refused to harm God's chosen king. As a result, he continued to live on the run, in fear for his life.

Sometimes David would recall that fateful day, so many years before, when Samuel the prophet had anointed him as the next chosen king. That day almost seemed like a faraway dream now, and David wondered if he would ever return to the security of home again, not to mention whether he would ever fulfill his role as God's chosen king.

In the meantime, the relationship between the Philistines and the Israelites had grown much worse. The two nations were on the brink of war, and the Philistines were preparing to attack. Another battle broke out between the two armies, and this time the Philistines went straight for the top, chasing King Saul and three of his sons. They eventually killed the three sons—including David's dear friend Jonathan—and soon had Saul surrounded.

When Saul saw the hopeless situation, he called for his armor-bearer. "I command you," Saul told him, "kill me with your sword so that the Philistines will not have the honor of killing me."

"I would do anything for you, my king," the armor-bearer answered, "but I can't do that."

Surrounded and filled with despair, Saul drew his own sword, leaned on it, and fell to the ground, dead.

A few days later, a man stumbled into David's camp. The man appeared to be in mourning: he had torn his clothes and covered his head with dust.

"Who are you? Where did you come from?" David asked the man.

"I am an Amalekite, escaped from the Israelite camp. They retreated from battle because so many of them died!" the man said, breathlessly. "And King Saul and his sons are dead!"

"His son Jonathan? How do you know?" David demanded.

"Yes! I saw them!" The man said, holding up a dusty crown. "Here is the crown from King Saul's head!"

David and his men tore their clothes and began to cry. They mourned for Saul. They mourned for Jonathan. They mourned for the army and the nation of Israel, for all the lives they had lost in battle.

After a while, David felt that it was time to return to his home. He asked God, "Should I return home to Judah?"

The Lord said, "Yes, go."

Then David asked God which city to go to specifically, and the Lord directed him to Hebron. Following God's direction, David and his family traveled to Hebron and settled there.

Soon after, the men of Judah came to David in Hebron and anointed him king over the tribe of Judah.

Over time, David's family grew stronger, while Saul's family grew weaker. Eventually, David became king over all of Israel. Finally, David saw the promise fulfilled that God had given him through Samuel.

When David became king of Israel, he captured the fortress on Mount Zion and named it David's City. He started to rebuild the city, and when King Hiram of Tyre heard about the new king of Israel, he wanted to be on good terms with him. Hiram sent cedar logs and builders and stonemasons to build a palace for David. God also helped David to defeat all of Israel's enemies. Soon, King David and his family settled into the grand palace and they were surrounded by peace.

King David decided to bring the ark of the covenant into the City of David and place it in a special tent that David had designed for it. A whole parade followed behind the ark, with dancing and celebration. As David looked around his beautiful new palace, however, he felt bad that God's holy ark was sitting in a simple tent.

"I'm going to build a house of God where the ark can be placed, and where people can come and worship You!" David declared to God.

God answered, "Haven't I always been with you? Have I ever asked you to build Me my own house of worship in Israel or complained about being in a tent? I will establish My own place to worship My Name, but it will be your son who builds it, during his reign as king. He will be My son and I will never take My love away from him, as I did from Saul. Your lineage and kingdom will be established forever. I will establish a home for my people Israel so that they too may live in peace."

"Who am I, God?" David replied, overwhelmed with gratitude. "Who are the members of my family that You would care so much for us? You have not only fulfilled Your promises this far, but You have also made wonderful promises for my family's future. There is no one like You, God. There is no one as trustworthy as You. You have fulfilled Your promises. You have made Your people Your own, and You will be their God forever."

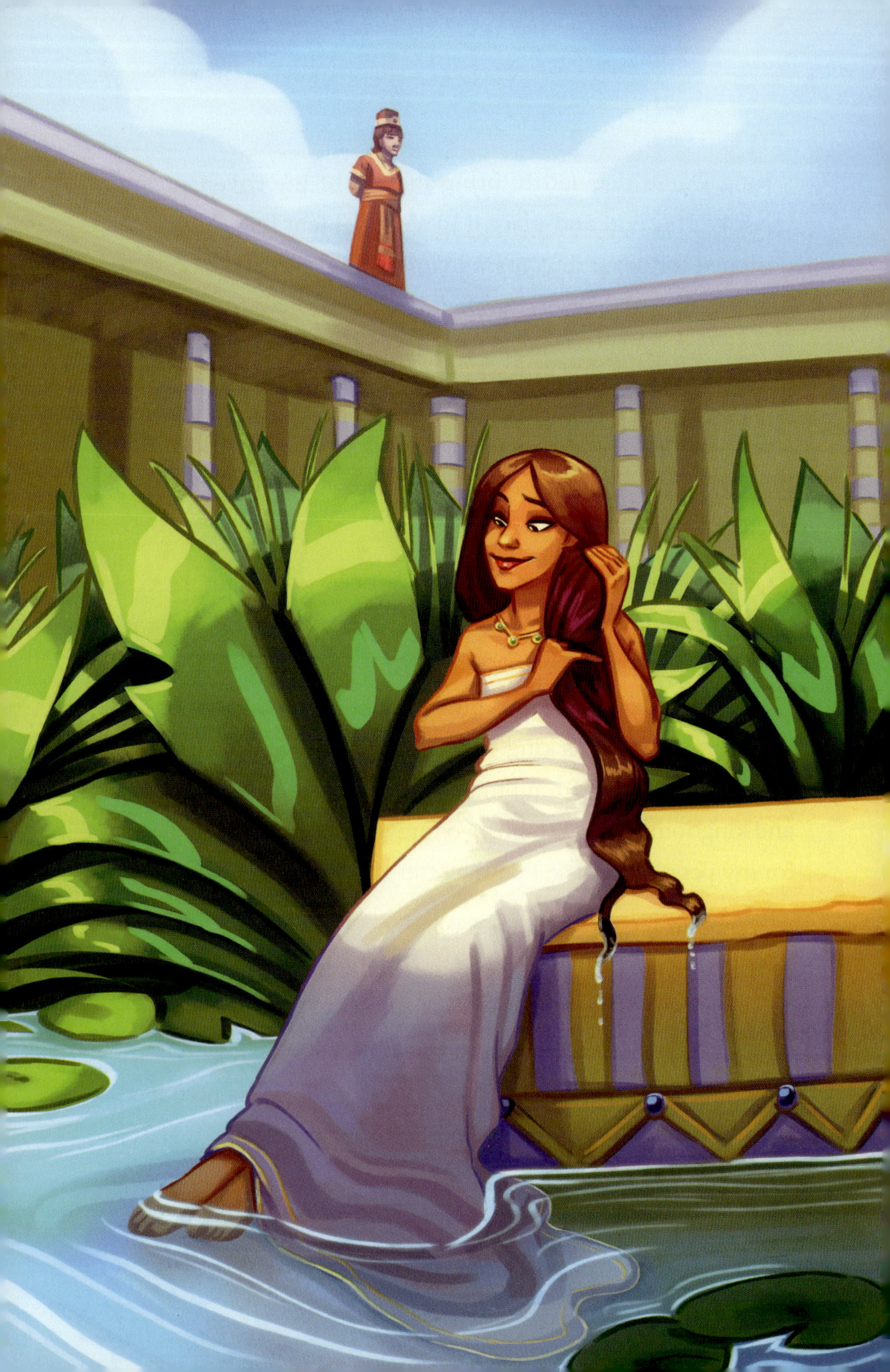

Although David was a good king, serving and following the Lord, he was not a perfect king. One evening, while many of the men were off at war, David was walking around the roof of the palace. From there, he could see a beautiful woman bathing down below.

"Who is that woman?" he asked one of his men. "Go, find out for me."

"That is Bathsheba, the wife of Uriah," the man reported.

David decided he didn't care that she was already married. He thought Bathsheba was beautiful, and he wanted her for his own. He brought Bathsheba to the palace to be with him, and then he wrote a letter to Joab, the commander of the army. "Put Uriah on the front line of the fighting," the king instructed. "Then withdraw from the fighting so that he will be alone and die."

That is exactly what happened. Soon, the news was brought to Bathsheba that her husband had been killed in the war, and she mourned the loss of her husband.

After Bathsheba had mourned her husband, David brought her back to the palace to become his wife. They had a son together, and everything seemed to be going well for King David. One day, however, the prophet Nathan came to David and told him a story about a rich man and a poor man. "The rich man had all kinds of sheep and cattle," Nathan explained. "But the poor man only had one little lamb. He had raised that little lamb with his children, just like another member of his family. The man fed the

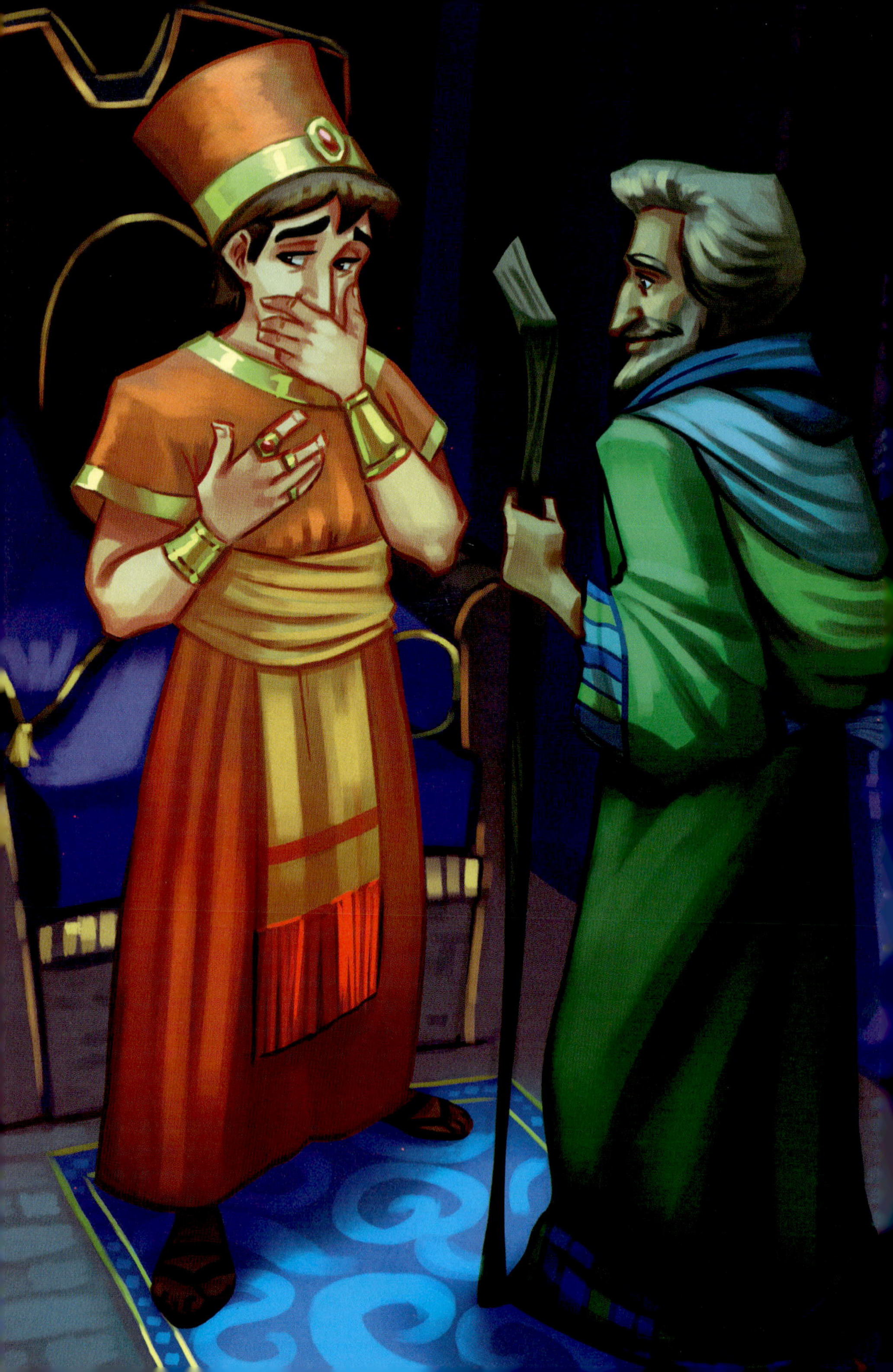

lamb from his own plate and even held it in his arms as it slept.

"One day, the rich man had a visitor. When it was time to prepare a meal, the rich man didn't choose one of his own sheep or cattle to serve. Instead, he went to the poor man and took the one little lamb that was like his child. He served the other man's lamb to his visitor."

This infuriated King David. "Who is this man?" he demanded. "I swear, whoever did this must die! Also, he must pay four times the cost of that lamb to the poor man!"

"That man," Nathan said, looking up at his king, "is you." David searched for the meaning in Nathan's words, and Nathan continued, "The Lord says, 'I made you king over all of Israel. I saved you from Saul. I gave you a family, a palace, and all of Judah and Israel. If that wasn't enough, I would have given you even more! With all that I have given you, why would you kill Uriah and take his wife as your own? For this reason, there will now be great conflict in your own family.'"

David shook his head, sad and ashamed. "I have sinned against God," he said.

Nathan stepped closer. "God has forgiven your sin," he said. "However, because of your actions, the son you have had with Bathsheba will not survive."

After that, David pleaded with God for his son's life. He wouldn't eat. He wouldn't get up. He just stayed on the ground, praying for his son. Despite all of David's pleading, however, after seven days King David's son died.

Even though God punished David for his sin, He also remained true to His great promises to David and his family. From David and Bathsheba another son was born whom they named Solomon. Through Solomon, David's name and service to the Lord would continue. Not only that, but one day from the line of David, just as God promised, a King like no other would be born—a King of kings, a Lord of lords, a Savior for the world.

> *Then David said to Nathan, "I have sinned against the Lord." Nathan replied, "The Lord has taken away your sin. You are not going to die. But because by doing this you have shown utter contempt for the Lord, the son born to you will die."*
>
> 2 Samuel 12:13-14

THE WISEST KING EVER

1 Kings 2–10

King David knew that his time on earth was coming to an end. Since he had other, older sons, he called in his son Solomon to name him as the next king. "I won't be on this earth much longer," he told Solomon. "So obey the Lord, and you will be successful in whatever you do. God has promised that if we are faithful to Him, our family will always have a king on the throne."

After King David was buried, King Solomon traveled to Gibeon to worship God by offering sacrifices. God spoke to Solomon there. "What is it that you want? Ask Me for whatever you want, and I will give it to you."

"Oh, God, you have been so good to my father because of his faithfulness," Solomon began. "But I have no idea how to be a king, how to serve all of Your people! Please guide me, show me how to be a just and righteous king."

"Solomon, you could have asked for anything," God answered, "for a long, healthy life, for all the riches in the world, or even for the destruction of your enemies. But instead, you asked to rule My people well. For that, I will give you all that you asked for and so much more—wisdom like no other and wealth with no equal. If you obey Me, you will also have a long life."

In that moment Solomon woke up. It had been a dream.

Solomon soon began to show the great wisdom that God had promised in his dream. People often came to have the king solve problems or make decisions in difficult situations. The king's word, his decision, was considered law.

One difficult case occurred when two women came before him, both claiming to be the mother of the same child. Solomon immediately knew what to do.

"Sword!" the king demanded. "Cut the child in half, and give one half to each mother."

"Fine!" one woman said. "Do it!"

"No, don't!" the other woman screamed. "Give the baby to her! Just don't kill him!"

"Stop! Don't hurt the baby. Give it to her," the king said, pointing to the woman crying for the baby's safety. "She is the real mother. She is the one who would give him up to save his life."

From that moment on, the people of Israel were impressed by Solomon's wisdom in judging his people. People from all over heard of his wisdom and would come to hear Solomon speak and hear his judgements. They would listen to his knowledge about plants, animals, and nature, from the tallest tree to the tiniest herb, from mammals and reptiles to birds and fish. Before long, they would all come to understand that Solomon's wisdom was from God.

Soon, Solomon began to make preparations for building the temple of the Lord that his father had wanted to build. He ordered cedar to be shipped from Tyre and stone to be cut from nearby quarries and brought in to build the temple. When all the materials had been gathered, Solomon oversaw the construction. He made sure that every beautiful detail was complete—from the olive-wood doors, carved with cherubim, palm trees, and flowers, to the gold overlays that covered the carvings. Finally, after seven years, the temple of the Lord was finished.

With the temple completed, King Solomon then built a palace for himself and his family. It seemed that there was no end to the wealth of Solomon's kingdom.

As word spread of Solomon's wealth and wisdom, kings and rulers would travel to spend time with him and hear his insights. From south of the Arabian Desert came the queen of Sheba. She had heard about the success that God had given Solomon, so she traveled to Jerusalem to see for herself. She brought camels with her carrying gold, spices, and precious stones. She questioned Solomon with riddles to test the depths of his wisdom.

After spending some time with Solomon, the Queen of Sheba told him, "When I heard about your wealth, wisdom, and all that you had accomplished, I didn't believe it. Now that I am here, however, I see that I hadn't even heard the half of it. It exceeds anything I had heard! I praise your God for His great love for Israel and for choosing you as king."

Throughout Solomon's reign, God fulfilled His promise to give Solomon not only great wisdom in ruling His people, but greater wealth than any other king on earth. In doing so, God brought glory to His name through Solomon.

> *"And observe what the L*ORD *your God requires: Walk in obedience to him, and keep his decrees and commands, his laws and regulations, as written in the Law of Moses. Do this so that you may prosper in all you do and wherever you go."*
>
> 1 Kings 2:3

FIRE FROM HEAVEN

1 Kings 16-19

After wise King Solomon died, other kings followed. Some were good and sought the Lord wholeheartedly, but many led the Israelites away from God. These bad kings allowed, and even encouraged, the Israelites to worship other gods and do things that were evil in the eyes of God. King Ahab was the most evil king yet.

King Ahab ordered the construction of another temple—a temple for worshipping Baal, not God. King Ahab's wife Jezebel worshipped Baal, and King Ahab started worshipping Baal too.

Building this temple to Baal was just one of the ways that Ahab led Israel down the evil path of idolatry. He even tried to make the worship of Baal the official religion of the land. Eventually, most of Israel turned away from God.

Because His people had turned away, God sent one of his prophets, a man named Elijah, to remind King Ahab that He was the one true God of Israel, not Baal. "As surely as the God of Israel lives," Elijah said, speaking for God, "a drought is coming!

There will be no rain, no dew, no water for your crops. This will last for years—from now until I say otherwise."

Because Jezebel was trying to kill off the prophets, God instructed Elijah to hide near a small brook. "You will have water here, and the ravens will bring you food," God told him. Each day, morning and night, ravens descended from the sky, carrying Elijah's meal of bread and meat.

At the end of the famine, God sent Elijah to confront Ahab and the people of Israel once again about turning their backs on God and worshipping Baal. God was going to do something big to get their attention and convince them to return to Him, the one true God.

Elijah sent for King Ahab to come meet him.

When King Ahab arrived, he said to Elijah, "Ah, look, it's the biggest troublemaker in Israel!"

"I am not the troublemaker," Elijah answered. "You are the one leaving God in order to worship Baal! Let's settle this matter once and for all. Call all of Israel, and all four hundred and fifty prophets of Baal, and meet me at the top of Mount Carmel."

The king sent word, and everyone assembled on Mount Carmel. Elijah stood before them and said, "How long will you try to serve both God and Baal? It's simple. If the Lord proves to be the true God, then follow him. If Baal is the real god, follow him."

The crowd stared at him in silence, but Elijah didn't falter.

"Let's get two bulls—one for me and one for Baal's prophets," he continued. "We'll each prepare our bull and put it on the altar, without setting fire to the wood. You call on your god, and I'll call on my God. Whichever one answers by bringing fire down on the altar is the one true God."

The crowd nodded, cheering their approval, and watched as the prophets of Baal prepared their sacrifice. When the sacrifice was ready, all four hundred and fifty prophets began to pray and call on the name of Baal. For hours they shouted and they danced, but no one answered.

"Maybe he's busy, or on vacation, or taking a nap," Elijah offered. "Shout louder!"

That's just what the prophets of Baal did. They shouted until their voices grew hoarse. They cut themselves with swords. They slashed themselves with spears. They spilled their own blood in exchange for the attention of their god.

Despite all of their efforts, nothing happened. No one answered. Baal didn't even show up for his own showdown, because he was a false god.

"Okay, okay, now, come over here!" Elijah called. All the people gathered around an altar to God that had previously been destroyed. They watched as Elijah stacked the stones, one for each tribe, until all twelve tribes of Israel were once again

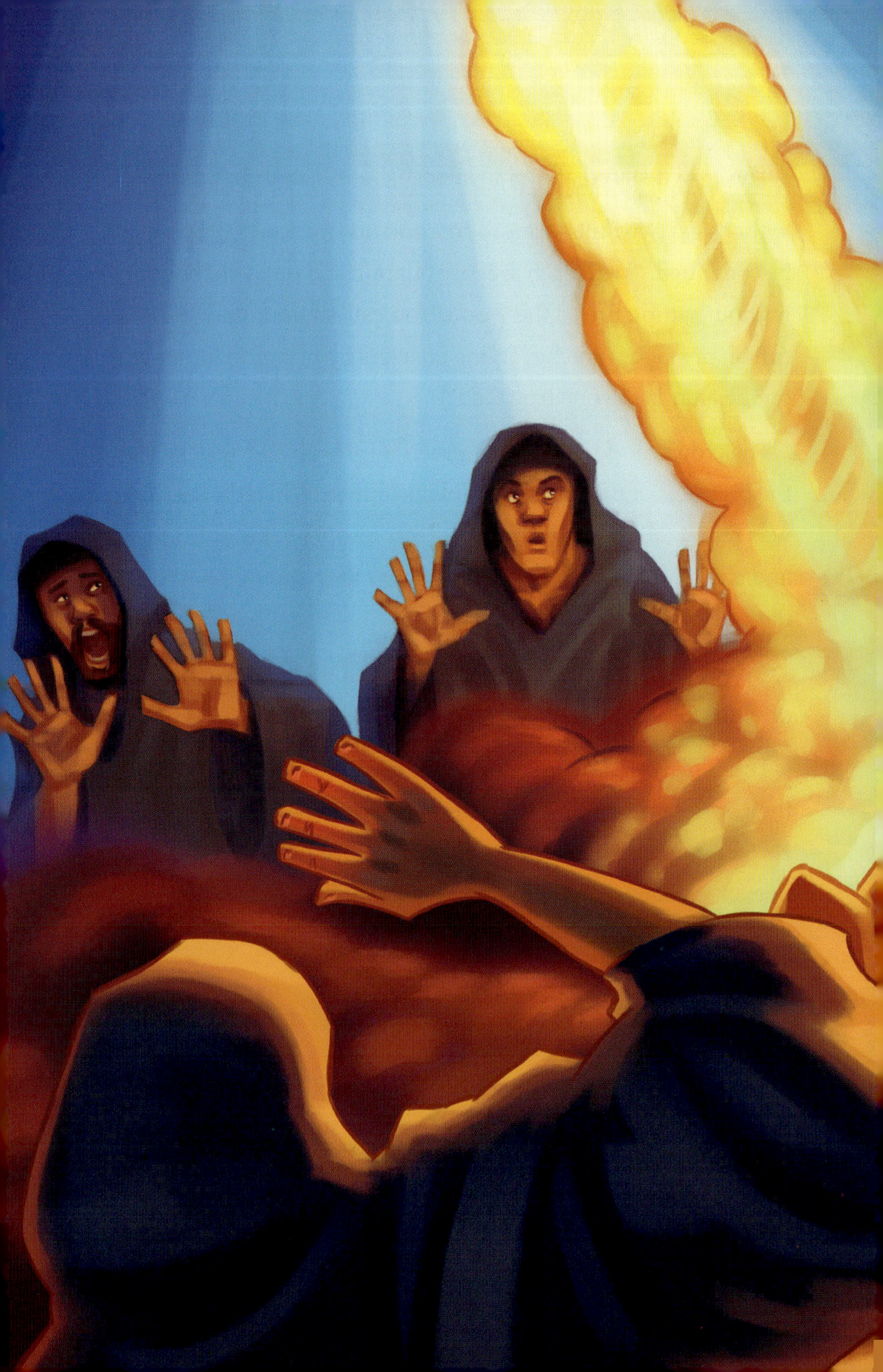

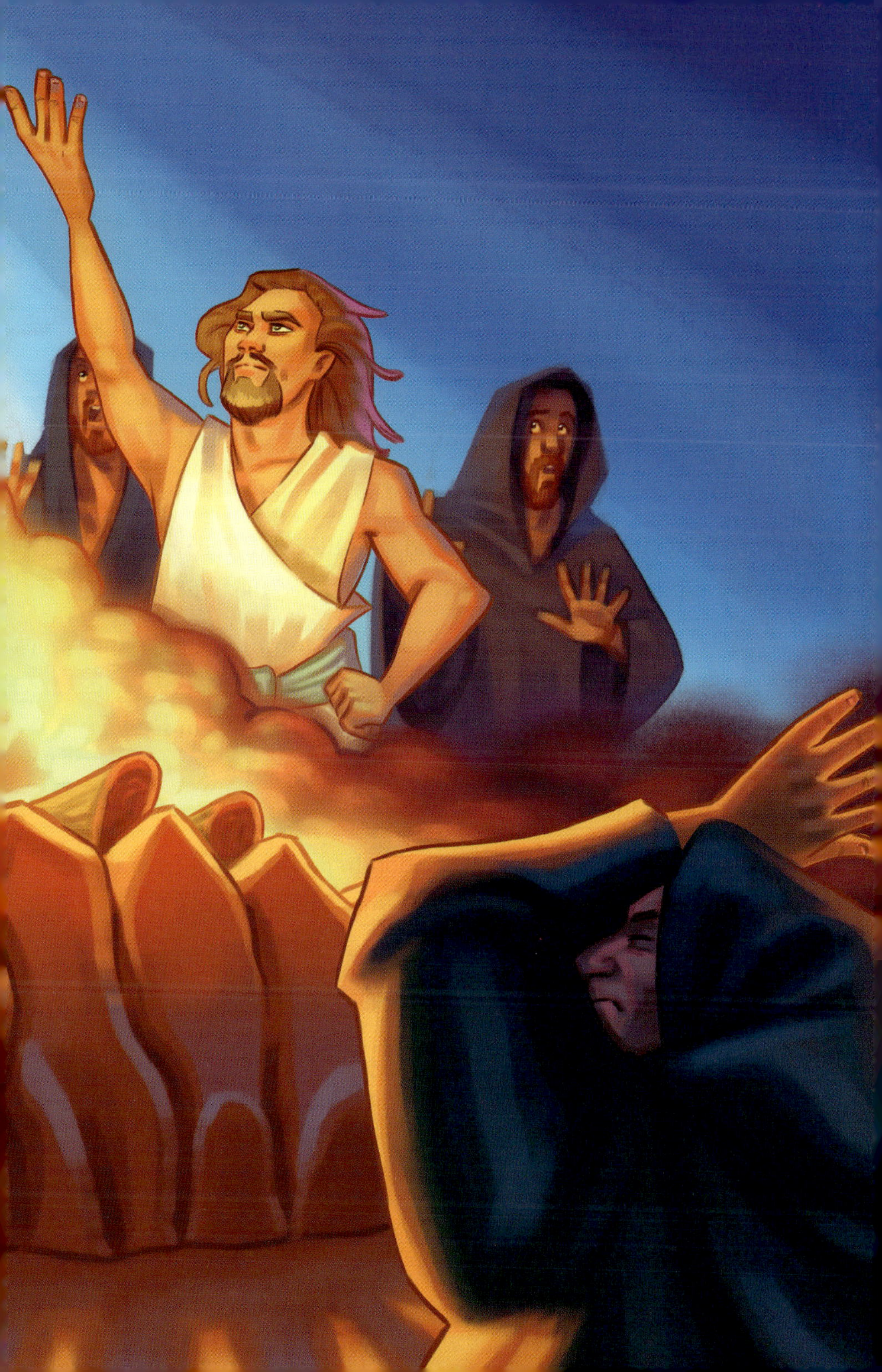

represented. He then dug all around the altar, creating a large trench. He placed wood on the altar, then placed the pieces of the bull onto the wood.

Elijah wasn't done yet, though. He sent someone to bring four large jars of water. "Now pour them on the offering and on the wood," he instructed. They did as he said, pouring water all over the altar, the wood, and the offering.

"Now do it again," he told them, so they did.

"Do it a third time," Elijah said, and they did. The water ran over the meat, drenched the wood, and filled the trench.

Every eye was on Elijah as he stepped toward the altar and began to pray. He said, "Oh, Lord, God of Abraham, Isaac, and Jacob, show these people your power today; let them see that You are their God and I am your servant. Answer me, God, so that they will all see You and serve You."

As the last word left Elijah's mouth, fierce fire fell from the sky. It burned up the sacrifice. It burned up the wood. It burned up the soil, the stones, and the water in the trench.

Immediately, the people fell on their faces in shock and wonder, crying, "He is God! The Lord is God—the one true God!"

The prophets of Baal didn't last very long after that, and neither did the drought. The praises from God's people rose with the wind and stirred among the clouds, delivering a refreshing rain on all of Israel.

There was one person who hadn't attended the show that day, however. When her husband told her what Elijah had done, Jezebel was furious. Then and there, she made a solemn oath to put an end to that troublemaker Elijah once and for all.

Elijah fled and went into hiding. He was crouched in a cave when the Lord came to him and said, "What are you doing here, Elijah?"

"I have served you wholeheartedly, Lord," Elijah began. "Now I am your only prophet left, and they're trying to kill me!"

"Return," the Lord answered. "Return the way you came and anoint Elisha as the next prophet. Anoint Jehu to be king over Israel and Hazael to be king over Judah. They will help to lead my people and restore them to me."

Elijah did as God told him. He anointed Elisha as the next prophet, knowing—just like the prophets before him and the prophets to come—that there is only one true God. The God of Israel, the God of everyone, is a God that loves, hears, and answers when people call on Him. He is there to love, guide, and even miraculously provide. He is a personal God who doesn't require blood in exchange for His attention. On the contrary, He offered the life of His own Son in exchange for those who have turned their backs on Him.

There is only one God, the one true God.

Elijah went before the people and said, "How long will you waver between two opinions? If the Lord is God, follow him; but if Baal is God, follow him." But the people said nothing.

1 Kings 18:21

"Answer me, Lord, answer me, so these people will know that you, Lord, are God, and that you are turning their hearts back again."

1 Kings 18:37

THE SULKING PROPHET

The Book of Jonah

One day, God asked the prophet Jonah to travel to the city of Nineveh, to warn them to turn from their wickedness. Jonah did not want to go to the Ninevites, the enemies of his people, and tell them anything! On the contrary, Jonah had his own plan: he would travel as far from Nineveh as possible.

Jonah had seen it happen time and time again, and he was tired of it: God would send someone to warn the most wicked people, and when that person did, the people would repent, stop being wicked, and God would forgive them. Jonah just wasn't going to do it. He wanted to see the evil people in Nineveh finally get what they deserved.

So, instead of going to Nineveh, Jonah boarded a ship that would take him to Tarshish, about two thousand miles in the opposite direction from where God had called him to go. Jonah paid the fee, climbed aboard, and went below deck to take a nap. While he slept, the wind began to howl, and the waves began to rise. A violent storm erupted, rocking and tossing the boat and threatening the lives of everyone aboard.

"Listen to that storm!" one of the sailors yelled. "It's ripping the boat apart!"

The men threw some of the cargo off the ship to lighten the load, but it didn't help. The storm continued to rage. Waves crashed over the bow, flooding the boat and throwing it back and forth in the angry sea.

While walking through the ship, the captain came upon a strange sight—it was Jonah, sleeping right through the storm! "How are you sleeping right now?" the captain yelled, waking Jonah. "Get up and pray to your God or we will surely die in this storm!"

The sailors had tried everything they knew to do, but nothing seemed to help. Finally, they decided that this must be the result of a god punishing someone on the ship. They decided to cast lots to see who was responsible. When they did, the lot pointed to Jonah as the one responsible for their distress. "Who are you?" they asked. "Where are you from? Why are you making all of this trouble for us?"

Jonah bowed his head. "This happened because I'm running," he told the crew. "I'm a Hebrew and I worship the Lord, the God of heaven, who made the very sea itself. This is happening to us because I am running away from Him."

"What should we do?" they asked him, terrified.

"Throw me in," Jonah told them.

"Throw you in where?" the sailors asked, exchanging glances.

"Throw me into the sea, and this storm will stop," Jonah shouted through the sound of the waves and wind. "I'm the reason for this storm. I'm the reason you are all in danger."

Instead of following Jonah's suggestion, the men tried to row back to land. When they did, however, the storm only grew stronger and tossed them harder. Finally, fearfully, they did what Jonah had asked. First they prayed to Jonah's God, asking Him not to punish them for this man's death. Then they threw him into the sea.

Immediately, the sea was calm. The sailors were awestruck. Everyone on the ship started worshiping the God of Jonah.

Meanwhile, Jonah sank beneath the waves and saw the dark shadow of death coming for him. Then he realized that it wasn't the shadow of death at all—it was actually a big fish, and it swallowed Jonah whole.

For the next three days, that's where Jonah would stay: in the belly of a fish. During that time in the dark, dank water of the fish's belly, Jonah gained a new perspective. He prayed, "Oh, God, thank You for hearing my cry. Even though the waves crashed around me, threatening to take my life, You heard my prayer. You rescued me. I deserved to die, but You saved me. Even if everyone else turns away from your love, I will praise you. I will serve you. I will remember and proclaim that salvation comes from you."

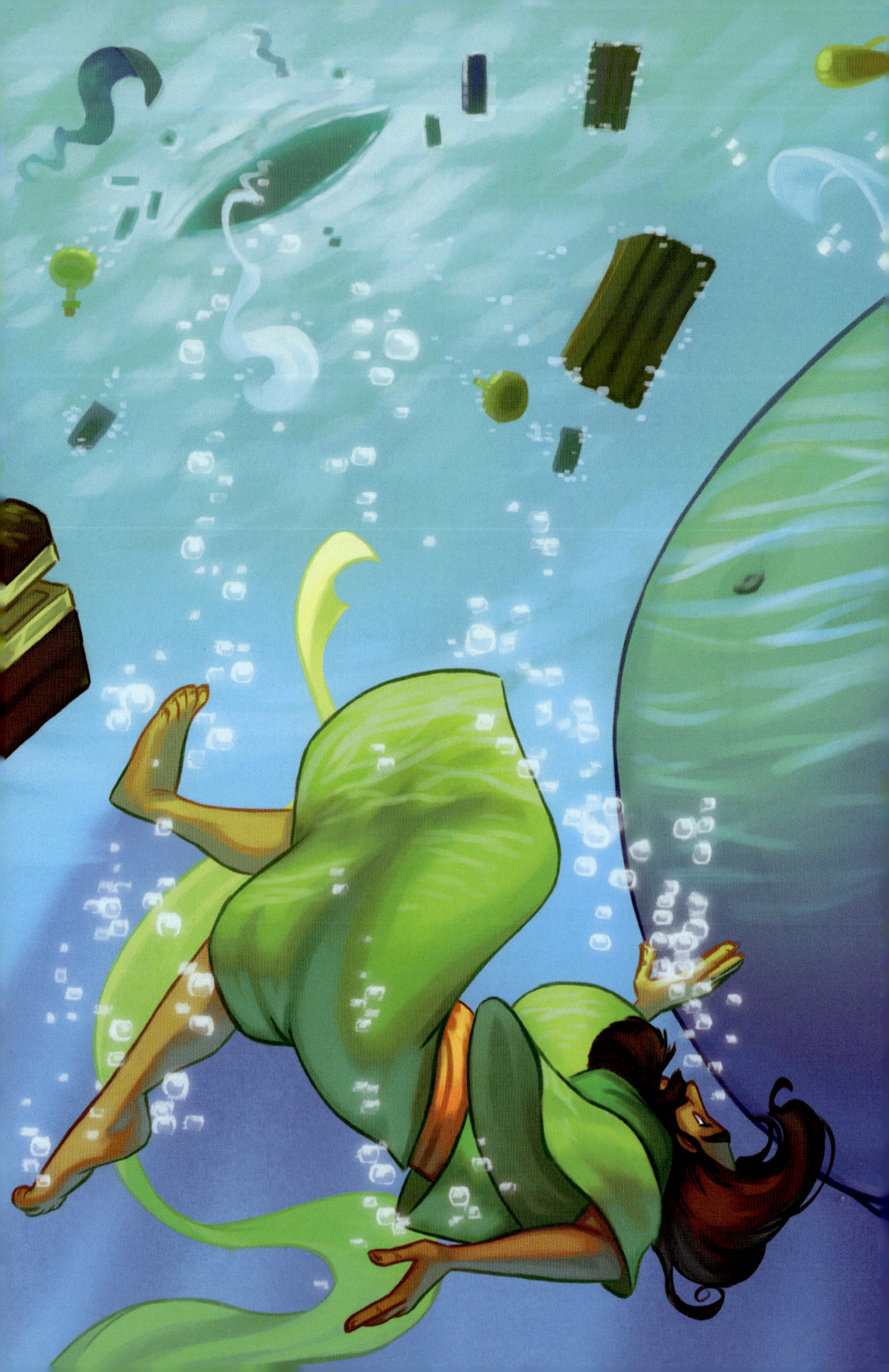

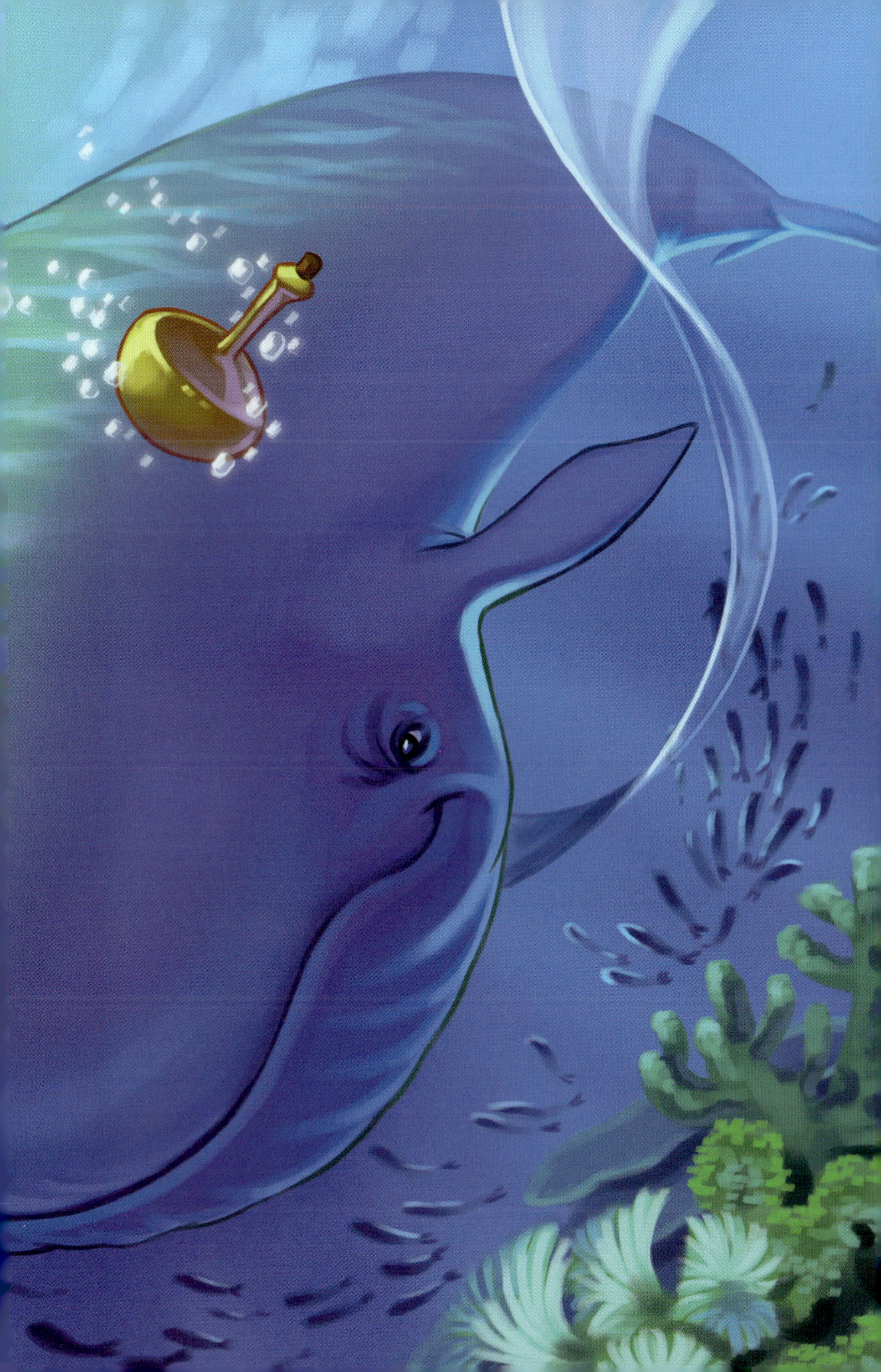

THE SULKING PROPHET

As Jonah's prayer ended, a rumbling began. A sloshing motion started pushing him forward and up, until, all at once, he exploded out of the fish's mouth and onto dry land again. Jonah sat for a moment to regain his senses, his eyes adjusting to the blinding sunlight.

"Jonah," God's voice called to him again, "go to Nineveh and deliver the warning I asked you to give them."

This time, Jonah stood up and headed directly where God was calling him. After Jonah had warned the people, delivering the message God had given him, the Ninevites mourned and turned from their wickedness. Because of God's warning, delivered by Jonah, the city of Nineveh was saved from destruction.

Instead of being happy that his message had saved the lives of the Ninevites, Jonah was angry. "See, God," he said, "this is why I didn't want to come! I knew that You would show them mercy."

"Why would you be angry about this?" God asked him. "You should be happy about my mercifulness."

Jonah sat outside the city and watched to see if anything would happen to Nineveh. While he waited, God made a plant grow above Jonah to shade him from the sun. The next day, when Jonah was still there, God had a worm chew on the plant, causing it to wither and die.

Again, Jonah was angry.

"You are angry about this plant," God said. "Yet you didn't plant it. You didn't water it. You didn't make it grow. Shouldn't I be more concerned about Nineveh, with well over a hundred thousand people inside, than you should be for this plant?"

That day, Jonah understood the great mercy of God, the great care He takes with His people. Because God sent Jonah to warn Nineveh, the people turned from their wickedness and were saved. Because God sent a giant fish to swallow Jonah, he was also shown mercy and saved.

Again and again throughout the stories of His people, God shows how much He loves them, how He rescues them, and how He longs for a relationship with them. Long before Jesus came to earth to offer everlasting grace, God was already giving grace to His people. Whether it was through a prophet, or a fish, or His very own Son, God would always find a way to save His people with His grace.

When God saw what they did and
how they turned from their evil ways,
he relented and did not bring on them
the destruction he had threatened.

Jonah 3:10

"And should I not have concern for the
great city of Nineveh, in which there are
more than a hundred and twenty thousand
people who cannot tell their right hand
from their left—and also many animals?"

Jonah 4:11

A MIGHTY KING'S NIGHTMARE

Daniel 1-2

Seeing that the Israelites continued to turn from Him to worship idols, God had to discipline them. He did this by letting foreign nations rule over them. It got so bad that, eventually, a great number of the Israelites were captured and led into exile in Babylon. King Nebuchadnezzar, the king of Babylon, attacked Jerusalem and destroyed it, taking many of its people back to Babylon with him. The king told his chief official, "Bring me the finest of the Israelite young men to serve in my court." So the official went to the Israelites and chose young men from the noble families who were handsome, intelligent, and able to serve.

Four of those young men were Daniel, Hananiah, Mishael, and Azariah. They were trained for years in Babylonian culture and customs in order to get them ready for their new positions. These young men were educated on the language, art, and religion of Babylon before being presented to the king for service. They were even given new names to remind them that they were no longer Israelites, the children of God, but that they belonged to Babylon now. Daniel they called Belteshazzar, Hananiah became

Shadrach, Mishael was renamed Meshach, and Azariah got the name Abednego. Over time, as the king spoke to these young men, he found that they were wiser than the magicians and enchanters—the wisest men already in his court.

One night, King Nebuchadnezzar was not able to sleep because of the dreams he was having. He urgently called all of his wisest men—his magicians and enchanters, astrologers and sorcerers.

"Tell me what my dream means!" he ordered. "In fact, if you are truly wise, you should already know what my dream was. If not, I'll know you're all lying to me. Therefore, if you can't tell me what I saw in my dream and what it means, I will cut you into pieces and tear your houses down!"

"But, your majesty," the wise men pleaded, "no one could do that! No one could possibly know your dreams, except the gods."

"Kill them!" the king ordered. "Kill them all!"

Immediately the officers went searching for all of the wise men in the king's court, including Daniel and his friends.

When they found Daniel and explained what was happening, Daniel said, "Wait! Don't kill all of the wise men! I will explain the king's dream."

The officials rushed Daniel to the king. "Well," the king asked, "are you able to tell me what I dreamed? Can you explain it to me?"

"No man, no matter how wise, could tell you what you have

asked," Daniel began. "However, God in heaven can. Allow me some time and I will interpret the dream for you."

Daniel went back and met with his friends. He told them what had happened, and together they prayed for God's help and mercy. That night, God revealed the king's dream to Daniel in a vision.

The next day, Daniel went back to the king and began to describe to him exactly what he had dreamed. Daniel said, "This is the dream, oh king, that you had: There was a large statue made of pure gold, with a chest and arms of silver, a belly and thighs of bronze, legs of iron, and feet of iron and clay. You saw a rock thrown, but not by human hands. The rock hit the statue's feet, smashing them and causing the entire statue to crumble. Then, the rock that was thrown grew into a mountain, filling the earth."

The king listened as Daniel went on to explain the dream. "You, King Nebuchadnezzar," Daniel said, "are the head of gold, but after you there will be lesser kingdoms until, finally, there is a kingdom as strong as iron. The feet of iron and clay are that kingdom once it becomes divided. The rock not made by human hands is a kingdom that God will raise up to end the other kingdoms. That kingdom will last forever."

King Nebuchadnezzar sat there in awe. When Daniel finished speaking, the king fell face down in front of him, saying, "Your God is the God of gods! He alone can reveal these mysteries to men!"

The king made Daniel the ruler over all of Babylon and its wise men. Daniel asked the king to also place Shadrach, Meshach, and Abednego in positions of power over Babylon, and Nebuchadnezzar did. Daniel did his work in the palace, and his three friends worked in the city of Babylon.

> *"In the time of those kings, the God of heaven will set up a kingdom that will never be destroyed, nor will it be left to another people. It will crush all those kingdoms and bring them to an end, but it will itself endure forever."*
> *Daniel 2:44*

THE FIERY FURNACE

Daniel 3

Not long after this, however, King Nebuchadnezzar made a huge golden statue and decreed that all of his officials must attend the dedication ceremony for it. "Whenever you hear the royal music, you must immediately fall down and worship this statue!" the king ordered. "If you don't, you will be thrown into a furnace of fire!"

So, of course, whenever the people heard the music, they fell down and worshipped the golden statue, just as they were told. Before long, some of the officials went to King Nebuchadnezzar with news of three Jews who were not obeying the king's orders.

The king was enraged and sent for these three men. When Shadrach, Meshach, and Abednego stood before the king, he asked them, "Is this true? Is it true that you will not worship the golden statue that I've set up? I'm going to give you one chance to prove your obedience. When you hear the music, bow down and worship the statue. If you don't, you will be thrown into the blazing furnace, where no god can save you!"

THE FIERY FURNACE

"Your Majesty, we know the law, and we know the punishment," they replied. "But we only bow to one God—the one true God who is fully capable of delivering us from anything, even your fiery furnace, if he so chooses. However, even if he does not, we could never bow down to your gods or to your statue."

This made the king so angry that he shouted, "Heat up the furnace! Heat it up seven times more than usual!"

The king called for his most powerful soldiers. They tied up Shadrach, Meshach, and Abednego and walked them to the furnace. The fire in the furnace was so hot that it killed the soldiers as Shadrach, Meshach, and Abednego fell in.

As the king watched the punishment being carried out, he jumped to his feet. "Wait a minute! Didn't we throw three men into the fire?" he asked.

"Yes, Your Majesty," the king's officials replied.

"Well then, who is that fourth man? He looks like a son of the gods," the king said, watching a figure standing alongside the three men. The king marched over to the furnace and said, "Shadrach, Meshach, and Abednego, get out right now!"

Just like that, the three men walked out of the fiery furnace— just as they had walked in. The king and his advisors could not believe what they saw. While the king's soldiers had died from the heat of the furnace alone, these three men had stood in the middle of the flames, but their clothes were not burned. Not only that, but their hair wasn't singed, and they didn't even smell like smoke!

When King Nebuchadnezzar finally found the words to speak, he shouted, "Praise the God of Shadrach, Meshach, and Abednego! They believed and trusted Him, and He saved them!"

THE FIERY FURNACE

THE FIERY FURNACE

After that, the king promoted Shadrach, Meshach, and Abednego yet again and swore to punish anyone who dared to speak against their God.

"If we are thrown into the blazing furnace, the God we serve is able to save us from it, and he will deliver us from Your Majesty's hand. But even if he does not, we want you to know, Your Majesty, that we will not serve your gods or worship the image of gold you have set up."

Daniel 3:17-18

IN THE LIONS' DEN

Daniel 6

When Nebuchadnezzar died, Daniel continued his work in the kingdom of Babylon under the rule of the next king. King Darius seemed to be just as impressed with Daniel as King Nebuchadnezzar had been. Darius had 120 rulers throughout the kingdom, and he put three men in charge of those rulers. Daniel was one of those three. In fact, Daniel was such an impressive ruler that the king planned to promote him as a leader over the entire kingdom. When the other rulers heard this, they were jealous.

"We have to find a way to bring Daniel down!" one of the rulers whispered.

"But how?" a second one asked. "He doesn't cheat. He doesn't lie. He never does anything wrong!"

"I think I know," a third one said with a smile.

Later, those rulers stood in front of King Darius with a proposal. "Oh, good and honorable King Darius," they began, "let's make a wonderful new law to honor you."

IN THE LIONS' DEN

"I'm listening," the king said.

"Let's make it a law that everyone should pray to you, and only you, for the next thirty days," one ruler suggested.

"If anyone doesn't," the second one chimed in, "he will be thrown into the lions' den!"

"Make sure to put it in writing so that it cannot be changed," the third one added. Without a second thought, Darius made the men's proposal into a law.

Daniel heard about the king's new law, of course, but he continued with his daily routine. Three times a day, he would walk quietly to his upstairs room and look out the windows that faced toward Jerusalem. He would get down on his knees and pray to God, thanking Him and asking Him for guidance.

Outside Daniel's window, listening to him pray, were those same rulers who had suggested the new law to the king. After they saw Daniel praying, they quickly went to pay the king another visit.

"Oh, King Darius," the first one began, "didn't you recently make a law that everyone should pray to you?"

"And only you?" the second one chimed in.

"And if not, he'd be thrown into the lions' den?" the third one asked.

"Yes," the king said. "Why do you ask?"

173

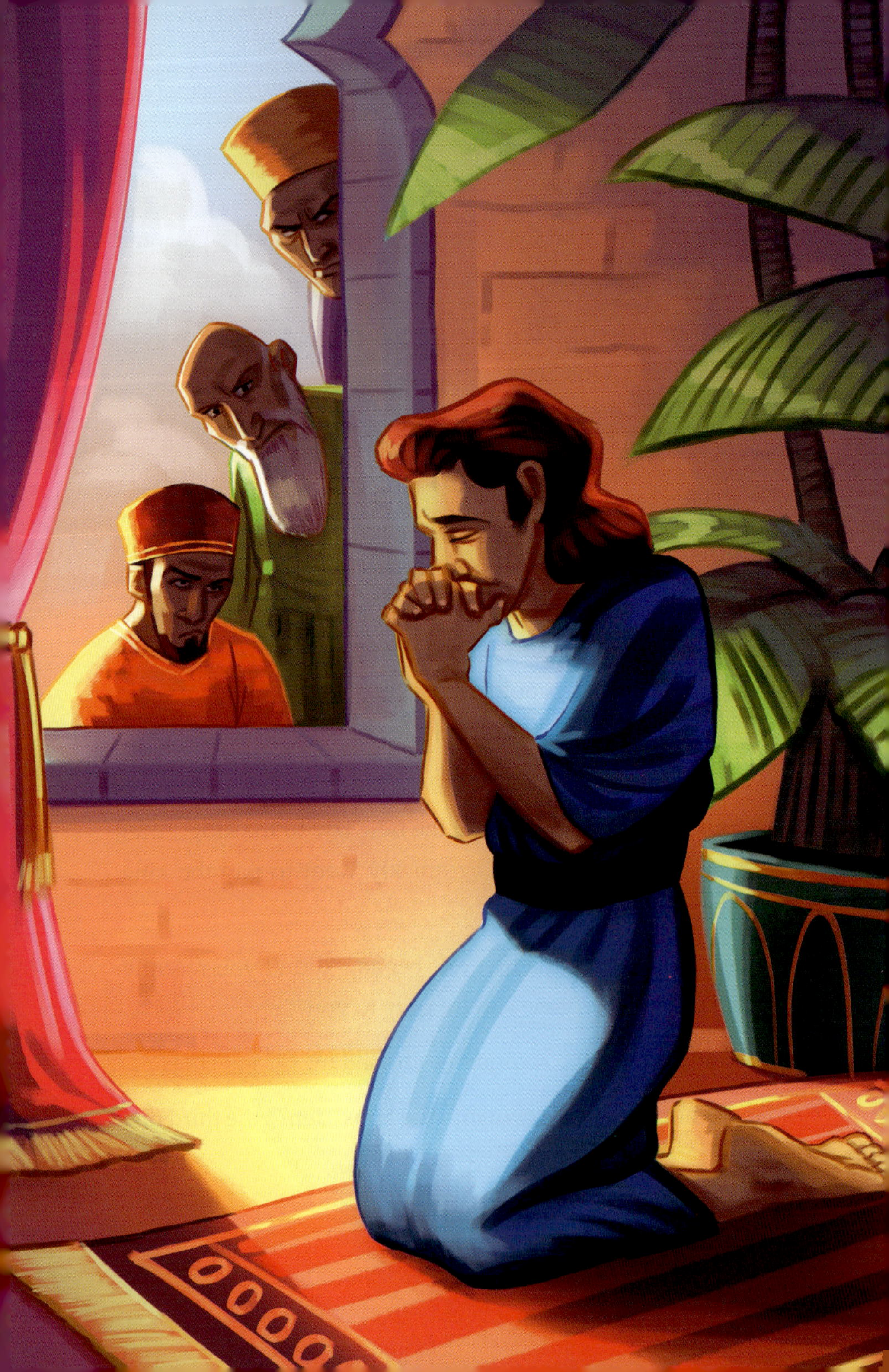

"Well, that ruler Daniel, he paid absolutely no attention to your law," the first ruler said.

"He still prays to his God," the second noted.

"Three times a day," the third added.

The king furrowed his brow and wrung his hands. Daniel was his most trusted and gifted ruler! Regardless, this law could not be changed! The king spoke with his advisors. He looked for loopholes in the law so that Daniel could be saved, but there was nothing he could do.

Finally, the king gave the order to bring Daniel out to receive his punishment. As Daniel was being thrown into the lions' den, the king called out to him, "I hope that the God you serve so faithfully will rescue you!" The king watched as the soldiers slid a heavy stone over the door of the den. Sad and frustrated, Darius went back to the palace to wait.

The king didn't eat. He didn't sleep. He just lay awake, waiting until morning, when he could go back and see if Daniel had survived. As soon as the sun peeked over the horizon, the king ran back to the lions' den.

"Daniel? Daniel?" the king called. "Has your God rescued you from the lions?"

"Your Majesty!" a voice answered from the lions' den. "God sent His angel to shut the mouths of the lions. He knew I was innocent!"

"Get him out of there!" the king ordered. "Get him out of there, now!" When Daniel came out of the lions' den, there wasn't a scratch on him.

"Now," the king said to his soldiers, "go find those men who tried to get rid of Daniel. Let them spend some time in the lions' den."

King Darius gave one more order. He said, "Let everyone in my kingdom honor the God of Daniel. He rescues, He saves, and He lives forever."

Just like his friends Shadrach, Meshach, and Abednego, Daniel had once again shown the entire kingdom of Babylon the power of his God. By simply being faithful, by doing what he knew was right, Daniel made the power of God known to those who had not known Him before.

Now when Daniel learned that the decree had been published, he went home to his upstairs room where the windows opened toward Jerusalem. Three times a day he got down on his knees and prayed, giving thanks to his God, just as he had done before.

Daniel 6:10

AN ORPHAN SAVES HER PEOPLE

The Book of Esther

After many years, the king of Persia conquered Babylon. This king, King Cyrus, allowed the Israelites to return home, back to their own country. By that time, however, many of the Israelites were thriving in the new country and didn't want to leave. Years later, there were still Israelites living in the Persian Empire.

Esther, whose family had chosen to stay behind and live in Persia, lost both of her parents when she was a young girl.

Esther's cousin Mordecai had stepped in to raise her as his own daughter after her parents died. She grew into a beautiful young woman as the two of them settled into a normal life in the city of Susa.

Elsewhere in Susa, there was a problem in the palace. King Xerxes loved to give huge parties with lots of food and drink. During one such party, he demanded that his servants bring his wife, Queen Vashti, to him. He wanted to show off her beauty to the crowd, but Queen Vashti refused.

The king's face burned with rage, and he demanded a conference with his wise men.

"What will we do with a queen who disobeys her king?" Xerxes asked.

"If word gets out," one of the wise men replied, "all of the women in the land will act the same way!"

As punishment, and to prevent an outbreak of rebelliousness, it was decided that Queen Vashti would be replaced. The search was on for a new queen! The king's servants brought young women to the palace from all over the region. These women would undergo beauty treatments for an entire year before they were presented to the king.

When the king's servants saw Esther, they were pleased with her beauty and invited her to the palace. Esther went with them to receive her year of beauty treatments and meet the king. She did everything she was told until it was finally time for her to be presented to the king. As the king spent time with her, he was taken by her beauty and grace. He favored her over all of the other young women.

"Bring the crown!" the servants shouted. "King Xerxes has found a new queen!" Sounds of celebration rang throughout the palace and all of Susa. The king threw a huge banquet, celebrating his new queen, Queen Esther. Xerxes even declared the day a public holiday and celebrated by giving gifts to all the people.

As Esther settled into her role as queen, Mordecai warned her not to tell anyone that she was a Jew. He knew that some people in Susa didn't like God's people and might make trouble for her if they knew. Mordecai himself was in the king's service, and he spent his days at the king's gate, witnessing the many business deals and meetings that took place there.

One day Mordecai overheard whispers of a plot to kill the king, so he reported it to Queen Esther. The men behind the plot were arrested, and the king was saved. Mordecai's loyalty and service to the king were recorded in the king's record book.

Also living in Susa was a man named Haman, one of the king's nobles. Haman had received the king's highest honors, and everywhere Haman went, the people were expected to bow to him. Everyone did as Haman expected—everyone except one man.

"Why do you not bow to Haman?" one of the officials demanded.

"Because I am a Jew," Mordecai answered. "I will only bow down to my God, the one true God."

When the official told him why Mordecai refused to bow, Haman was so angry at this act of defiance that he decided to kill not only Mordecai but all of the Jews in the entire kingdom.

Haman went to the king and said, "Some people in this kingdom do not only have different customs and worship a different god, but they don't obey the king's commands either." Haman was so persuasive that he convinced the king to sign a decree ordering the destruction of all the Jews in Persia. What King

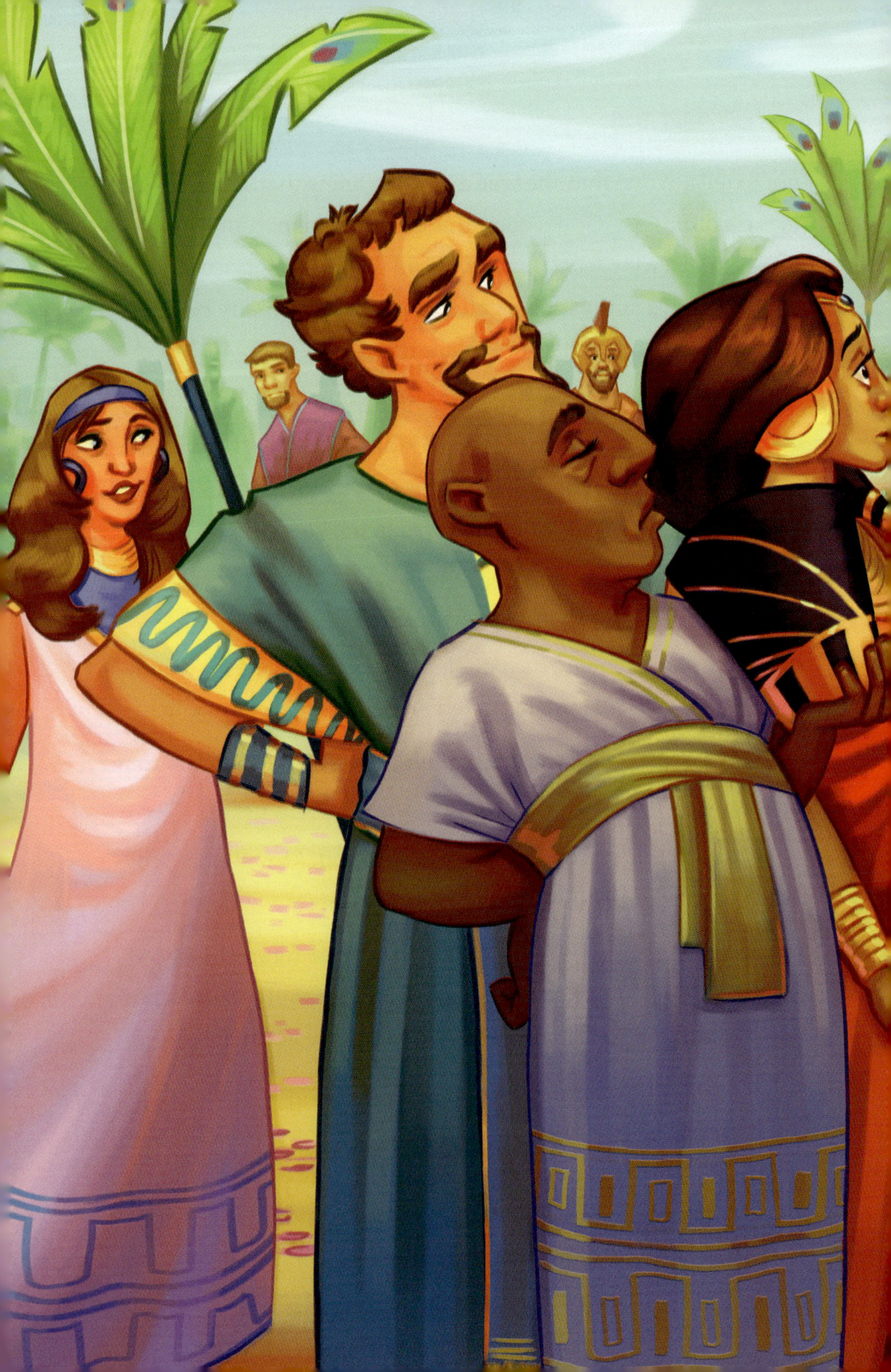

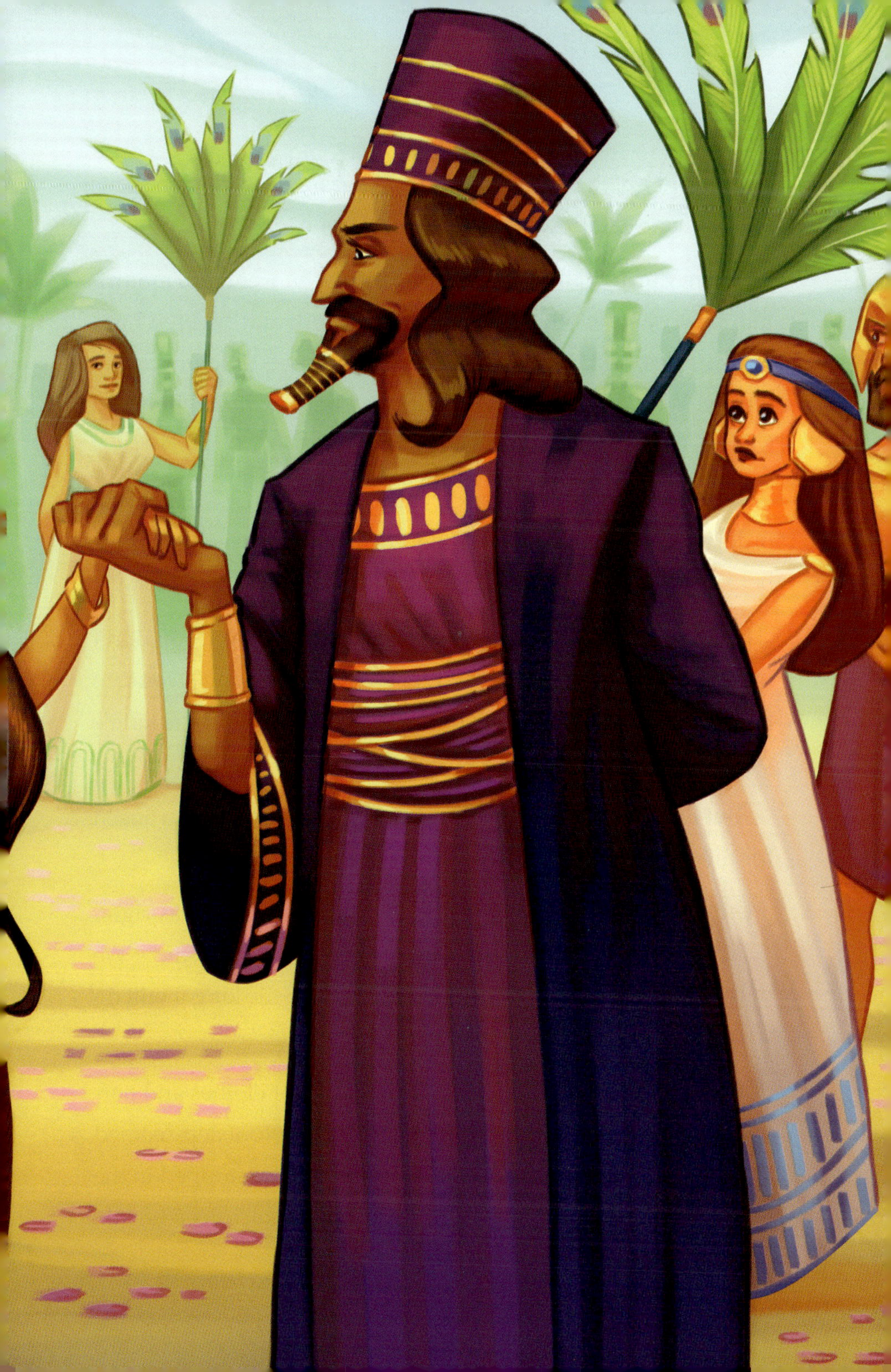

Xerxes did not know, however, was that he had just signed his own queen's death sentence.

When Mordecai heard about the decree, he went into mourning. He tore his clothes. He put on sackcloth and covered himself in ashes, and he walked through the streets of town, crying loudly. When Esther heard about this, she sent clean clothes to Mordecai, asking what was wrong.

Mordecai simply sent back a copy of the decree—the decree ordering their death as Jews—and he begged Queen Esther for help.

Esther immediately sent word back to Mordecai. "You don't understand!" she said. "I can't just go into the king's court to talk to him! I have to be called in to see him. If I enter the king's presence without permission, he can kill me!"

"But Esther," Mordecai pleaded, "maybe God made you queen for this very time, for this very purpose."

Esther was terrified, but she knew that Mordecai was right. "Gather all of the Jews to fast and pray for me," she said. "We will do the same. After three days, I will go to the king. I will do what I can to save my people, but if I die, I die."

After three days, Esther dressed in her finest clothes and nervously walked toward the king's court. Each footstep seemed to echo with foreboding: *Boom! Boom! Boom!* She stopped in the inner court, where the king could see her, and took a deep breath.

AN ORPHAN SAVES HER PEOPLE

When King Xerxes noticed her, he was happy to see her and called her to him. "What is it, Esther?" he said. "What can I give you? I'd give you half the kingdom if you wanted it!"

"Well my king," she began, "I was hoping that perhaps you and Haman could join me for dinner."

"Go!" the king called to his servants. "Bring Haman so that Esther may have what she wants!"

As they were eating dinner, the king asked Esther, "Now, tell us, what can we do for you?"

Esther looked at the king. "Well, I was hoping that maybe you would come back to eat with me tomorrow?"

The king raised an eyebrow, then smiled. He said, "Tomorrow it is! Right, Haman?"

Haman could not believe his luck. First, the king had given him the highest honors, and now the queen herself was inviting him to a second private dinner with the king. That night, he went home and bragged to his friends and family about his good fortune.

"Still," Haman admitted to them, "all of my happiness disappears when I see that Jew Mordecai sitting at the gate."

"So, get rid of him," his wife and friends suggested. "Set up a huge pole to hang him on, and in the morning ask the king to hang him. Then you can go enjoy your dinner with the queen." Haman loved the idea and gave orders to have the pole erected.

About the same time that Haman was having the pole set up to hang Mordecai, the king was having trouble sleeping. He called for his records to be read to him. As the king listened, the records told of a man who had informed him about a plot to kill the king.

"Wait!" the king interrupted. "What was ever done for this man, the man who saved my life?"

"Nothing, Your Majesty," the attendant answered.

Just then, Haman scurried into the king's court. "Haman, my man," the king asked him, "what should I do for a man I would like to honor?"

Haman grinned, thinking, *Who else would the king like to honor but me?* He cleared his throat and answered, "Well, first of all, I would clothe him in the king's own royal robe. Then, I would give him the king's own royal horse—you know, the one that wears the little royal crest on its head? That one." Haman closed his eyes, walking as he talked, imagining it all. He continued, "And I would let him wear the robe and ride the horse through the streets while someone proclaims ahead of him, 'Look everyone! This is how the king treats those he wants to honor!'"

"Yes! Perfect!" The king exclaimed, clapping his hands. "Now go and do all of those things—every last detail—for Mordecai, the Jew!"

Haman stood in horror as he realized what the king had just ordered him to do. He was trying to get rid of Mordecai completely, and now the king wanted Haman to honor him? Haman had never felt so humiliated. The next day, however, just as planned, Haman had to join the king and queen for dinner.

"Tell me," the king asked Esther again, "what is it that you wish? Whatever it is, you can have it."

"Your Majesty," she looked up at him, "I really just have one request—please spare my life, and spare my people. Someone is trying to get rid of us, to kill us all."

"What do you mean?" The king asked, and stood up quickly. "Who would dare to do such a thing?"

Esther pointed a quivering finger and said, "He would! Haman!"

Haman cowered before the king and queen. He begged for forgiveness and pleaded for his life, but it was too late. That very night, Haman would be hung on the pole that he had built himself—the pole on which he had intended to hang Mordecai.

The king issued a new law, overruling Haman's order and protecting his queen's people. The Jews would be free to defend themselves from anyone trying to hurt them because of Haman's law. They would be safe from all harm.

A brave young queen had spoken up for her people. She had spoken out against evil, and in doing so, she saved generations of Jews and fulfilled the very purpose that God had given her.

"For if you remain silent at this time, relief and deliverance for the Jews will arise from another place, but you and your father's family will perish. And who knows but that you have come to royal position for such a time as this?"

Esther 4:14

THE NEW
TESTAMENT

PREPARING FOR A SAVIOR

Luke 1, 3

A long time had passed since God made the world. People had chosen sin over and over again, making it so they couldn't have a relationship with their Creator. But God had a plan to save the people He had created—the people He loved. God's plan centered around a person, but not just any person. God's plan involved His own Son, who would give new life to the world.

The prophet Isaiah foretold it years ago. God knew it from the very beginning. Now, it was time for the whole world to see.

But before God unveiled his plan, preparations had to be made.

A priest named Zechariah and his wife Elizabeth were both faithful and obedient to God. Even though they loved God and each other, they still had not been blessed with a child. By this point, now that they were old, they had little hope of that ever happening, but they remained faithful in their service to the Lord.

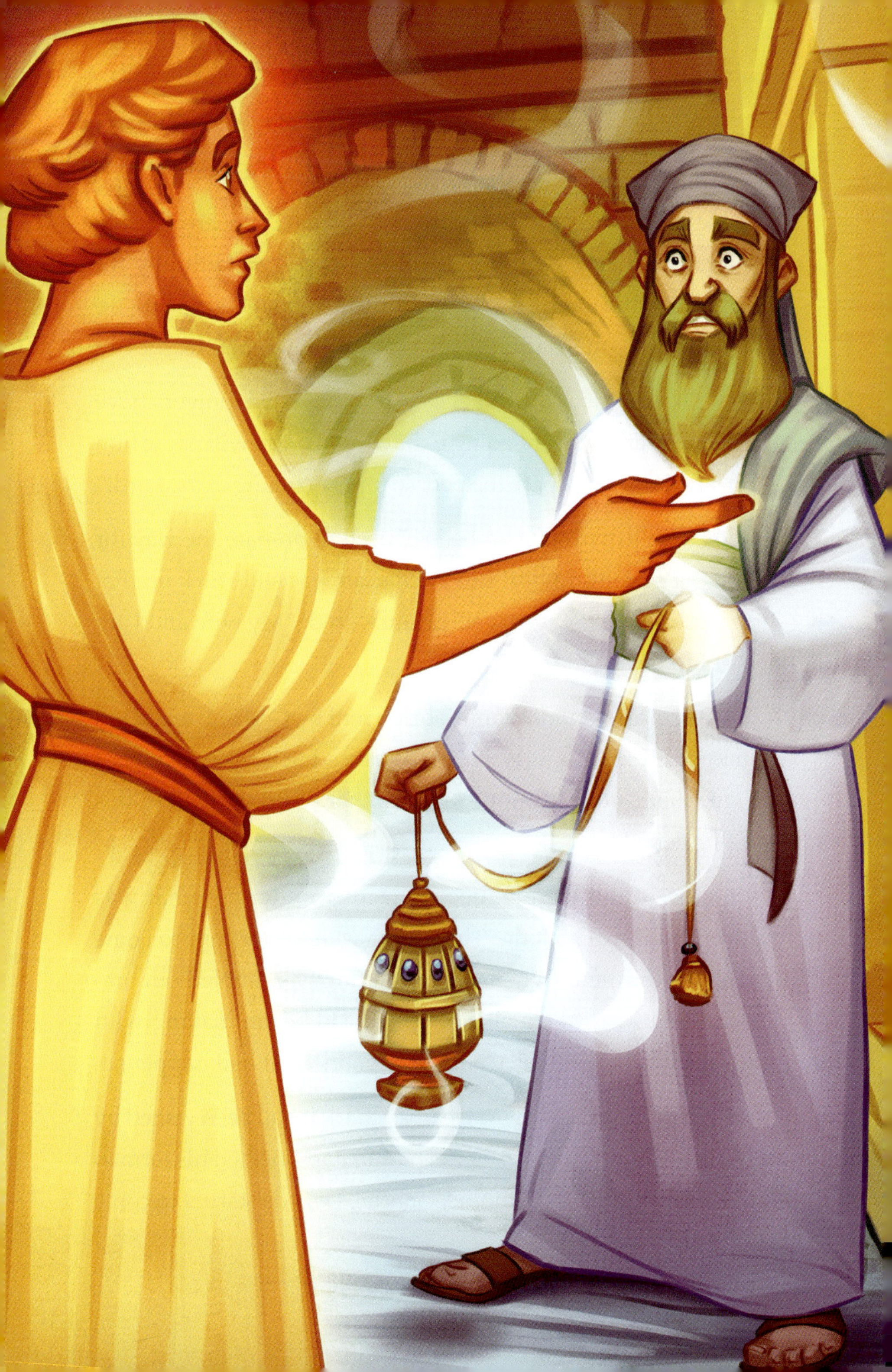

One day Zechariah was performing his priestly duties, burning incense in the temple, when suddenly, an angel appeared beside the altar. Zechariah froze in fear. He had served faithfully for many years, but Zechariah was not used to angels showing up in the temple—this had never happened to him before.

"Don't be afraid," the angel said to him. "Your prayers have been heard, and you are going to have a son. You will name him John, and he will prepare the people for the coming of the Lord."

Zechariah's own son had been chosen to prepare the way for Jesus, the coming Savior! But Zechariah was still stuck on that first part. "This can't be true!" he answered. "My wife and I are too old to have children!"

The angel answered, "I am Gabriel, sent by God himself to tell you this news. My words will come true—but since you did not believe them, you will not speak another word until all of this has happened."

Outside of the temple, people were wondering what was taking Zachariah so long. They were waiting for him to come out and bless them. When Zechariah finally stumbled out into the sunlight, he was unable to speak. He began making wild gestures with his hands, trying to explain what had happened.

After a while, it all became clear: Zechariah had been visited by an angel. Not very long after Zechariah had finished his term in the temple and returned home, Gabriel's words started to come true! They discovered that Elizabeth was going to have a baby. She and Zechariah were overwhelmed with joy.

When Elizabeth had the baby, Zechariah gazed upon his newborn son, and he was filled with joy. All of their friends and family gathered around to celebrate, and when it came time to name the baby, everyone wanted to name him Zechariah, after his father. But Elizabeth said, "No, his name is John!"

Everyone looked to Zechariah, who motioned for a tablet to write on. Zechariah, still unable to speak, wrote, "His name is John." With those words, confirming what the angel Gabriel had foretold, Zechariah's voice came back. He immediately began to sing and praise God for His precious gift of a son—a son that would prepare the way for the Savior.

That little baby grew into a bold young man. And when he was grown, John began telling everyone about the world's coming Savior: the Savior that Isaiah had foretold, the Savior that existed even before the world began, the Savior that the world had been waiting for.

Despite John's boldness, when that Savior came, few would recognize Him. Even though John preached and taught, preparing the way, few would understand. Despite all of God's preparations, the world just wasn't ready for the Savior to come like *this*.

> "And he will go on before the Lord,
> in the spirit and power of Elijah, to
> turn the hearts of the parents to their
> children and the disobedient to the
> wisdom of the righteous—to make
> ready a people prepared for the Lord."
>
> Luke 1:17

AN UNEXPECTED GIFT

Luke 1; Matthew 1

A few months after Elizabeth learned that she was pregnant, her nearby relative received some exciting news of her own. Elizabeth's younger cousin Mary was engaged to marry a man named Joseph. To everyone else, they were just another young couple in the small town of Nazareth. To God, on the other hand, they were His chosen ones for a very special task.

Mary was alone, minding her own business, when suddenly, a voice exclaimed, "Greetings, favored one! God is with you!"

Mary looked up, startled to see an angel standing before her. She stepped back, quivering in fear.

"No, no—don't be afraid, dear Mary," said the angel. "My name is Gabriel. I've been sent by God to tell you that He has chosen you."

Chosen? For what? Mary's mind was racing as she tried to take it all in.

"You will give birth to a baby boy, and you will name Him

Jesus. God will make Him a king, like David before Him, but this king will reign forever. His kingdom will never end."

"How—how can this happen?" Mary asked. "I'm not even married yet."

Gabriel answered, "The power of God will come over you and give you a son. He will be God's Son. Just as God has made it possible for Elizabeth to have a child in her old age, he will make this possible too. Nothing is impossible for God!"

"I am God's servant," Mary said, bowing her head. "Let it be done just as you said."

Mary gathered a few supplies and started the journey to Elizabeth's house. When she arrived, Mary called out, "Elizabeth! Elizabeth! You'll never believe what—" Mary stopped as Elizabeth came into the light. What the angel had said about Elizabeth was true. Mary's cousin smiled, proudly placing her hand on a very round belly.

Before Mary could say another word, Elizabeth exclaimed, "Blessed! You are so blessed, Mary! Blessed more than every other woman on the earth! Blessed is the child that you carry! Why am I so honored that the mother of my Lord is visiting me?"

Mary didn't know what to say. Elizabeth was like an aunt to her—why was she suddenly honoring her? How could Elizabeth already know that she was carrying the Son of God?

AN UNEXPECTED GIFT

Elizabeth answered the questions spinning in Mary's head. "As soon as I heard your voice, I felt my own baby jump for joy! You are blessed, Mary, blessed for believing the Lord's promises."

Elizabeth knew, and Mary knew, that she would soon give birth to the Son of God.

Mary couldn't help wondering about her future husband, though. What would Joseph think?

Joseph was a good and honorable man, a descendant of King David himself, and he had asked Mary to be his wife. When he found out that she was pregnant before they were married, it's safe to say that he was more than a little disappointed. He would be frowned upon if he married her now, but he also didn't want Mary to be publicly shamed for being pregnant without being married. So Joseph planned to do the only thing he thought he could. He would divorce Mary as quietly as possible, without making a public spectacle of it.

After making his decision, however, Joseph had a strange but very persuasive visitor. As Joseph drifted off to sleep, his dreams became odd and surprising. There was a man in his dreams—a man unlike any he had seen before. As the man spoke, his words were seared into Joseph's memory. He said, "Joseph, descendant of David, don't be afraid to take Mary as your wife. The child she carries is the Son of God. You will name Him Jesus. He will be a Savior to the world, saving people from their sin."

AN UNEXPECTED GIFT

Joseph woke up and sat there in amazement. Could it be true? Was the Savior really coming? Had he really been chosen to be the earthly father of the Savior of the world?

Although Joseph was stunned, he went to Mary and they got married right away. Together, strengthened by the hand of God,

Mary and Joseph would soon welcome the Son of the Almighty God into their little family, and He would be the Savior of the world.

But the angel said to her, "Do not be afraid, Mary; you have found favor with God. You will conceive and give birth to a son, and you are to call him Jesus. He will be great and will be called the Son of the Most High. The Lord God will give him the throne of his father David, and he will reign over Jacob's descendants forever; his kingdom will never end."

Luke 1:30-33

AN UNLIKELY KING

Luke 2; Matthew 2

As the baby grew inside Mary's belly, so did her anticipation. Each day held a new excitement for Mary and Joseph as the day drew closer that He would be born, and Mary and Joseph would meet their Savior—God's own Son. But When they heard the news that Caesar Augustus, the Roman Emperor, was requiring all families to register in their hometowns, they were not very excited about that. Joseph's hometown was Bethlehem, meaning that Mary and Joseph would have to travel about eighty miles—a journey that would take several days—to obey the decree.

Joseph packed everything they may need for the journey, placed it on a donkey, and helped Mary onto the donkey's back. Together they headed south for their destination. As they traveled, however, Joseph realized that their family would not only be registering in Bethlehem, it would also be increasing there—the baby was on His way.

The more uncomfortable Mary became, the more urgently Joseph searched for a place to stay, but it was no use. *What would*

God think of this stable? Joseph thought. True, there was no room in the inn, where he had expected to stay—he wanted Mary to be able to rest in a comfortable bed so God's son could be born in the place that He deserved. But this? A lowly manger? A chorus of animal sounds? This was no place for a king.

Or was it?

Beneath the steady glow of a bright-shining star, Mary wrapped her tiny baby in cloth and laid Him on a bed of hay, unable to take her eyes off of Him. His eyelashes fluttered. His cheeks were so soft, His fingers so tiny and new. To the world, He may have looked like a helpless baby, but Mary knew different. When she looked up at her husband, she saw that he knew it too.

He was here. He had finally arrived.

The King of kings, the Lord of lords, the Savior of the world was here.

Just outside of Bethlehem, a group of shepherds were enjoying the peacefulness of the rolling fields. Together they quietly recapped the events of the day and noted the unusually bright stars that filled the night sky. After a while, they began settling in for a restful night under the stars.

It was not to be a very restful night, however, because heaven above just could not contain its excitement! Suddenly an angel burst forth, lighting up the field like it was morning. The shepherds cowered at the sight of this heavenly visitor.

"Don't be afraid!" the angel said. "I have good news! Great news! Wonderful news! For everyone! For all the people!"

The shepherds squinted at the brightly glowing angel.

The angel continued his proclamation. "On this very day, a Savior has been born! He is the Messiah, the promised king! He is the Lord! And He's right here in Bethlehem! Go see for yourselves! Just look for a baby wrapped in cloth and sleeping in a manger."

Before the shepherds could say a word, the sky was filled with more angels, with the glory of God, and with a bright, shining light. All together, the angels began to praise God with one voice, singing:

"Glory! Glory! Glory to God on high!

Peace! Peace! Peace to His people!"

The shepherds could still hear the angels' praises as the heavenly choir disappeared back into the heavens. After a few moments of stunned silence, the shepherds looked at each other. They nodded in agreement and headed straight for Bethlehem.

It didn't take them long for them to find the baby in the stable.

The child's young mother smiled warmly, welcoming them in. The father watched closely as they stepped toward the manger. The baby, sleeping peacefully, didn't look like a king at all—He had a manger full of hay instead of a throne.

Even so, there was something about Him. A calm holiness filled this place. The peace the angels had spoken of was surely here.

The shepherds' knees bent in humility, in worship, in wonder at this tiny Messiah, this unlikely king. They told the new parents about what they had seen in the fields, about the announcement from the angels. As the shepherds returned to their fields and wandered around with their sheep, they told everyone they met all about the wonders they had seen, of the Savior born in a stable.

Mary watched it all unfold, these shepherds—these strangers—worshipping her infant son. She would remember it always. Little did she know, there were more visitors on their way.

Far in the east, when the bright star appeared, another journey had begun. A group of Magi—star studiers, dream interpreters, wise men who served kings—set out to find the new king, the King of the Jews. They loaded their camels up with gifts and headed west. It would be a long journey, but their time would be well rewarded.

When the Magi were nearing their destination, they stopped at the palace in Jerusalem. It seemed like the best place to find a king. Excitedly, they left their camels and approached the throne.

"Where is the new king, the child who was born King of the Jews?" the Magi asked King Herod. "We saw His star, and we followed it here. We have come to worship Him."

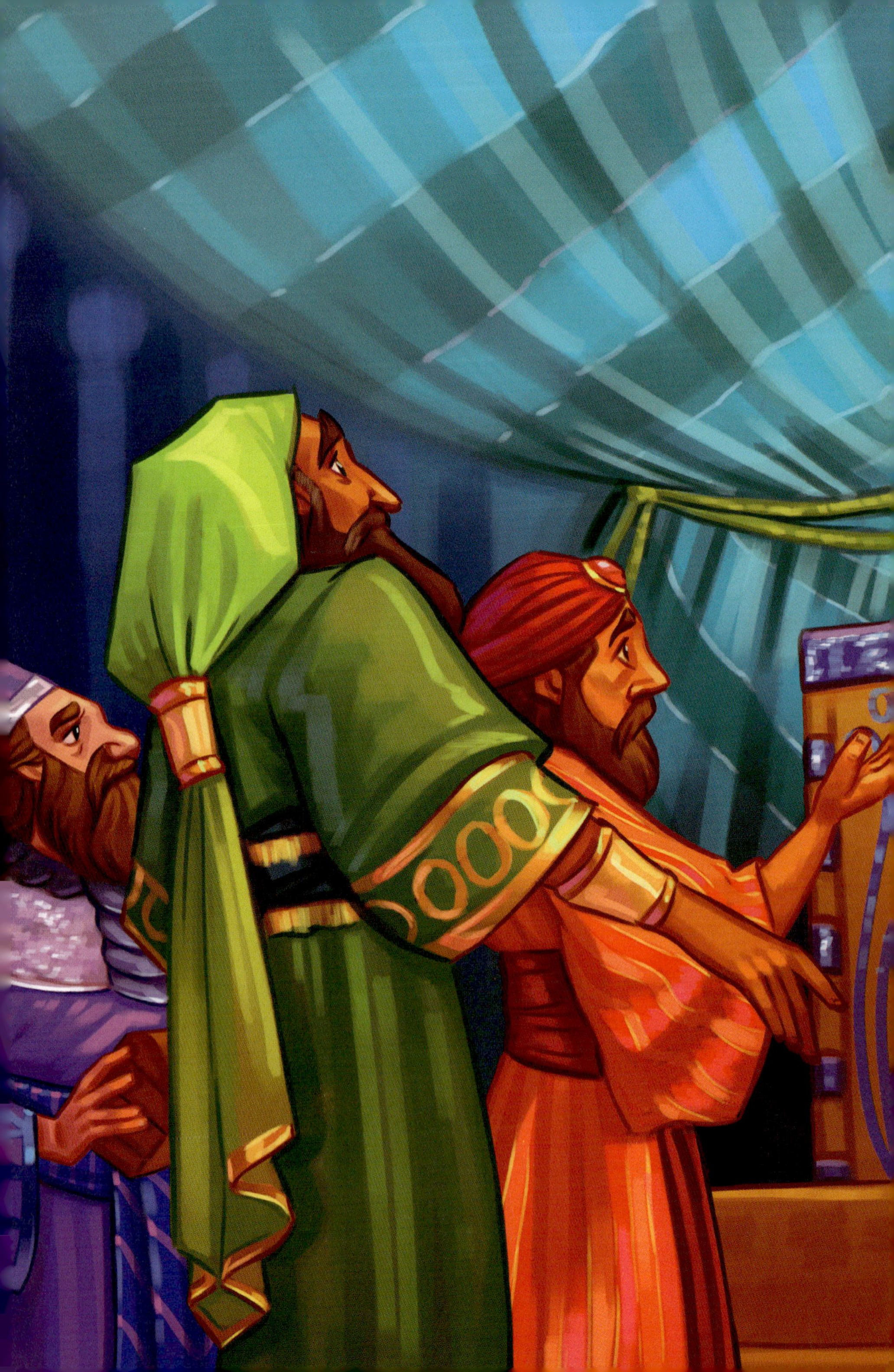

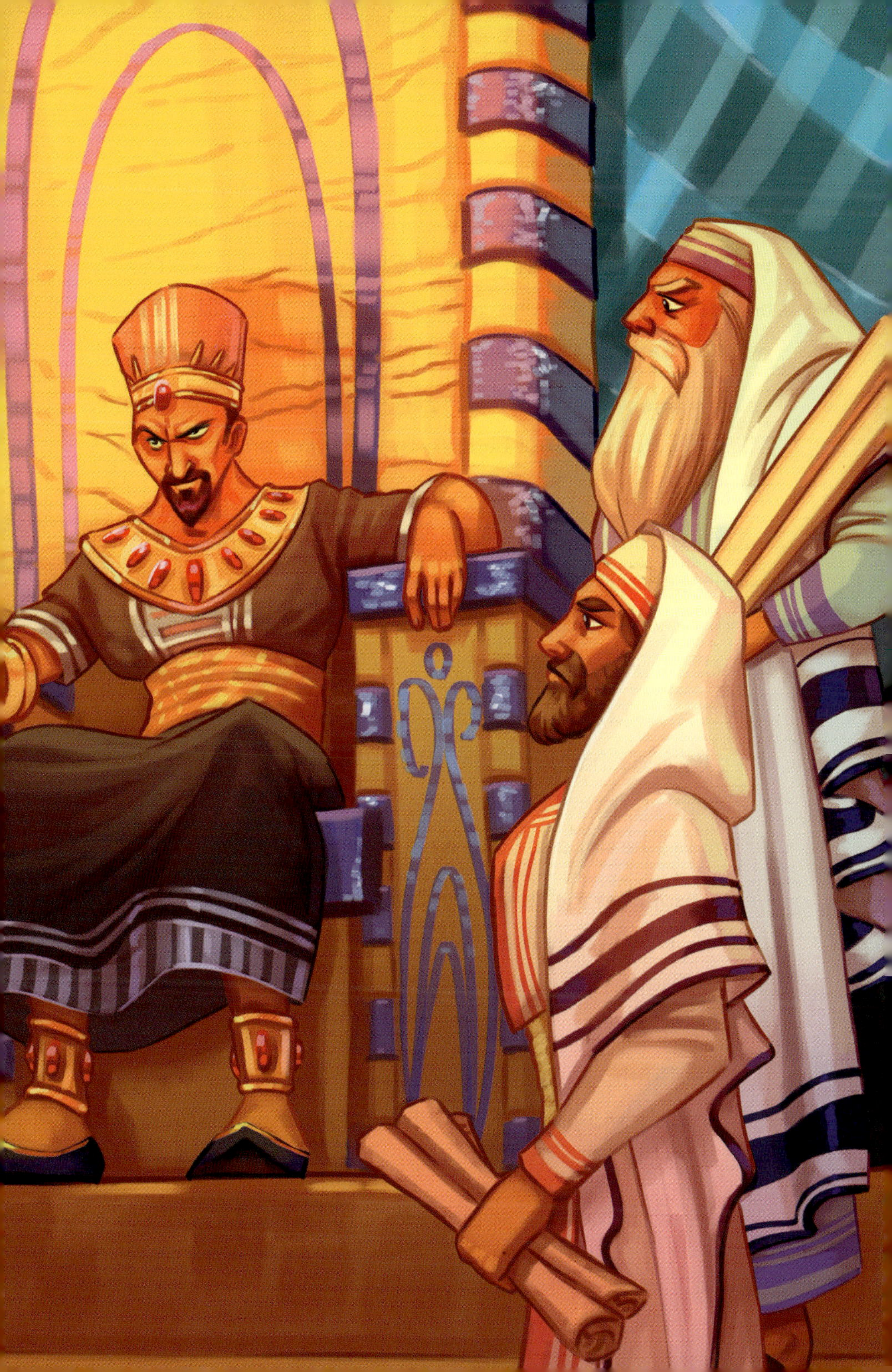

AN UNLIKELY KING

King Herod was furious. *He* was the only king worthy of worship—and he would destroy anyone who got in his way! He was concerned, however, that what the Magi said could really be true. To make sure, he called his advisers and said, "Tell me, what do the scriptures say? Where is the Messiah to be born?"

"In Bethlehem," one of his advisers answered. "The prophet Micah foretold, 'Out of Bethlehem will come a ruler for God's people.'"

King Herod smiled sweetly at the Magi from the East. After asking them when exactly they had seen the star, he said, "Good, good. Now go and find this child for me, and as soon as you do, tell me where He is. I, too, want to go and... *worship* Him."

"Yes, Your Majesty," the Magi said. They bowed low and left the palace. As they went on their way, they were amazed to see the bright star once again, leading them on. They followed it until, finally, the star came to rest over a small home in Bethlehem.

The people in the streets stopped and stared as the caravan passed. They watched and wondered as colorfully decorated camels, laden with supplies and gifts, stopped in front of the humble home.

"What in the world?" the townsfolk whispered. "Isn't that where Mary and Joseph live? What is the reason for such regal visitors?"

The Magi had waited so long for this moment, to finally meet this Messiah, to see the King they had been seeking for so long—the Savior of the world.

The Magi from the east bowed low, offering gifts to Mary's young son. The child watched as these prestigious men laid a box of gold at His feet. The strong aroma of fine spices filled the room as they presented Him with jars of frankincense and myrrh. Most remarkable of all the gifts were the visitors themselves: these wise and regal men who had traveled so far to worship a child named Jesus.

Filled with wonder, the Magi turned to head back toward the palace and tell King Herod that they had found Him, the Messiah, the King. But before they could, a dream stopped them in their tracks, warning them not to go back to King Herod. Instead, they returned home a different way, staying far away from the palace.

Of course, that didn't stop King Herod. In fact, he ordered all of the boys two years old and under to be killed—just to be sure he got rid of that little "King of the Jews." After an angel warned Joseph in a dream, he took his family to Egypt where they would be safe, at least for a while.

It wouldn't be the last time that someone tried to hurt Jesus. He would be rejected and mocked, beaten and bruised. Time and time again, people proved that the world just did not understand a Savior like this, an unlikely King of kings, a lowly Lord of lords.

AN UNLIKELY KING

It just didn't make any sense. Why was the greatest of all kings born in a stable instead of a palace? Why was His birth announced to faraway Magi and lowly shepherds instead of by royal proclamation? Why would God send the Savior to earth in a way that few expected and even fewer believed?

But God's ways are not like the ways of this world. He knew that the last thing the world needed was another pompous king. He knew that true salvation would only come through the power of this kind of Savior, and He knew that, ultimately, even the Savior's rejection would lead to the world's redemption.

An all-knowing God knew what the world did not: the world's greatest hope had arrived, and it was this tiny, unlikely king.

"But the angel said to them, "Do not be afraid. I bring you good news that will cause great joy for all the people. Today in the town of David a Savior has been born to you; he is the Messiah, the Lord."

Luke 2:10-11

"MY FATHER'S HOUSE"

Luke 2

Forty days after Jesus was born, Mary and Joseph dedicated Him in the temple according to the Jewish custom. As Jesus grew, His earthly parents raised Him carefully, making sure to follow the law of the Lord. Throughout the years that followed, Mary and Joseph regularly attended the Jewish religious festivals with Jesus.

When Jesus was twelve years old, He and His family set out for the Passover festival in Jerusalem, just as they had done every year before. It took several days to travel from the town of Nazareth to the city of Jerusalem, but crowds of people made the journey along with them. The festival was a time of great celebration, a time to remember God's faithfulness to His people.

When the celebration was over, the family prepared to return home. Mary and Joseph gathered their belongings and headed back toward Nazareth.

After traveling for about a day, they realized that they hadn't seen Jesus in a while. At the age of twelve, He was old enough to walk with His friends or the relatives who had traveled with them, but when Mary and Joseph checked with the families in front of them and behind them, Jesus wasn't there. They turned and started heading back toward Jerusalem, checking with everyone they passed to find out if they had seen Him. In spite of their searching, there was still no sign of Jesus. When they finally got back to Jerusalem, they checked the place where they had stayed, but Jesus wasn't there.

Mary began to panic. She had lost her son—not only that, she had lost the *Son of God*. She had been entrusted with the most precious person in the universe, *and she lost Him.* Now He was all alone in this big city. He wouldn't know where to find His parents. He wouldn't know how to get home. Mary's thoughts raced, *What will He eat? He must be starving by now!* "Mary!" Joseph's words broke through her frantic thoughts. "Let's check the temple. Maybe He's there."

They had been looking for three days now. What were the chances that He'd be in the temple? Mary followed along but didn't even look up until she heard a precious and familiar voice.

Mary couldn't believe what she saw. Sitting among the teachers of the law and the priests of the temple was her son, Jesus. Everyone around her seemed to share in her astonishment. Who was this twelve-year-old boy, asking questions of the teachers in the temple and discussing the ancient truths of the scriptures with them?

"MY FATHER'S HOUSE"

"Jesus!" Mary called, running to Him and throwing her arms around her son. She took a step back and quickly brushed away the tears in her eyes. People were staring at them now, but she hardly noticed. "Why would You do that to me?" she asked. "Don't You know we've been looking for You everywhere? We were worried sick!"

Jesus looked up calmly into His mother's eyes. "Why would you be looking for Me?" He asked with a warm smile. "Didn't you know that I had to be right here, in my Father's house?"

Speechless, Mary looked at Joseph. Joseph shrugged and gave her a slight smile. Unable to say another word, Mary just threw her arms around Jesus again, thankful to have found her son. Over the years, time and time again, she would be amazed as He continued to grow in wisdom, gaining the favor of both God and man.

> *"Why were you searching for me?" he asked. "Didn't you know I had to be in my Father's house?"*
>
> Luke 2:49

THE LAMB OF GOD

Matthew 3; Luke 3

John, the son born to Zechariah and Elizabeth late in their life, grew up to prepare the way for the coming Savior, just as the prophet Isaiah had predicted. John was a voice to the people, telling them about Jesus, the Messiah.

To the outside world, John appeared a bit odd. He wore camel's hair for clothes, he ate locusts and wild honey, and he would often spend time in the wilderness alone. As strange as it may have seemed, it was there in the wilderness that the word of God was revealed to him.

People flocked to John from Jerusalem and the whole area of Judea. They came out to the desert to hear him preach the messages God had placed on his heart. He taught them to turn away from their sins and turn back to God and His forgiveness. He taught people to share what they had with those who had nothing, and he taught the tax collectors to be fair. He taught the people not to take more than what they needed and to be content with what they had. Through it all, he taught them that repentance and wholeheartedly seeking God was the only way to have an eternal life with Him.

Even the religious rulers came to hear John speak. He urged them not to simply rely on their religious heritage, but to do what was right and good—instead of only talking about it.

Down in the Jordan River, John baptized everyone who came to him wanting to know the way to God.

When people asked if he was the Messiah, John would tell them, "No! I only baptize you with water. Someone else is coming, One who is far greater than I am. In fact, I am not even worthy to untie His sandals. When He comes, He will baptize you with the Holy Spirit." One day, that *One* did come. John pointed and said, "Look! There is the Lamb of God who takes away the sin of the world!" Jesus stood in line, waiting to be baptized. The perfect, holy Savior waited behind sinners, waited for His turn to be obedient to His Father's word.

When Jesus' turn came and He asked to be baptized, John tried to refuse. "No, Master," he said. "If anything, *You* should baptize *me*. Why would You want to be baptized by me?"

"Because this is the right thing to do," Jesus answered. "This is how it must be."

John didn't understand. He knew that Jesus was free from sin, and that He had nothing of which to repent. He had no sins to wash away. Later, John would come to realize that Jesus was showing the way, setting an example for believers now and yet to come.

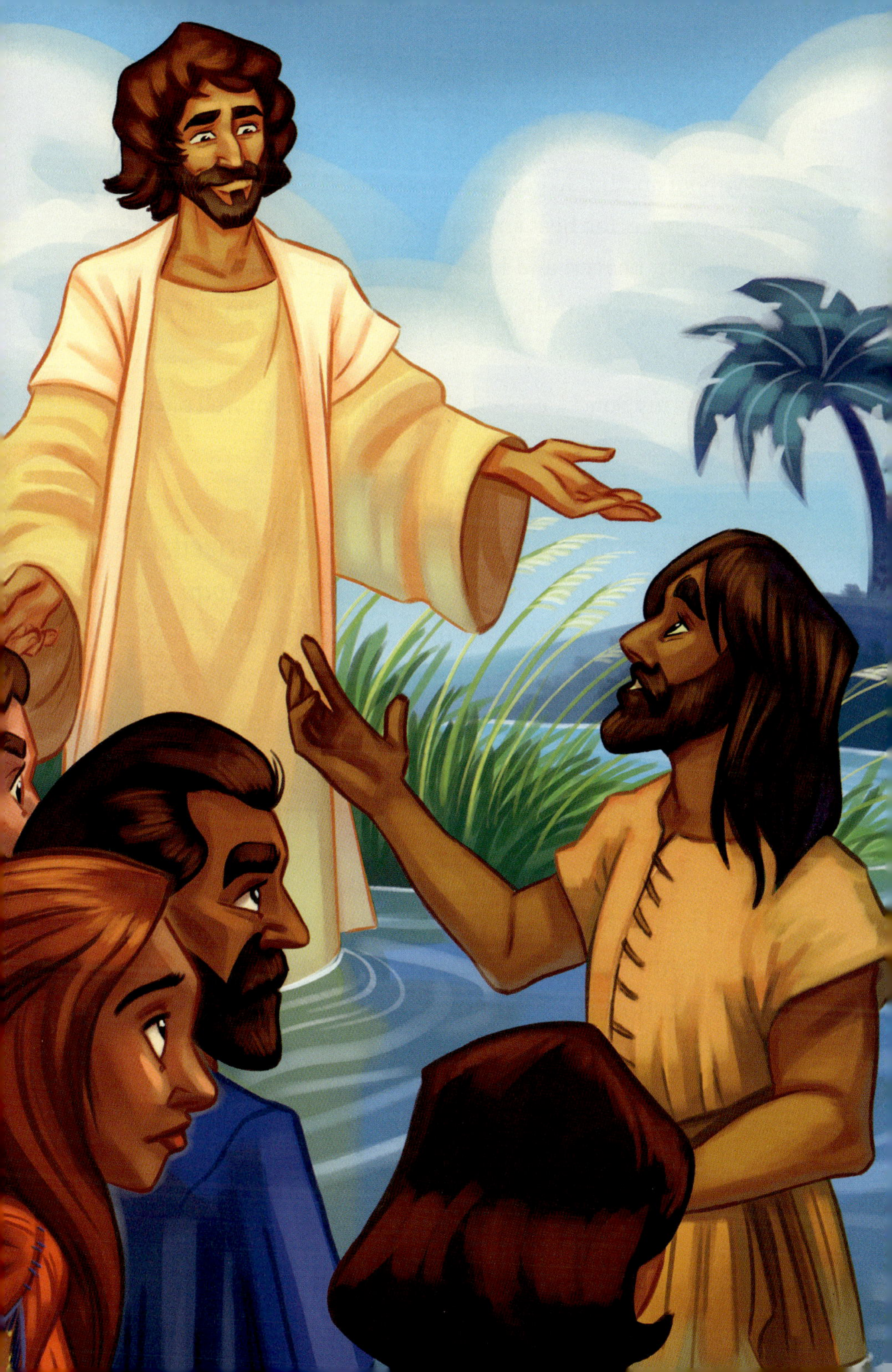

Without another word, John baptized Jesus. As the water rolled off Jesus' face, the heavens opened up. A Spirit like a dove flew down from heaven and hovered over Jesus, and a voice came from above, confirming to the crowd what John the Baptist already knew.

"This is my Son," God said, "and with Him I am well pleased."

When all the people were being baptized, Jesus was baptized too. And as he was praying, heaven was opened and the Holy Spirit descended on him in bodily form like a dove. And a voice came from heaven: "You are my Son, whom I love; with you I am well pleased."

Luke 3:21-22

The next day John saw Jesus coming toward him and said, "Look, the Lamb of God, who takes away the sin of the world!"

John 1:29

THE DEVIL TEMPTS JESUS

Matthew 4; Luke 4

After Jesus was baptized, He was led by the Spirit deep into the wilderness. For forty days, Jesus fasted there, and by the end of this time He was very hungry. That's when Satan came to tempt Him.

"Well, hello there, Jesus," Satan said, smiling slyly. "You look like you're just *starving*." He picked up a stone and tossed it in the air, catching it, and continued, "I mean, if you really are the Son of God, you could just turn one of these stones to bread—*couldn't you?*" Satan held the stone up, encouraging Jesus to imagine the satisfying taste of bread on His tongue.

"It's written in the Scriptures," Jesus replied, "that man shouldn't live on bread alone. He should nourish himself with God's Word, on every word that comes from the mouth of God."

Satan rolled his eyes. *The Scriptures.* Of course, Jesus' parents had taught Him the Law and taken Him to the temple. But out here, starving in the wilderness, anything could happen.

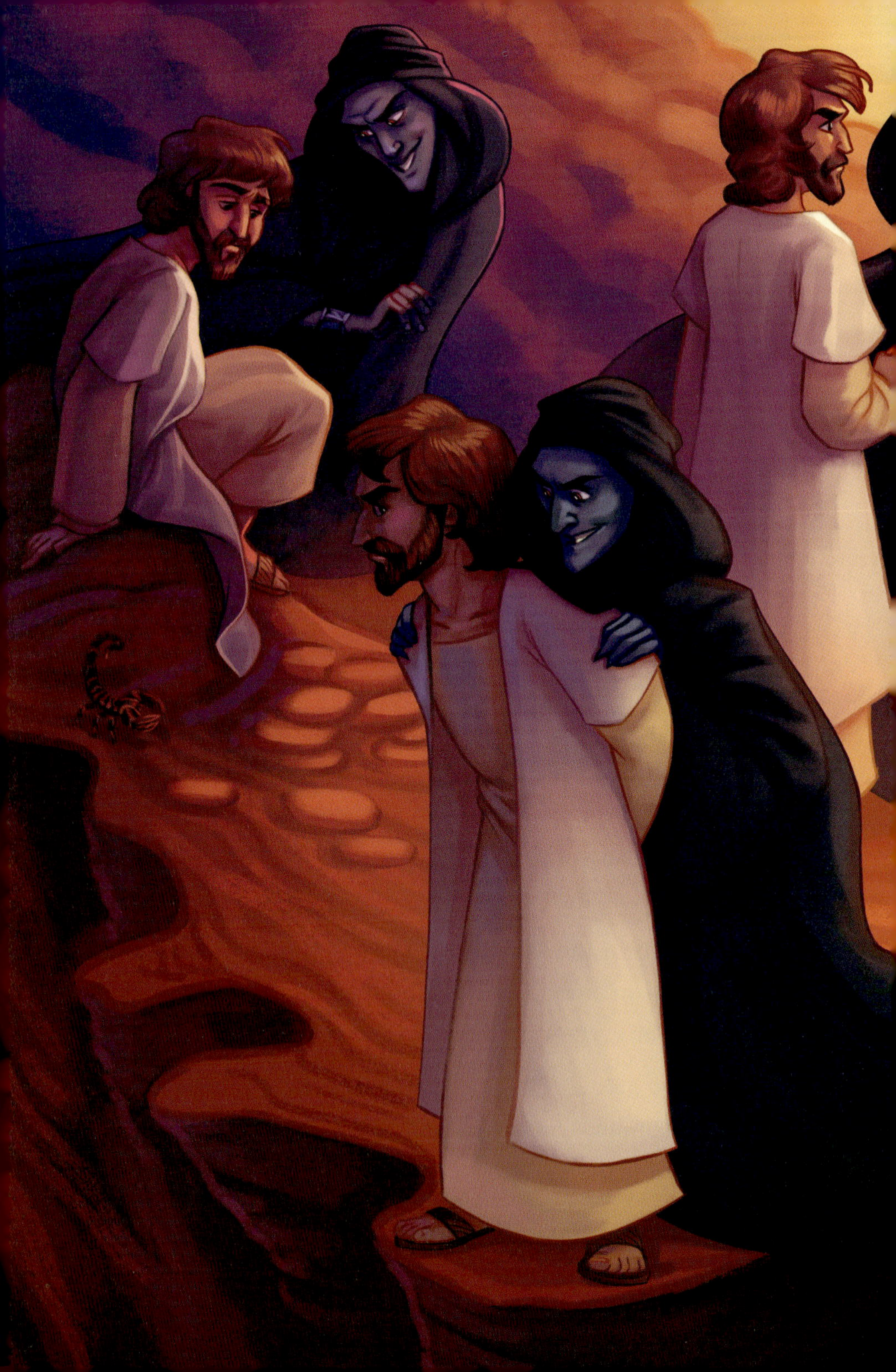

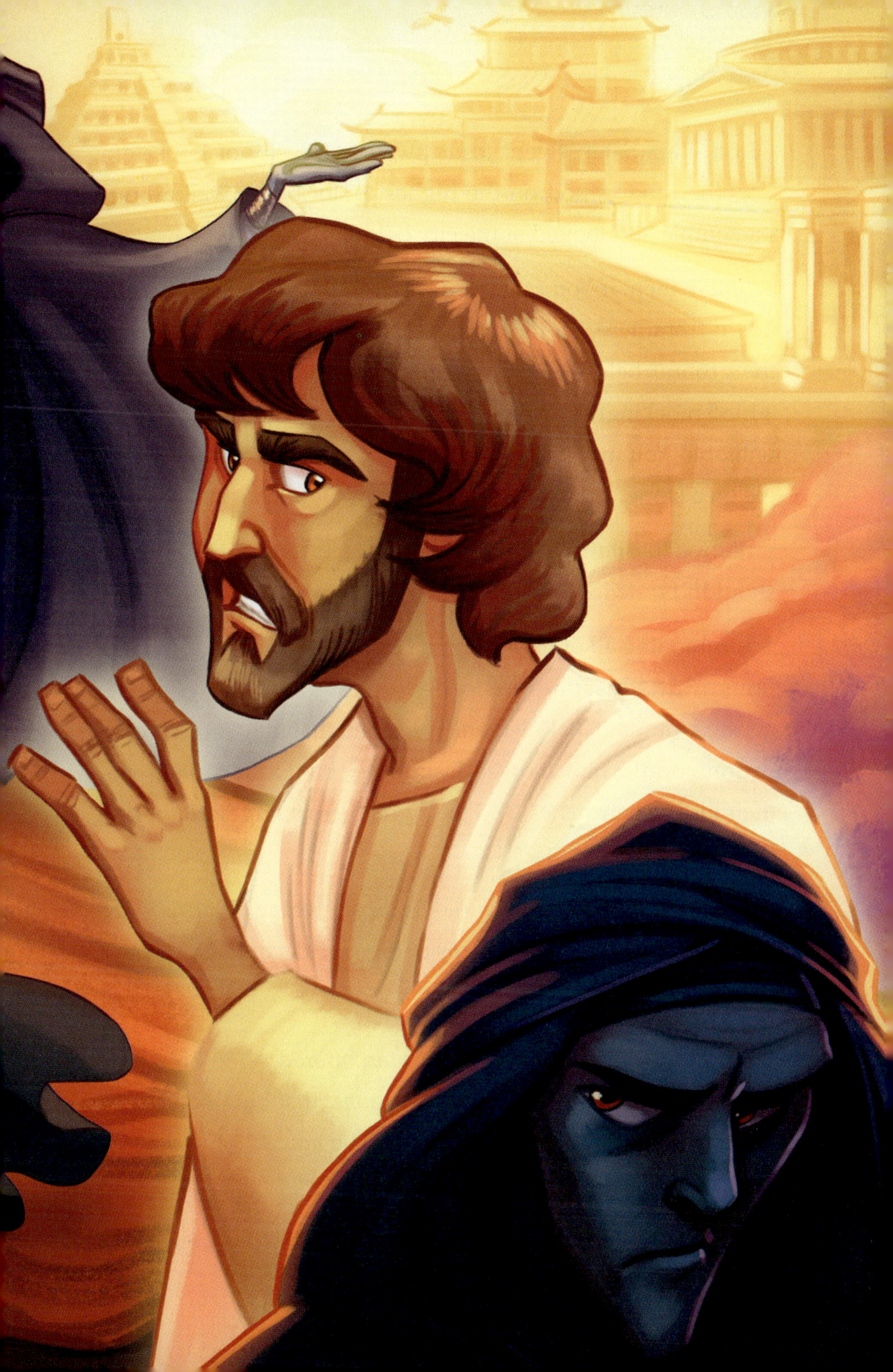

In a snap, Satan swept Jesus away to the city of Jerusalem. Together, they stood on the highest point of the wall around the temple and looked at the city below.

"Okay then, if You really are the Son of God, throw Yourself down from here," Satan said, whistling as he looked down at the ground below them. "Because, after all, *it is written*," he added mockingly, "that God will send His angels to You. They will hold You in their hands, so that You won't even stub Your toe on a stone."

Without hesitation, Jesus answered, "It is also *written* that you shouldn't test God."

Summoning all of his strength and power, Satan again swept Jesus away. This time, he stood with Jesus at the top of a staggering mountain. Below them, it seemed that they could see the entire world! Satan showed Jesus all of the Earth's kingdoms, their glory, their riches, and their greatness, lying right there at their feet.

"Look at all of this," Satan told Jesus, stretching his arms wide. "All of this, all of the kingdoms of the world, could be yours."

Jesus didn't respond.

"I will give all of this to you," Satan offered. "You only have to do one thing: bow to *me*. Worship *me*. Just bow down now and worship me here, and this will all be yours."

"Away from me, Satan," Jesus answered. "I will never serve you." Again, Jesus felt the power of God's Word surging inside of Him. He looked Satan straight in the eye and firmly said, "It is written: Worship the Lord, your God. Serve no one but *Him*."

Satan had nothing to say. He had been rebuked. He had sought Jesus out when he thought Jesus would be at His weakest, in order to tempt Him with what he thought Jesus would want the most. What Satan *hadn't* considered was that Jesus was God Himself, filled with the knowledge of God's Word, and willing to be led by the Holy Spirit. What Satan could never understand was a hunger, a desire for something other than food or power or the riches of this world: a desire to be totally obedient to the will of His Father.

For now, Satan would retreat to his lair, waiting for another chance to present itself. The angels came to comfort Jesus and attend to His needs.

Satan would never stop trying. He would always be there, waiting for people's weakest moments to offer the most tempting satisfaction. He would never stop trying to overthrow the power of the Almighty God or the plans of Jesus' gracious and loving Heavenly Father.

Jesus said to him, "Away from me, Satan! For it is written: 'Worship the Lord your God, and serve him only.'"

Matthew 4:10

FISHING FOR PEOPLE

Luke 4-5

After Jesus had been tempted in the desert, He returned to Galilee, filled with the power of the Spirit. There, He proclaimed the Good News that the kingdom of God had come to earth.

One day Jesus was preaching by the Sea of Galilee. As the crowd grew larger and larger, Jesus saw a couple of fishing boats by the shore. The fishermen had left the boats there while they were washing their nets. Jesus climbed into one of the boats and asked Simon, one of the fishermen, to pull it away from the shore a bit so that there would be more room for the crowd to see and hear Him. Simon did as Jesus asked, and Jesus continued to teach the people from the boat.

When He was finished speaking, Jesus told Simon, "Sail out into the deep water over there and let down your nets."

Simon shook his head and laughed. "Oh, teacher," he said, "we've tried all night and haven't caught a thing. But if you say so, we will try it one more time."

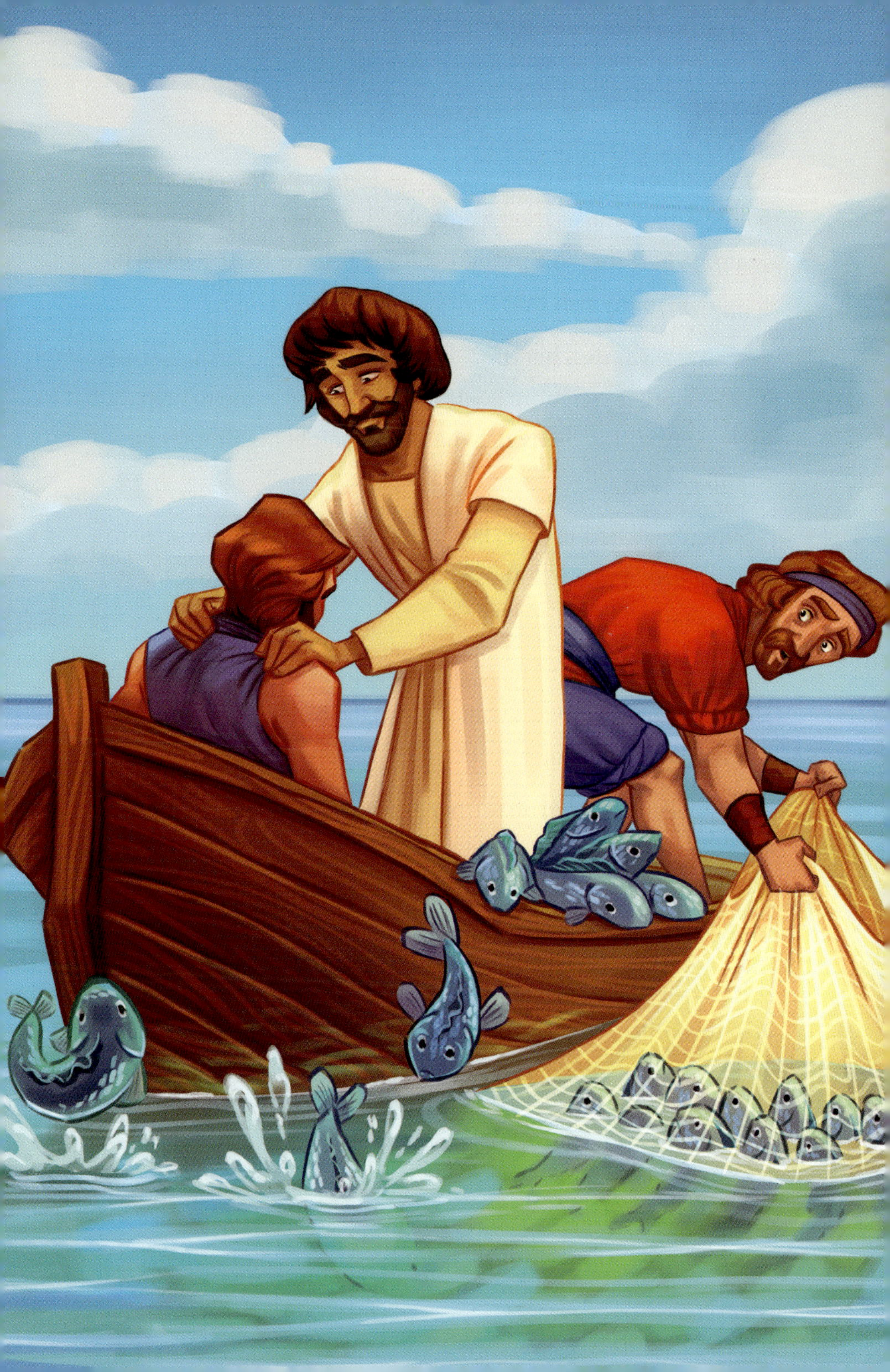

The other fishermen were tired and frustrated—what was the point? But, doing as they were told, they lowered their nets yet again. When they did, they couldn't believe their eyes! They caught so many fish that their nets began to break!

"Guys! Give us a hand!" they shouted back to the fishermen on the shore. Even more boats and fishermen came to help, but there were still so many fish that all of their boats almost started to sink!

Simon watched in awe. He knew that he was in the presence of the Lord, so he fell at Jesus' feet. "Please leave me, Master. I'm a sinner," he said.

"There's nothing to fear," Jesus said to him. "You think this is something? From now on, you will be called Peter and we're going to fish for people."

Simon Peter needed no further explanation. Whatever this man Jesus was doing, he wanted to be a part of it. In that moment, Jesus gained His first disciples: Simon Peter, his brother Andrew, and their two fishing partners, James and John.

Jesus didn't just call fishermen, either. He called Philip on His trip to Galilee, and Nathanael from under a fig tree. Matthew was in a booth, collecting taxes, when Jesus told him, "Follow me." Altogether, He chose twelve men to be His disciples, His followers.

Together these men would witness the unthinkable, the unbelievable, the unexplainable miracles of Jesus, as he preached about the kingdom of heaven and called everyone who would listen to follow Him. The disciples would witness Jesus' miraculous ministry until His dying day, and even after that. They would be faithful to the task Jesus left to them, the task given to all of Jesus' followers: to carry the Good News to the ends of the earth, to all people.

> *Then Jesus said to Simon, "Don't be afraid; from now on you will fish for people." So they pulled their boats up on shore, left everything and followed him.*
> Luke 5:10-11

JESUS, THE MIRACLE WORKER

Matthew 6; Luke 6, 8, 10, 14, 17-19; John 2, 6, 9

Jesus had not yet begun His ministry or performed any miracles when He was invited to a wedding in the city of Cana. During that wedding, an embarrassing situation suddenly presented itself: the host had run out of wine to serve his guests. What could he do?

When Mary, Jesus' mother, heard of the situation, she knew exactly what to do—or rather, she knew exactly *who* could help. She found her son and whispered in His ear, "They're out of wine!"

"Mother, what do you want me to do? It's not yet my time," Jesus said.

But Mary was already talking to the servants, pointing Jesus' way. "Just do whatever He tells you," she instructed them.

"Take these jars and fill them with water," said Jesus.

The servants exchanged confused looks but obeyed, filling the jars to the top.

"Now take some of it to the master of the banquet," Jesus instructed.

Again, they obeyed, watching curiously as the master of the banquet took a sip. A look of surprise, followed by a smile, spread across his face. He went to the groom, and said, "Most people only serve the good wine at the beginning of the party and start to serve cheap wine later. But you have saved the best wine for the end of the feast!"

It would be the first of many signs that Jesus did, one of many miracles to come.

Soon after the wedding, Jesus began his public ministry. He traveled around, preaching to the crowds that gathered in the towns and surrounding countryside. Crowds started following

Him from one town to the next, meeting Him eagerly when he arrived. One such time, as the crowd gathered, a leader of the synagogue named Jairus came and fell at Jesus' feet.

"My daughter, she's dying!" Jairus said. "She is my only daughter and just twelve years old!" He begged Jesus to come to his house and lay hands on the girl to heal her.

By this time, the crowds had grown chaotic from everyone pressing in on Jesus and trying to get to Him. In all of the chaos, Jesus turned around and asked, "Who touched Me?"

Peter answered, "Everyone is crowded all around, and any number of people could be touching You."

"Someone touched Me," Jesus insisted. "I felt power go out from Me."

A woman fell at Jesus' feet. "It was me!" she said. "I have been sick for twelve years and no one could heal me. I simply touched the hem of Your cloak, and now I am healed!"

"My daughter, your faith has healed you," Jesus answered her. "Now go in peace."

As Jesus was speaking to the woman, someone came from Jairus's house with bad news. The messenger told Jairus, "I'm sorry, sir, but there's no need to bother Jesus anymore. The girl has... She is... *gone*."

As Jairus folded over in grief, Jesus turned to him and said, "It's okay; she'll be fine. Don't be afraid. Just believe."

As they neared Jairus's house, they could hear a great commotion inside: people wailing and crying. Family and friends had already gathered to mourn the death of the little girl.

"Why are all of you crying?" Jesus asked them. "She's not dead. She is only sleeping."

The people laughed at Jesus. They had watched the color drain from her face. They had felt her cold, lifeless hands. They *knew* that she was dead.

Still, Jesus took Peter, along with John, James, and the girl's parents, with Him to where the girl lay. Jesus held the little girl's hand and said, "Little girl, get up!"

Immediately, the girl's eyes opened, and she swung her legs off the bed and stood up. Her parents couldn't believe it—their daughter was alive! Those who had laughed at Jesus now watched in awe as He left the house with His disciples.

After Jesus and his disciples left Jairus's house, two blind men started following them. They shouted, "Please! Have mercy on us!"

When the blind men approached Jesus, He asked them, "Do you truly believe that I am able to give your sight back to you?"

"We do, Lord," they both answered.

Then Jesus reached out and touched their eyes. "Then by your faith, let it be done," He said.

Just like that, the men could see again!

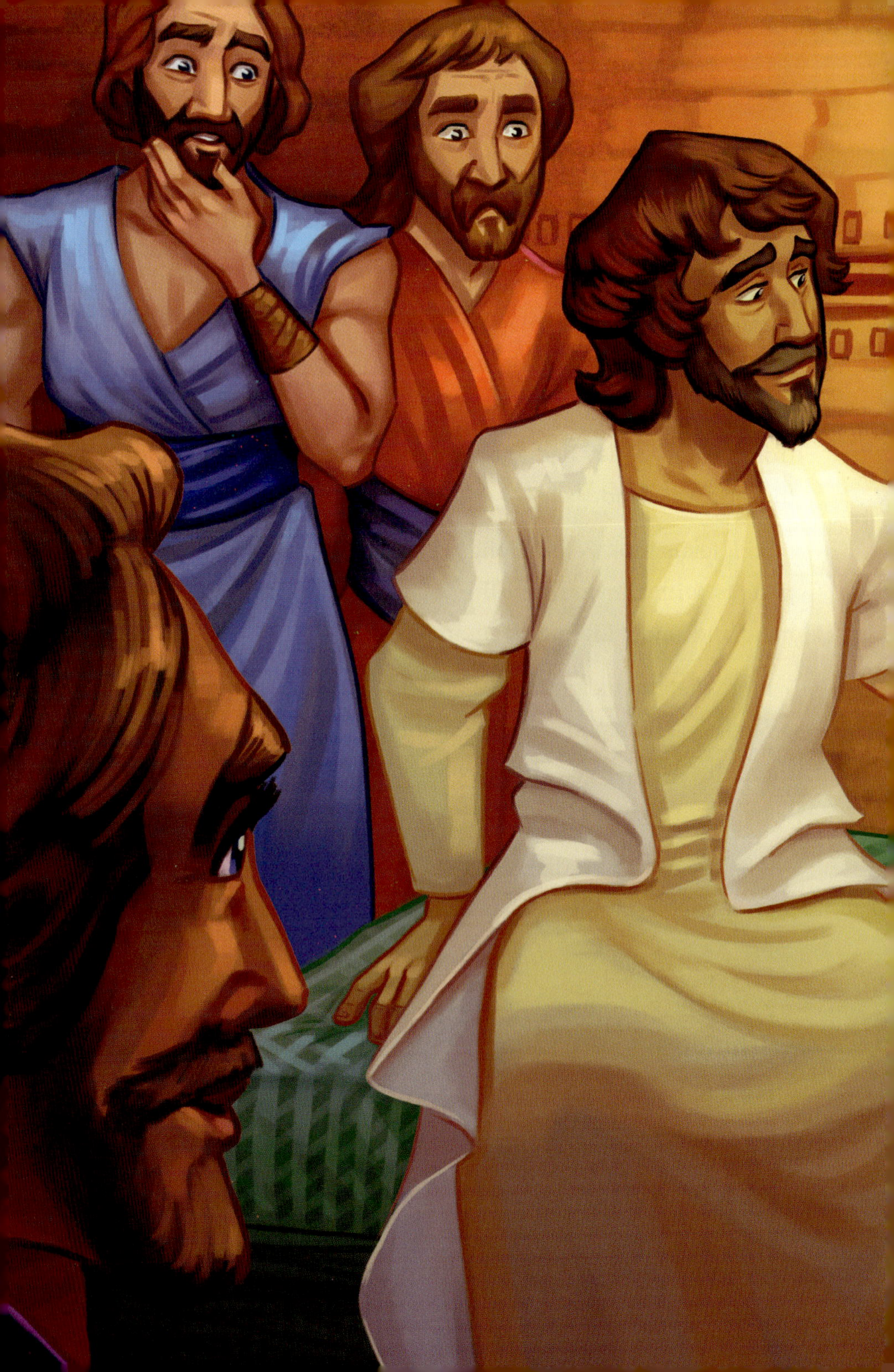

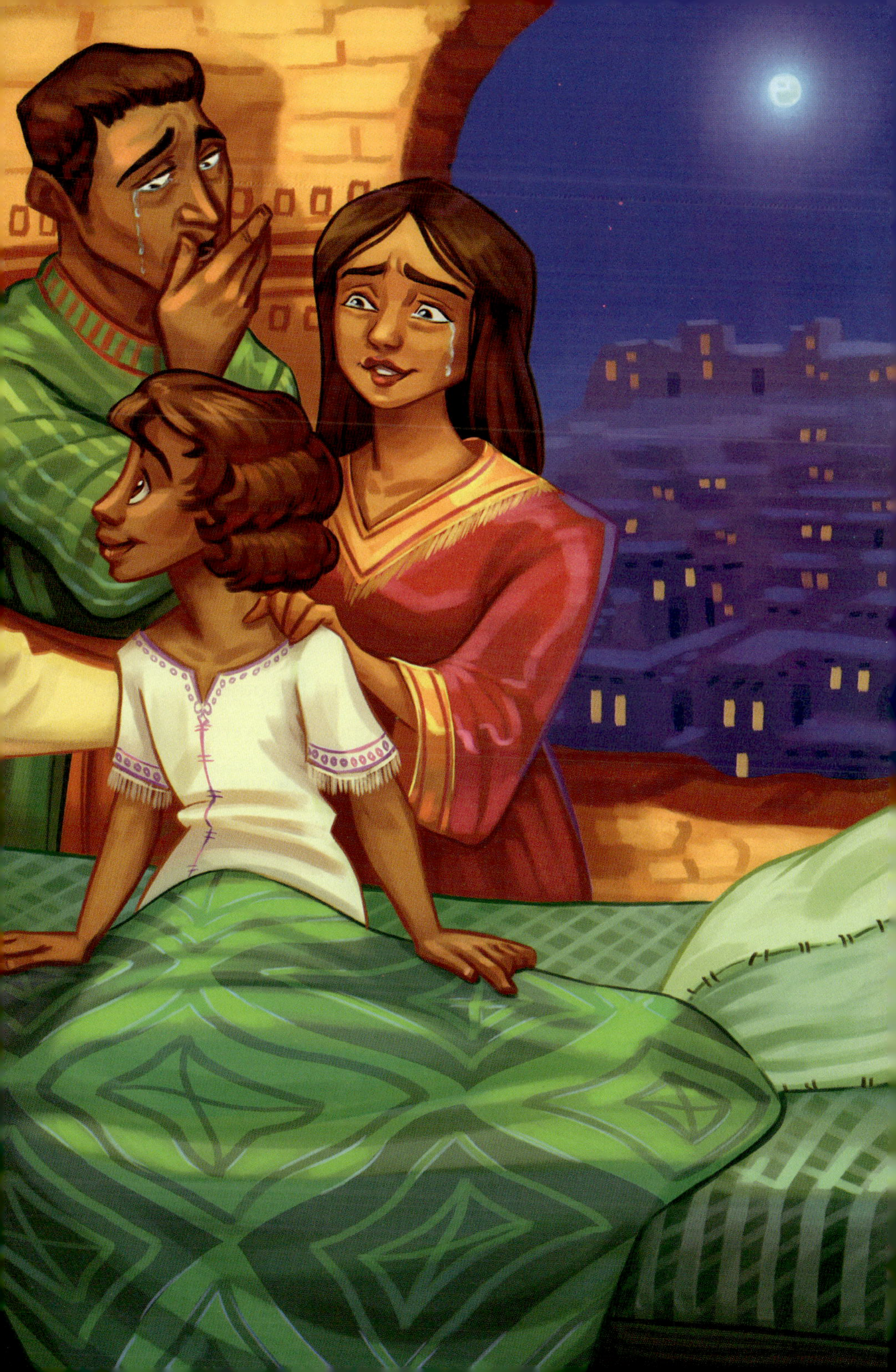

Another time, on His way to Jerusalem, Jesus entered a village and met ten men who were leaving it. Because these men had leprosy, a terrible skin disease, they stood at a distance and pleaded with Him. "Please, Jesus!" they called out. "Please, help us!"

"Go back to the priests and show them your skin," Jesus instructed. The men did as Jesus told them, and as they walked away, their skin became clean. They were healed!

One of the men came back to Jesus, shouting and praising God. He fell at Jesus' feet and said, "Oh, thank you! Thank you!"

Jesus asked the man, "What about the other nine? Were they not healed also? Only you have returned to give praise to God?"

The man stood and looked back toward the other nine, who hadn't given Jesus a second thought once they were healed.

"Go," Jesus told him. "Your faith has made you well." And Jesus continued on His way.

By this time, thousands of people gathered around Jesus wherever He went. At times, He would try to find a place to be alone with just His disciples. But people would still find them or follow them, even to remote places. One time in particular, Jesus welcomed the people, teaching them about the Kingdom of God. As it grew later and later in the afternoon, Jesus knew that the people must be getting hungry, and there was no place nearby for them to get food.

Although Jesus already knew the answer, He asked His disciples, "Where will we get food for all of these people?"

"We'd have to work for six months to buy enough for each person just to have a bite!" Philip answered.

Andrew offered another solution, but it was almost as strange as the first. He said, "This boy has brought his lunch. There are five small loaves of bread and two little fish, but they won't go very far with *this* crowd."

Jesus smiled and said, "Just have the people sit down."

The disciples looked at one another, eyebrows raised. They had seen some miracles, but Jesus couldn't really feed all of these people with that tiny amount of food, could He? Impossible as it seemed, they also knew by now to expect the unexpected as far as Jesus was concerned. As the disciples roamed the crowd, asking everyone to sit, they realized that there were at least five thousand people there—and that was only counting the men!

Jesus took the five loaves of bread and the two little fish and thanked God for the food that they had been given. After His prayer, He began to pass the food around. Every single person got plenty of food that day. In fact, everyone ate until they were full!

When everyone had enough to eat, Jesus told His disciples, "Now, gather up what's left. Let's not waste anything."

Waste anything? It seemed silly, really. How could anything at all be left over? Five thousand people had eaten five loaves of bread and two fish! Even so, as the disciples gathered, they filled an entire basket, and another, then half a dozen. By the

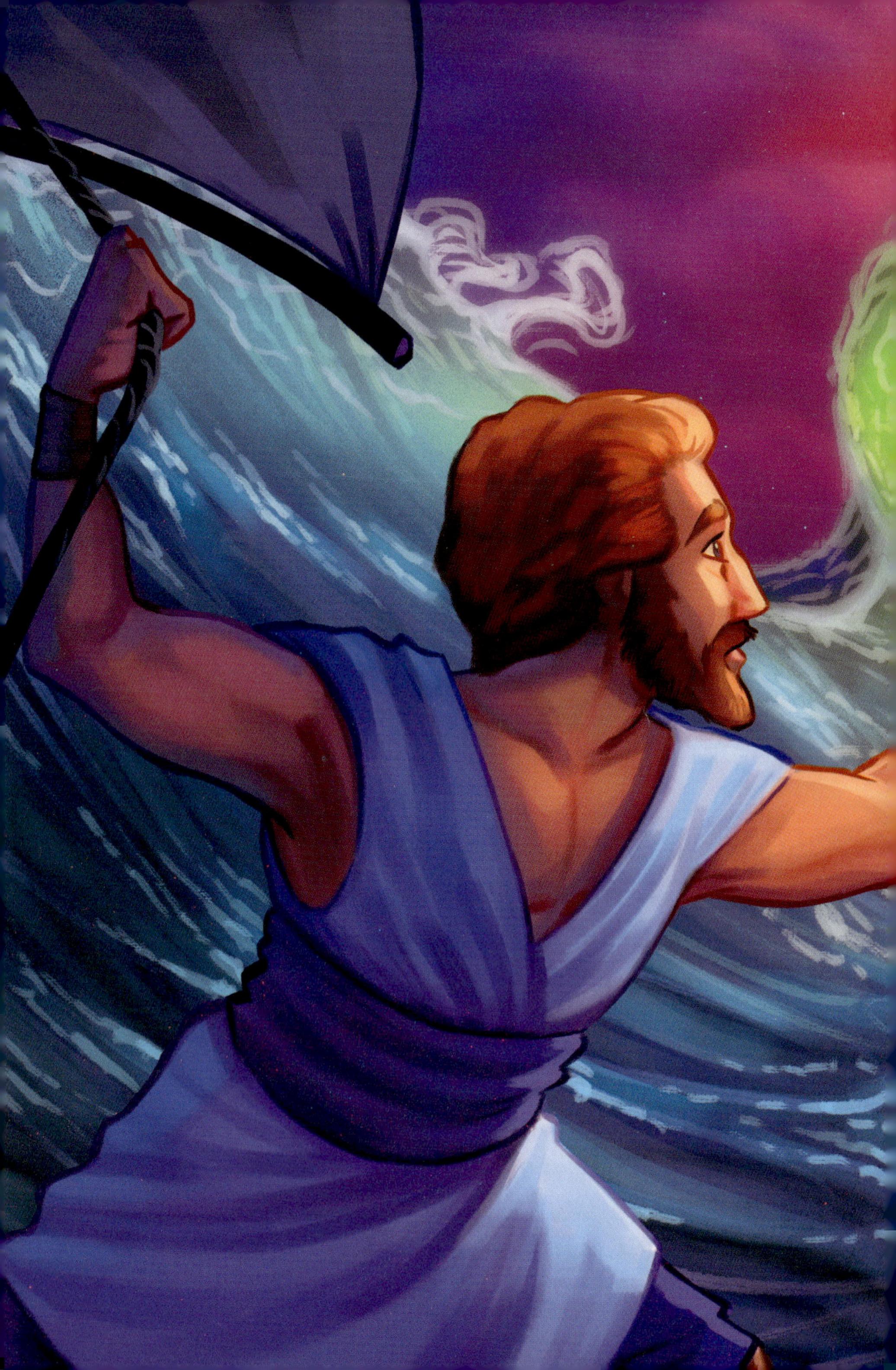

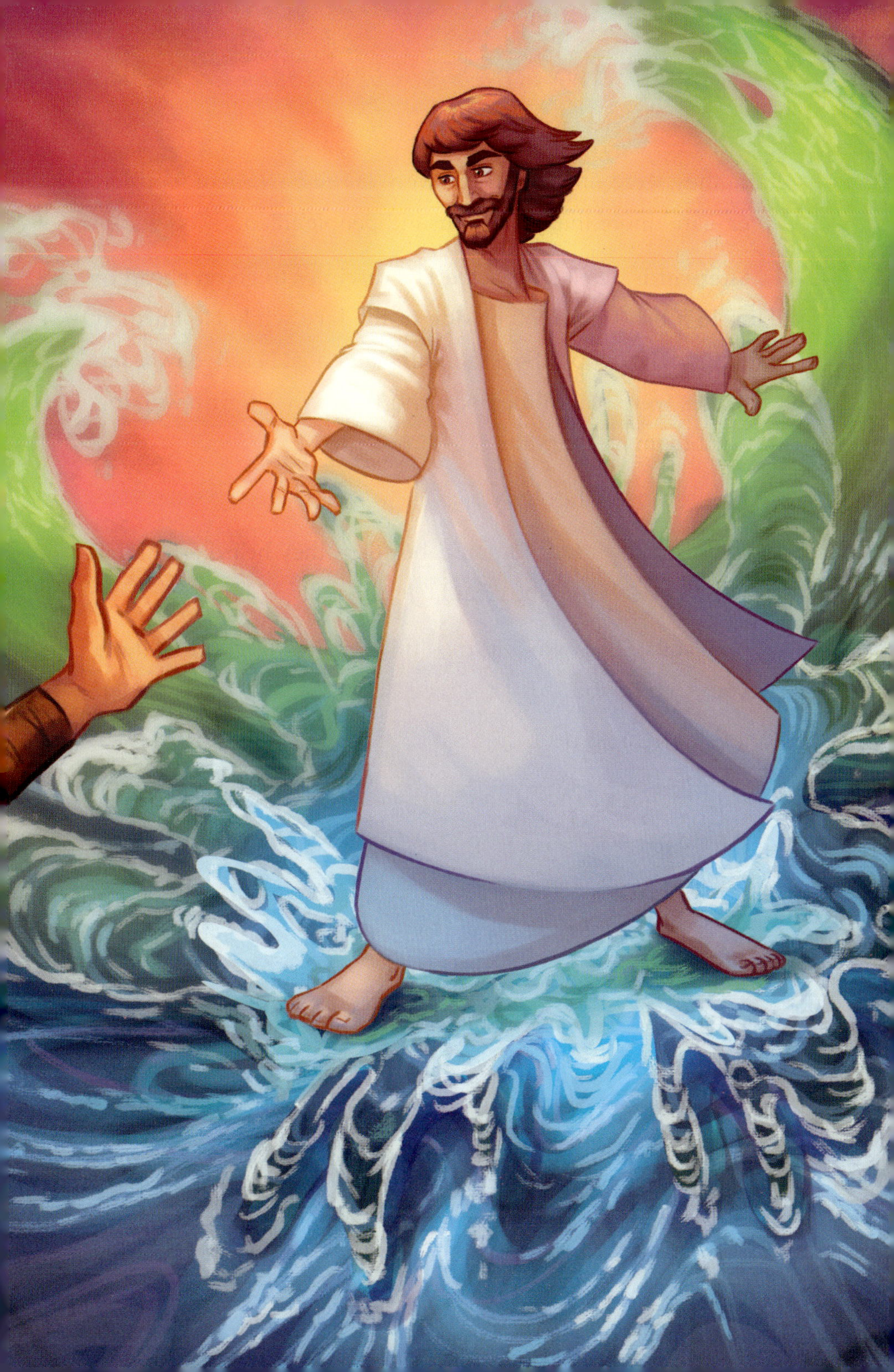

time they were finished, there were *twelve* baskets of food left over—and more than five thousand people filled.

Afterwards, Jesus instructed His disciples to go on ahead of Him in a boat to the other side of the lake while He finished talking to the people. Several hours later, just before dawn, the disciples were still in the boat, and they saw a figure walking toward them on the water.

"It's a ghost!" they cried.

The disciples began to panic, but then they heard a familiar voice. "It's Me! Don't be afraid," Jesus said.

Peter called out to the figure, "If it's really You, Lord, tell me to come out to You."

"Come!" Jesus answered.

With that assurance, Peter stepped over the side of the boat and onto the water. There, on the surface of the water, he took one step after another toward Jesus, but then he heard the wind and saw the waves. As he let fear begin to set in, Peter started to sink. "Save me!" he cried.

Jesus simply reached out His hand and held Peter securely above the waves. "Oh you of little faith," Jesus said, "why did you doubt?"

As Peter and Jesus climbed into the boat together, the other disciples exclaimed, "You are truly the Son of God."

In His short time on earth, the Son of God would heal countless illnesses, feed countless people, cast out countless demons, and forgive countless sins. Jesus did far more than just calming a stormy sea and walking on its waters or raising a little girl who had just died and curing a woman who had been troubled for years by a disease! For friends and strangers, young and old, Jesus breathed life into the dead, caused the lame to leap, lepers to be clean, and helped the blind to see—again, and again, and again.

About the many miracles of Jesus, the apostle John wrote that even the whole world could not contain all of the books that would have to be written to tell all of the works that Jesus had done.

> *Then he said to her, "Daughter, your faith has healed you. Go in peace."*
> Luke 8:48

> *But when he saw the wind, he was afraid and, beginning to sink, cried out, "Lord, save me!" Immediately Jesus reached out his hand and caught him. "You of little faith," he said, "why did you doubt?"*
> Matthew 14:30-31

THE MOST IMPORTANT THING

Luke 10

Because Jesus and His disciples traveled almost constantly, they didn't really have homes of their own. They mainly depended on the hospitality of friends or strangers when they needed a place to stay. Fortunately, many people were eager to welcome Jesus, the healer and teacher that they had heard so much about.

Mary and her sister Martha were two of those people. When Jesus and His disciples came to their village, Martha invited them to stay with her family.

When Jesus came to Mary and Martha's home, Martha was busy in the kitchen, preparing an elaborate dinner. Mary, on the other hand, was drawn to Jesus and found herself simply sitting at His feet, soaking up every word and relishing every moment in His presence. Finally, Martha had had enough. She was tired of rushing around and doing everything while Mary just sat there on the floor, enjoying the company of Jesus.

"Lord!" Martha said, stomping into the room and wiping her hands. "Don't you even care?! Can't you see that I've been

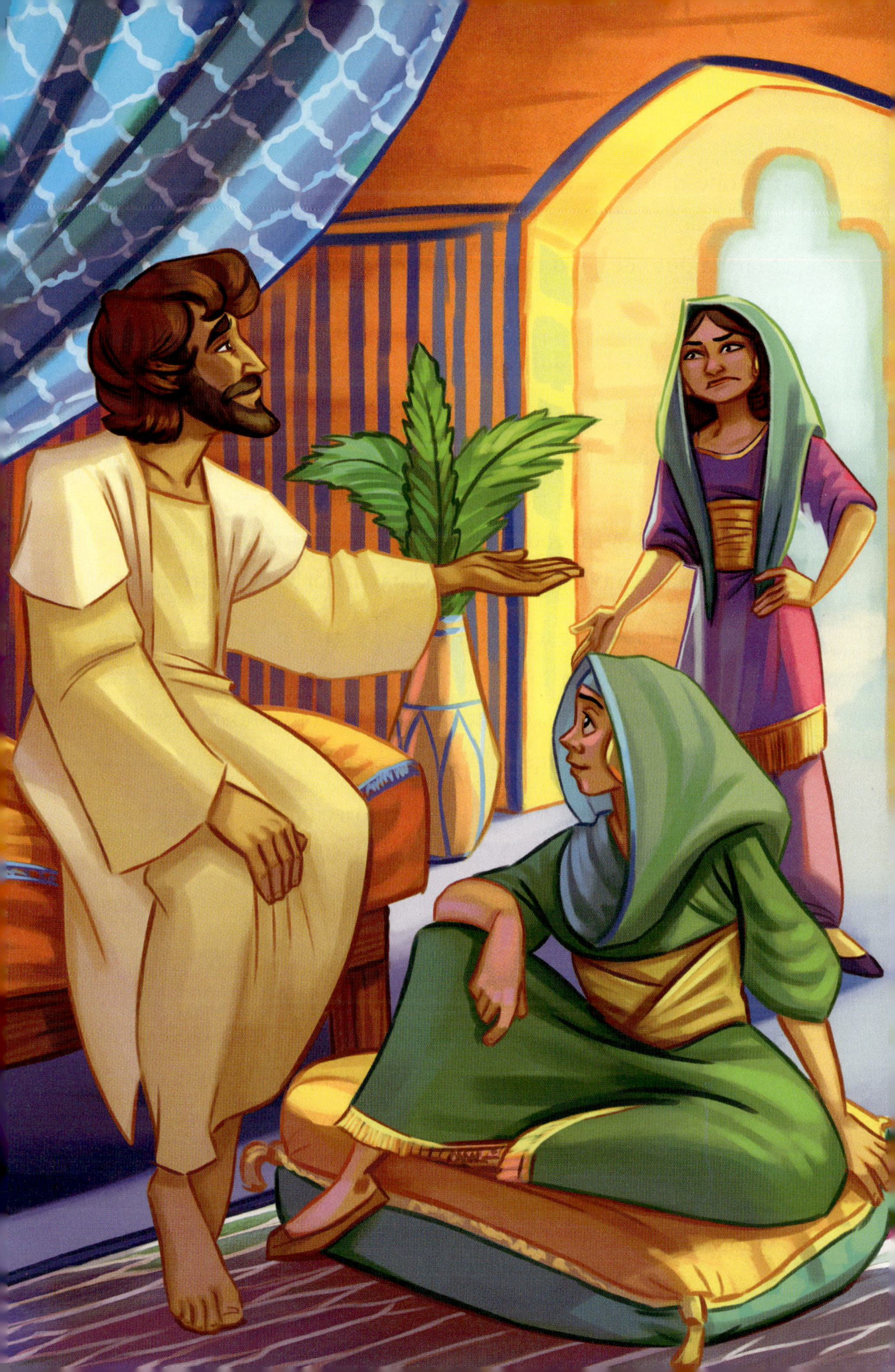

the one doing all the work around here? I've been cooking and cleaning and trying to make everything perfect and neat!" Martha put her hand on her hip, and said, "Tell her, Jesus. Tell her to help me."

Martha glared at Mary and waited for Jesus to scold her sister.

"Oh, Martha," Jesus said, smiling at her, and then at Mary, "you worry about these little things and you let them upset you. But these things don't really matter. A clean house and dishes, bedding, and even food, aren't really what is important. Mary is doing what is most important, and it will not be taken from her."

Jesus stood and reached out to Mary, still at His feet. "Mary has chosen to listen to My words, and that is something that will truly last. Don't scold her for choosing the most important thing over lesser things."

Could it be true? Could all of this worrying and fussing have been in vain? What had Martha missed while she was so concerned about doing good works?

Jesus had taught this lesson to thousands in His Sermon on the Mount, and now He was sharing the same lesson one-on-one with His friend. He wanted the focus of His disciples, His followers, His friends not to fall on the temporary things of this earth: what you will eat or what you will wear. He doesn't want us to worry about these things because, as Jesus explained, the body is more than the clothes you put on it, and life is more than what you eat. Your focus should be on God.

THE MOST IMPORTANT THING

"Martha, Martha! You are worried and upset about so many things, but only one thing is necessary. Mary has chosen what is best, and it will not be taken away from her."

Luke 10:41-42 CEV

THE WIND AND WAVES OBEY

Luke 8; Mark 4

Jesus and His disciples had just finished teaching a crowd by the sea of Galilee, and they left to go to the other side of the lake. After they had started on their way, however, the clouds began to grow thick and dark. The winds started whipping through the sails, and the waves grew large and powerful.

It wasn't the first storm the disciples had seen on the lake. After all, several of them were fisherman before they became disciples, and had spent almost more time on the water than they had on land. Together, they tried everything they knew to navigate the boat and push through the storm.

Soon, however, the winds picked up and the storm howled. Finally, when the waves started crashing over the boat, filling it with water, the disciples looked at each other and cried, "Jesus!"

They looked around and saw their teacher, lying on a cushion in the back of the boat. While the disciples had been scrambling and the storm had been howling and the waves had been crashing, Jesus had been peacefully sleeping. *How could He be sleeping?!*

"Jesus!" one of the disciples yelled. "We're all going to drown! Don't You even care?!"

Jesus stood up in the back of the boat and shouted over the storm, "Winds, be quiet! Waves, be still!"

Immediately, the water became smooth like glass, and the wind was silent.

"Why were you so afraid?" Jesus asked them. "Don't you have any faith?"

The disciples stood, staring at Jesus in awe.

"Who is this guy?" one of them finally whispered. "What kind of man can make even the wind and waves obey him?"

It was a question that would not be answered that day. Although the answer was standing right in front of them, the disciples would not fully understand what kind of man Jesus was until they had walked with Him and finished out the course of His life on this earth. Even then, the answer would be hard to believe.

THE WIND AND WAVES OBEY

So they went to Jesus and woke him up, "Master, Master! We are about to drown!" Jesus got up and ordered the wind and waves to stop. They obeyed, and everything was calm. Then Jesus asked the disciples, "Don't you have any faith?" But they were frightened and amazed. They said to each other, "Who is this? He can give orders to the wind and the waves, and they obey him!"

Luke 8:24-25 CEV

THE GOOD SAMARITAN

Luke 10

One day while Jesus was teaching, a question came from the crowd. "Teacher, how do I get eternal life?" a man in the crowd, an expert in religious law, asked.

"What does the law say?" Jesus replied. "And what do you think it means?"

"Ahem, well, the law says to love God with all your heart and soul and with all your mind and strength," the man answered. "And to love your neighbor the way you love yourself."

"Exactly," Jesus answered. "That's what you need to do."

"Well, wait a minute," the man continued, wanting to give Jesus a more complicated question. "Who is my neighbor?"

Jesus answered the man with a story that had a lesson in it: a parable. He told the crowd about a man who was robbed as he was traveling down the road from Jerusalem to Jericho. The robbers took everything the man had and beat him, leaving him barely breathing and lying on the side of the road.

A little later, a priest came walking down the same road. When

THE GOOD SAMARITAN

he saw the injured man lying there, hurt and clinging to life, the priest crossed to the other side of the road, getting far away from the man. The priest just kept walking.

After the priest, a Levite, a man who worked at the temple, came down the same road where the man lay. When he saw the man, he did the same thing as the priest, passing him by on the far side of the road.

Finally, Jesus told about a Samaritan who came down the road. Everyone knew that Samaritans and Jews despised each other. There was a long-standing hatred between the two groups of people. The first two passersby were Jewish, but the third, the

Samaritan, was certainly the last person anyone would expect to help a Jew lying on the side of the road.

Still, when *this* Samaritan saw the Jewish man lying there, he ran over to him. He cleaned the man's wounds, put oil on them, and bandaged them. Then he helped the man onto the back of his donkey and carried him to the nearest inn. The Samaritan checked the man into the inn and even cared for him overnight. The next morning, the Samaritan paid the innkeeper and asked him to look after the man, offering to pay for anything else he may need.

Finishing His story, Jesus looked at the expert in religious law and asked him, "Which of these three men do you think acted as a neighbor to the man who was robbed?"

"The one who cared for him," the man answered.

"Then go," Jesus said, "and do the same."

Then Jesus asked, "Which one of these three people was a real neighbor to the man who was beaten up by robbers?" The teacher answered, "The one who showed pity." Jesus said, "Go and do the same!"

Luke 10:36-37 CEV

THE SMALL AND THE LOST

Luke 15

Once Jesus taught a parable about a lost sheep to teach people about the Kingdom of God—to describe the lengths He would go to in order to save the lost, the broken, and the outcast. He said, "Think about it. If you had a hundred sheep, what would you do if you lost one? Wouldn't you leave the other ninety-nine in the field to go find that one lost sheep? Then, when you finally found it, wouldn't you carry it home on your shoulders, cheering all the way? This is how heaven rejoices when one sinner repents."

Jesus made it clear that in the Kingdom of God, every single soul matters. Every single person who was lost and comes to know Him is celebrated—even more than those who already believe. Like a shepherd finding his lost sheep, God wants to bring every person into His Kingdom, to live in the security of His love forever.

To strengthen his point, Jesus gave another example. He said, "If a woman has ten silver coins and loses one, what does she do? She lights a lamp! She sweeps the house! She searches carefully until she finds that one coin. When she does find it, she calls everyone together to celebrate with her because she has found her lost coin. This is how the angels in heaven rejoice over just one sinner who comes to God."

Using these parables, Jesus tried to show the people just how much they were loved and valued by God. God's love and care don't just apply to adults, either. He loves and values everyone, old and young alike.

Once when Jesus was teaching, some parents brought their children to see Him. They wanted Jesus to put His hands on the children and bless them, but as the children got close to Jesus, the disciples turned them and their parents away. Wasn't Jesus much too important and busy to be spending His time with these little kids?

No, He was not. He made that very clear.

"Don't stop them," Jesus corrected His disciples. "Let the little ones come to Me. The Kingdom of God belongs to them, and to people like them, who have open hearts and depend on Me."

With that, the disciples stepped back and let the children spend time with Jesus. They watched in wonder, realizing that the Son of God was like no one else and His kingdom was unlike anything they had ever seen or heard of.

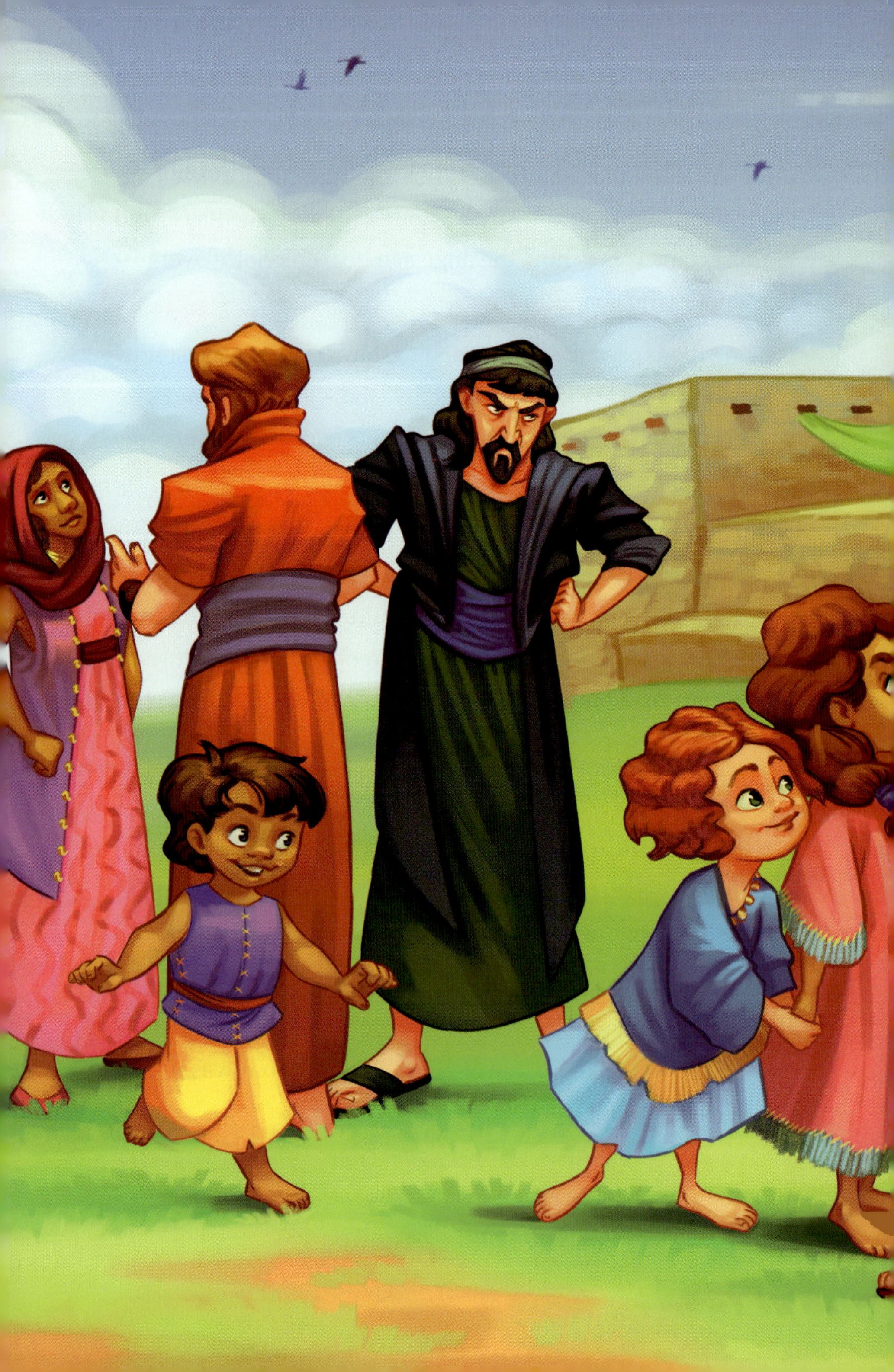

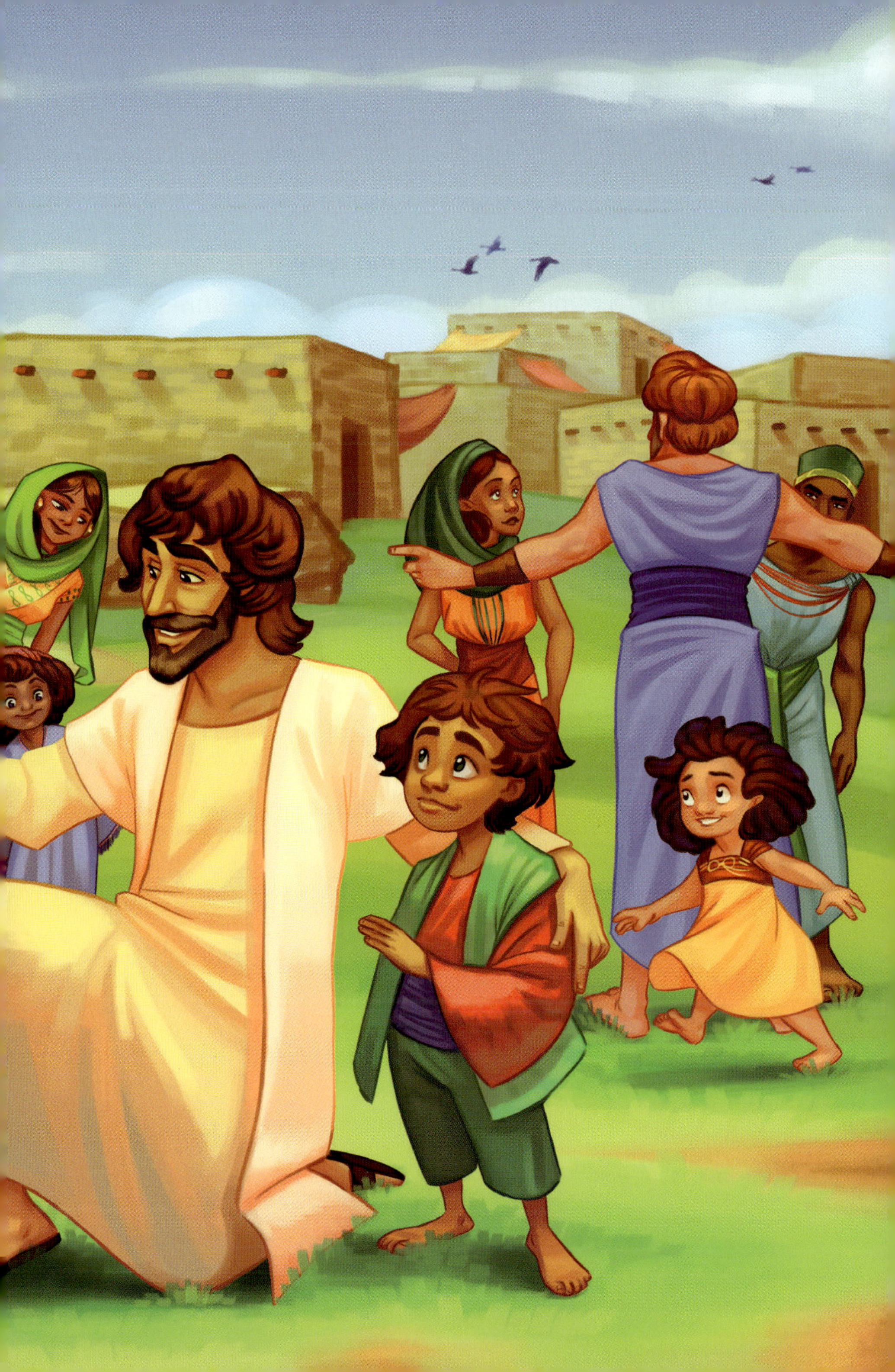

"I tell you that in the same way there will be more rejoicing in heaven over one sinner who repents than over ninety-nine righteous persons who do not need to repent."

Luke 15:7

"Truly I tell you, anyone who will not receive the kingdom of God like a little child will never enter it."

Luke 18:17

THE PRODIGAL SON

Luke 15

While explaining just how much God values each person in the Kingdom of God, Jesus told a parable about a father and his two sons.

One day, the younger son asked his father to give him the inheritance that was due to him when his father would eventually die. The father granted his son's request and divided his property, giving the younger son money for his share.

The older son stayed at home and continued to work for his father, while the younger son took off, traveling to faraway places. He lived a wild life, doing whatever he wanted, whenever he wanted, and spending all of the money than he had inherited.

Unfortunately, at that same time, a famine—a severe shortage of food—hit the country he was living in. He eventually got a job feeding pigs for a local man, but by then the son was so starved that he was tempted to eat some of the food that he was slopping out to the pigs!

At that moment, he finally realized just how foolish he had been and what a mess he had made of his life. "Even my father's

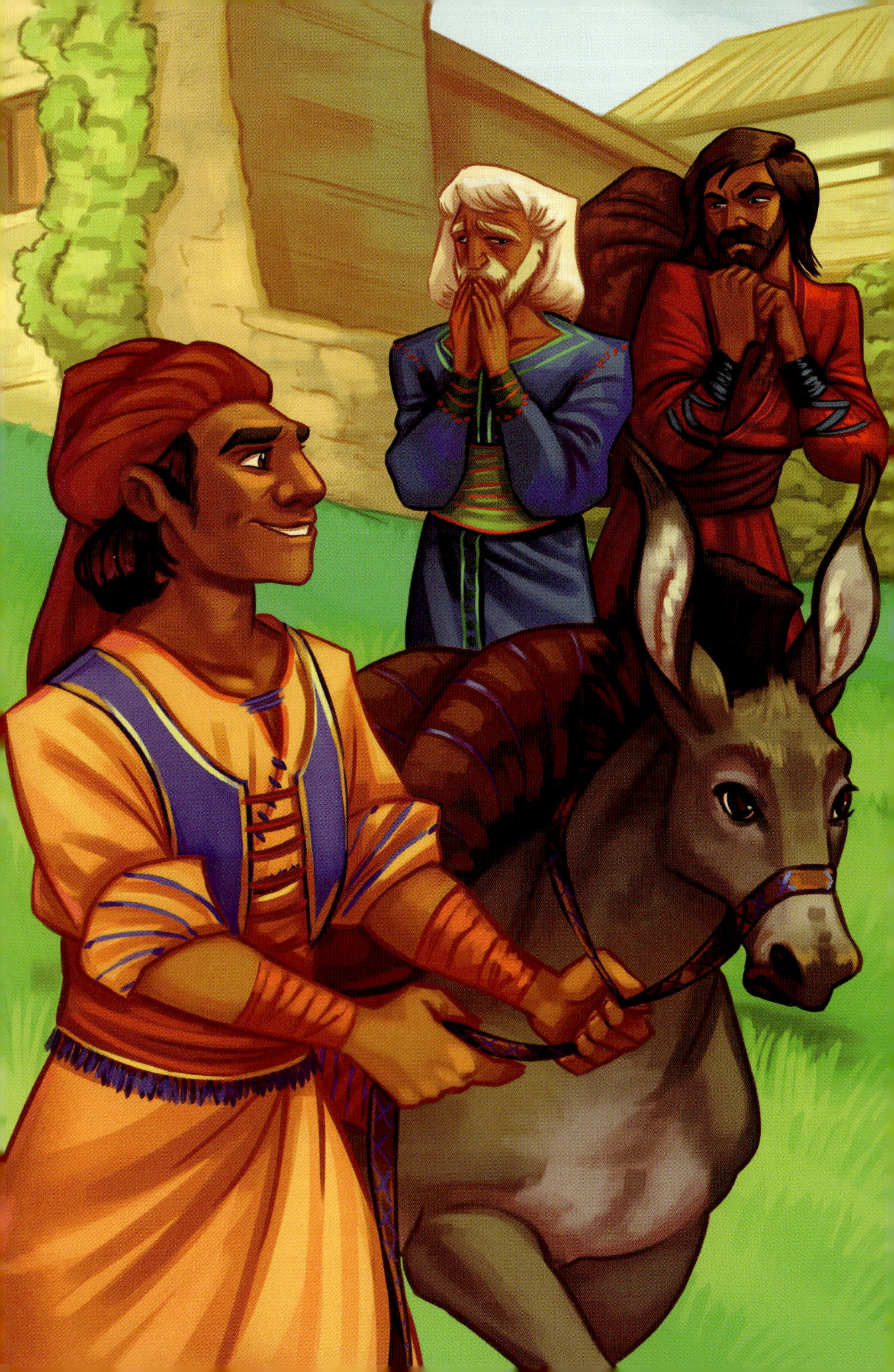

servants have more food than me," he thought. "They even have food to spare, and I am starving!"

With that realization, the son began the long journey back home. He hoped that his father wouldn't turn him away when he arrived, even though he knew that he deserved it. He didn't dare to hope that his father would take him back as a son and heir, but if he could just become one of his father's workers, that would be enough.

As the younger son neared his father's house, he squinted at the shape of the home he had abandoned on the horizon. Looking ahead, he could just barely make out the figure of a man in the distance. The son stopped. Should he even try to go home? After all that he had done—squandering his inheritance, not to mention what he had squandered it on—why would his father even speak to him again?

Nervously, and more slowly now, the son walked toward the figure in the distance. He knew that he was unworthy of being called his father's son, but he had nowhere else to go.

Suddenly, the son saw the figure in the distance move. It started running toward him. It was his father! Was he angry? Would he be happy to see him?

The son walked cautiously toward the figure of his father, but his father just kept running toward him. The father ran until he could finally throw his arms around his son. He kissed him and welcomed him home.

The son bowed his head. "Father, wait, I need to tell you something," the son said, hanging his head in shame. "I've sinned against God and I've sinned against you. I'm not worthy to be called your son, but if you could only use me as a servant"

His father didn't seem to hear him at all. "Hurry!" he called to his servants. "Bring the best robe you can find. Bring a ring and new shoes for my boy! Go prepare a huge feast! Let's celebrate!"

Celebrate? the son thought. *Didn't he hear anything I just said?* "My son—my son who I thought was dead!" the father shouted. The servants and family gathered around to see what all of the shouting was about, and the father continued, "Look! Here he is! Alive! He was lost, but now he is found!"

Everyone cheered, wrapping the younger son in their loving, welcoming arms. The servants served up the feast, and a great celebration began.

The older brother was returning from the field when he heard something. Music? Were they dancing? He called one of the servants to him. "What's going on?" he asked.

"Your brother—he's come home!" the servant cheered. "We're having a party!"

The older brother could not believe it. He pushed past the servant and stomped toward the house. When he got there, he just stood outside the party, watching angrily and refusing to join the celebration.

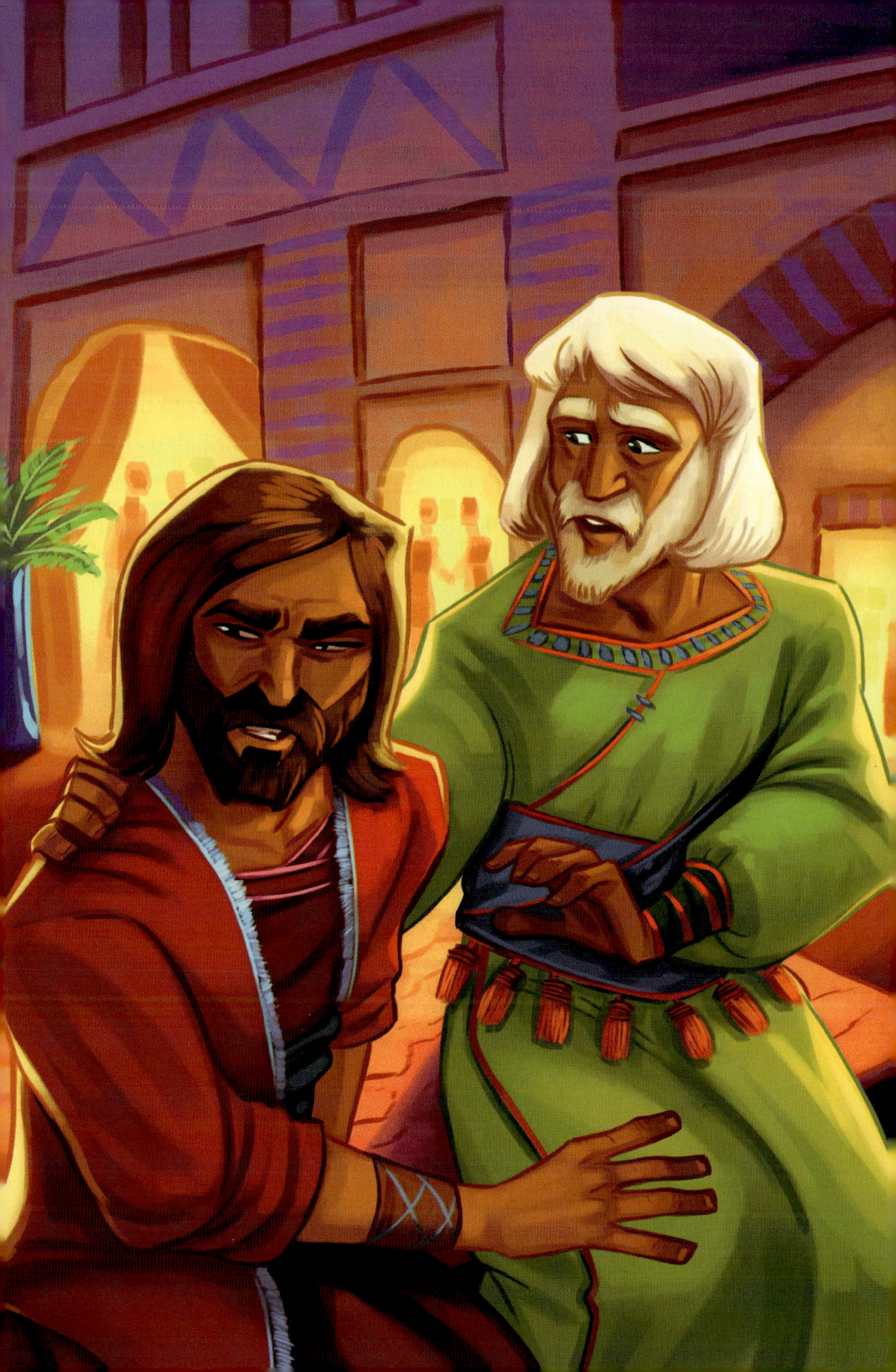

His father went out to him. "Come on in! Join us!" he said. "Your brother is finally home!"

"Are you kidding me?!" the older brother asked. "I have worked for you, slaved for you, all these years! I've never disobeyed you, *not once*! And you've never given *me* a party!" He gestured angrily toward the party before continuing, "But this?! He has wasted the inheritance you gave him on scandalous living and who knows what else! And you are *celebrating him?!*" The older son crossed his arms, fuming with rage, and looked away disapprovingly.

"You're right," the father said, smiling and wrapping an arm around his older son. "You have been with me all this time, and all of this—everything I have—is *yours*. But your brother was gone. He was lost. He was as good as dead to us and is now alive again! He has been found—he has returned! How could we *not* celebrate that?"

With this story, Jesus made it very clear: No matter where we've been, what we've done, or what we've been through, our Father will always lovingly, excitedly welcome us home, forgiving us and wrapping us in his loving arms.

I will set out and go back to my father and say to him: Father, I have sinned against heaven and against you. I am no longer worthy to be called your son; make me like one of your hired servants.'

Luke 15:18-19

While he was still a long way off, his father saw him and was filled with compassion for him; he ran to his son, threw his arms around him and kissed him.

Luke 15:20

THE FIRST STONE

John 8

Early one morning, right at dawn, Jesus made his way into the courtyard around the temple. As He walked, people began to gather around Him like they often did. Seeing the crowd forming, Jesus settled in, finding a spot where He could sit to teach them and talk with them.

As Jesus was speaking, He was suddenly interrupted by the sound of an uproar in the crowd. The Pharisees, some of the strictest religious leaders, were pushing their way through to Jesus, pulling a woman behind them. The woman's head was down, her hair was tousled, and her cheeks were streaked with tears.

"Teacher!" the Pharisees shouted. "See this woman? She was caught in bed with someone who was not her husband! According to the Law of Moses, we are to stone her to death—but what do *You* say?"

Jesus' knowledge of God's Word, His power to work miracles,

and His growing popularity throughout the land were a threat to the religious leaders. In response to that threat, they were willing to try anything to make Jesus say something against the law of Moses, or against the Roman authorities and their laws, in order to trap Him.

This time, they had dragged a woman through the streets and into the temple courts to test Jesus' knowledge and compassion. Would He follow the law that God gave to Moses and stone this woman in front of everyone, going against the kindness and compassion He always preached? Or would He go against God's law, declaring Himself a fraud?

Fully God and fully human, Jesus could see right through their schemes. He loved and understood people more than any mere human could ever imagine.

A hush fell over the crowd as they awaited Jesus' response to the Pharisees' challenge.

Jesus didn't say a single word. He simply knelt on the ground and started writing in the dirt with His finger.

"Well, come on, *teacher*! What do you say?" the Pharisees demanded.

Jesus stood up. He looked at the trembling woman, then out at the crowd, and then straight at the religious leaders. "Okay," he said. "Anyone among you who has never sinned, come on up here. You get to be the first one to throw a stone at her."

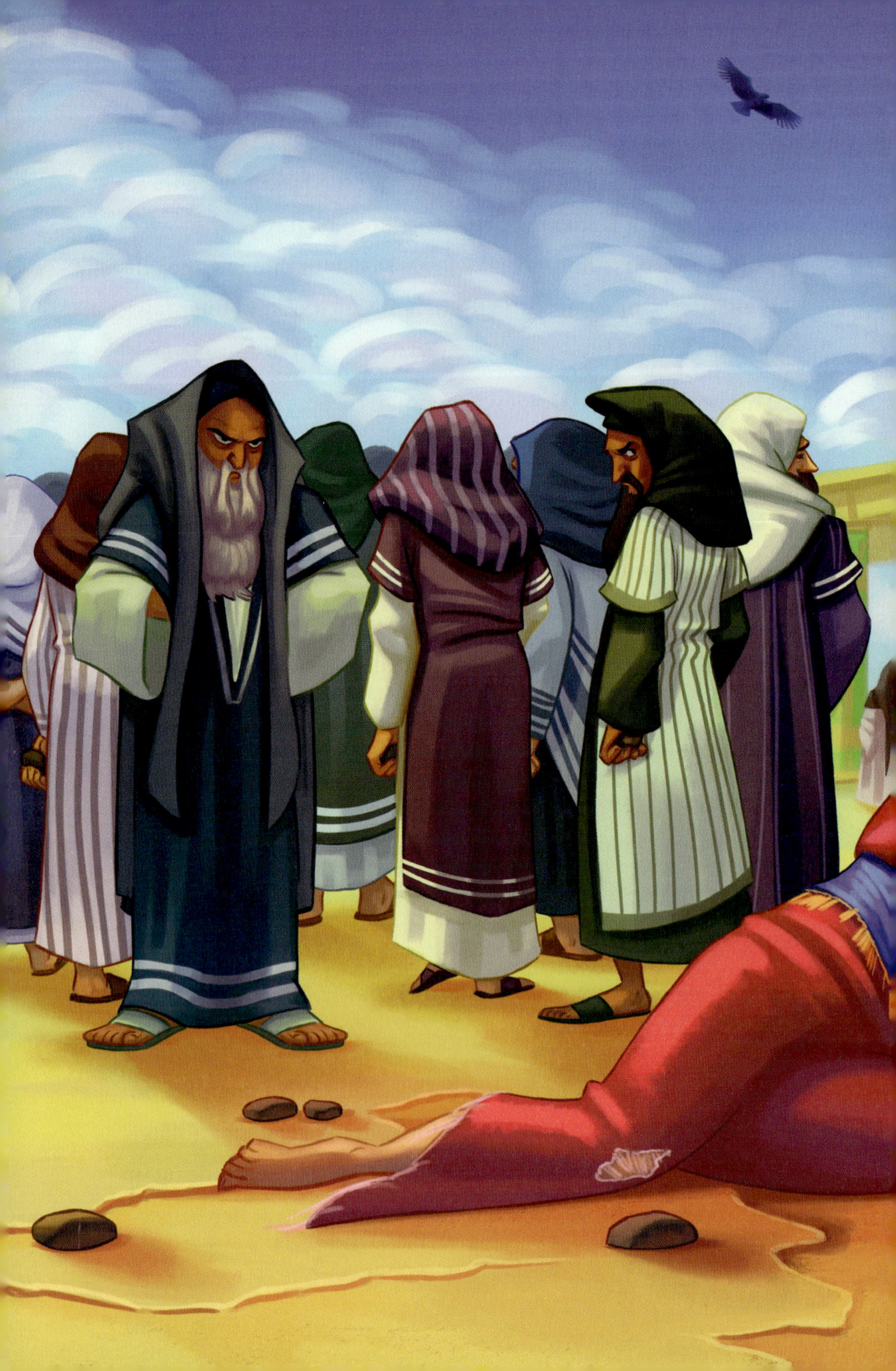

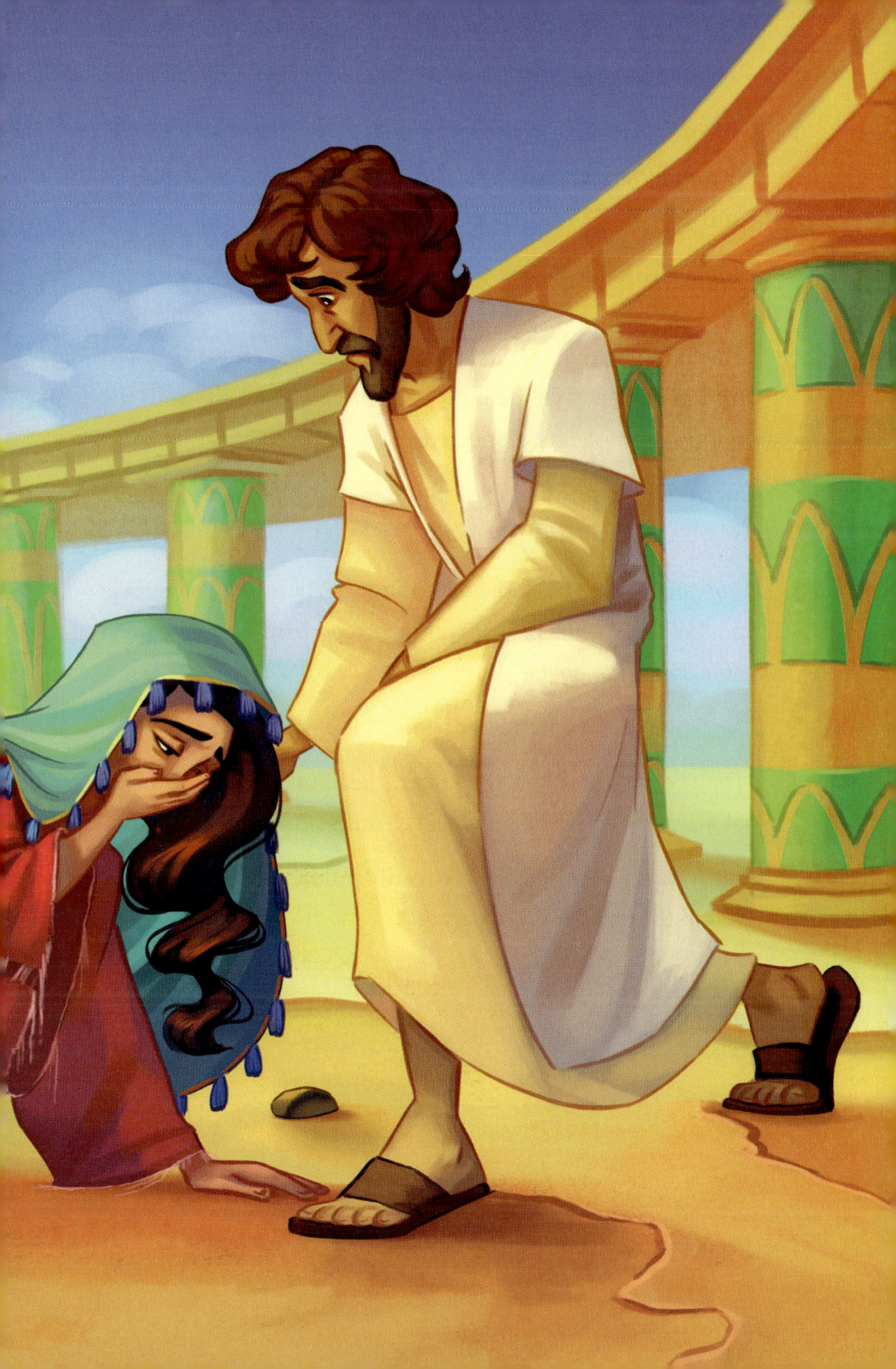

With that, Jesus knelt back down and continued writing in the dirt.

After an awkward silence, an older man shuffled away. Then the woman beside him left. A Pharisee walked away, and then another. One by one by one, all the people, the oldest first and then the younger, every single person walked away, until the crowd had completely dispersed.

Only the woman remained. Still awaiting her sentence, she stood obediently beside Jesus.

Jesus stood up and looked around. "Where are they?" He asked. "Where are the people waiting to condemn you, to punish you? Is there no one left?"

"No," She said, shaking her head. "No one, sir."

"Then I don't condemn you either," Jesus answered with compassion. "Now go, and forever leave your sinful life behind you."

This woman, at the brink of a deadly punishment, was pulled back into the arms of God's grace.

*Jesus stood up and asked her,
"Where is everyone? Isn't there
anyone left to accuse you?"
"No sir," the woman answered.
Then Jesus told her, "I am not going
to accuse you either. You may go
now, but don't sin anymore."*

John 8:10-11 CEV

"LAZARUS, COME OUT!"

John 11

Jesus was out traveling with His disciples when He received a message: "Your friend Lazarus is sick." The message was from Mary and Martha, the sisters who had welcomed Jesus and His disciples to stay in their home. Lazarus was their brother, and they all lived in Bethany, a town outside of Jerusalem. When Lazarus became seriously ill, Mary and Martha sent for Jesus, knowing that He would make their brother well again.

But when Jesus got the news, He didn't hurry to get to Bethany. He simply said, "This will not end in death; it will end with God being glorified."

The disciples didn't understand. Jesus loved Mary and Martha and Lazarus. Why wouldn't He go to them immediately to do something about this illness? Why wasn't He going to check on Lazarus?

Finally, after two days had passed, Jesus told His disciples, "Let's go back to Judea. Lazarus has fallen asleep, and I'm going to go wake him up." So Jesus headed in that direction.

"LAZARUS, COME OUT!"

The disciples followed Him, exchanging confused glances. Eventually, one of them spoke up. "Um, Jesus, if Lazarus is just sleeping, he's going to be fine. Why should we go all the way there to disturb him?"

Jesus stopped and turned to face them. "Lazarus is dead," he said, slowly this time so they could understand. "I am glad I wasn't there when he died so that you can see what will happen. Let's go see him, and then maybe you will believe."

Jesus continued on His way, and the disciples followed, thinking about Jesus' words. What was He going to do now?

As Jesus and His disciples neared the village, someone saw them and ran to tell Martha. "He's coming!" the person called. "Jesus is coming!" Martha ran out of the house and went to meet Jesus just outside of the village. Mary, however, stayed at the house with those mourning the loss of her brother.

When Martha saw Jesus, she hugged Him and cried, "Oh, Lord, if only You had been here, I know that You could have saved him." She shook her head in sadness, then looked up at Jesus hopefully and said, "Yet, even now You could ask for whatever You want, and God would give it to You, wouldn't He?"

Jesus gave her a gentle smile. "Your brother will be raised again," he promised.

"Yes, yes, I know," Martha answered, a tinge of disappointment in her voice. "He will be raised from death on the final day."

"LAZARUS, COME OUT!"

"Martha?" Jesus said gently.

"Yes, Lord?" she replied.

"I am the resurrection. *I am* the life. When someone believes in Me, they will live on, even when they die. When someone believes in Me, they *never* die," Jesus said, looking Martha in the eyes. "Do you believe this is true?"

"Yes, Lord," she answered, nodding sincerely. "I believe—I know that You are the Messiah, the Son of God."

He pulled her close into a hug. "Okay, now where's Mary?" He asked.

Martha quickly made her way back to the house. "Mary! Mary, come on," she called. "Jesus is here, and He wants to see you."

Mary jumped up and ran to meet Jesus. A crowd of people had gathered at the house with her; they had come from all around Jerusalem to pay their respects to Lazarus. When the people saw her leave so quickly, they thought she was going back to Lazarus' tomb, so they followed her.

When Mary saw Jesus, she collapsed at His feet in tears. "Oh, Jesus," she cried, "my brother would not have died if You had been here." The others who had come with her began to weep too, and Jesus was deeply moved by their sadness.

"Where is he?" Jesus asked them.

"This way," Mary and Martha answered, leading the quiet,

somber group to the tomb where Lazarus lay. Jesus followed close behind them. He wept, sharing in the sadness Mary and Martha felt at the loss of their brother, His beloved friend, sharing in the pain that death causes for the world.

"Look how much He loved Lazarus," one person whispered.

Another one said, "If this guy can work miracles, why couldn't He keep Lazarus from dying?"

"LAZARUS, COME OUT!"

When they arrived at the tomb, everyone gathered around. The tomb was built into the side of a mountain. It was a cave, with the opening covered by a huge stone.

"Move the stone away," Jesus said.

"But, Jesus," Martha interrupted, "he's been in there for four days already. It's going to smell really bad if you open the tomb."

Jesus looked at her and said, "Remember what I told you? If you believe, you will see the glory of God."

Martha stepped back. She watched some of the men move the stone away from the opening of the tomb.

Jesus looked to the heavens and said, "Father, I know that You've already heard My prayer. I know that You *always* hear Me, but I want everyone else to hear Me so that they can believe that You sent Me."

Then Jesus shouted, "Lazarus, come out!"

The crowd gasped at the boldness of the command.

There was a shuffling sound from inside the tomb. The shadow of a figure appeared in the opening of the cave. A hand reached out, with strips of cloth hanging from it, feeling its way toward freedom. The figure was wrapped in linen from head to toe.

"Unwrap him. Set him free," Jesus said.

Slowly, the removal of the cloth they had buried him in

"LAZARUS, COME OUT!"

revealed the impossible. Lazarus, the man who had been dead and buried, was now alive!

This one life-giving act would eventually lead to the death of Jesus. Hearing about this miraculous act, the Pharisees decided, once and for all, that they must get rid of Jesus. They decided then and there to find a way to kill Him.

Jesus was showing the world, little by little, the miracle of Himself—the Savior of the world. Some would believe Him. Some would reject Him. But all would have the choice to unwrap and receive this gift from heaven, presented to the world by a loving God.

> *Jesus said to her, "I am the resurrection and the life. The one who believes in me will live, even though they die; and whoever lives by believing in me will never die. Do you believe this?"*
>
> *John 11:25-26*

THE LAST SUPPER

Matthew 21, 26; John 13

Jesus' days on earth were coming to an end. He knew it. He felt it.

Jesus also knew that His disciples did not yet understand that He was going to be taken from them. Even though it would be hard, He knew that, in the end, it would be what was best for them all—for the whole world. With the little time that He had left, Jesus continued to teach and prepare His friends, His followers, for what was to come.

As Jesus and His disciples entered Jerusalem one day, a spirit of excitement was in the air. The Passover was quickly approaching, and Jesus would celebrate it in the city with His disciples.

Jesus had sent His disciples into town to get a colt, one that He would ride into Jerusalem. By doing so, He knew that He was fulfilling the prophet Zechariah's words that the King would come riding into Jerusalem on a donkey's colt.

As Jesus neared Jerusalem, He most certainly received a king's welcome. The crowds got bigger and their excitement grew

THE LAST SUPPER

greater and greater as Jesus made His way into the city. His path was paved with cloaks, as people laid their own clothes on the ground to make a road fit for a king. Others pulled palm branches from the trees and laid them on the ground for Jesus and His colt to travel over, or waved them in the air, shouting their welcome to Jesus.

By the time He got close to the city, a crowd had formed around Jesus, leading the way in front of Him, following behind Him, and lining each side of the road. They were all shouting, "Hosanna! Hosanna! Blessed is the One who comes in the name of the Lord!"

As the celebration moved through the town, people came out to see what all the shouting was about. "Who is it? What are they shouting about?" they asked.

The crowds answered, "It is Jesus."

Not everyone was happy to see Jesus entering Jerusalem. When the people's shouts reached the ears of the religious leaders, they were infuriated with Jesus and demanded He put a stop to this noisy celebration. Jesus knew that they were plotting against Him, but He still had work left to do on this earth.

When it was time to celebrate the Passover, Jesus told His disciples, "There is a certain man in the city. Go to him and tell him that the teacher wants to celebrate the Passover at his house." The disciples did just as Jesus said and got the Passover dinner ready.

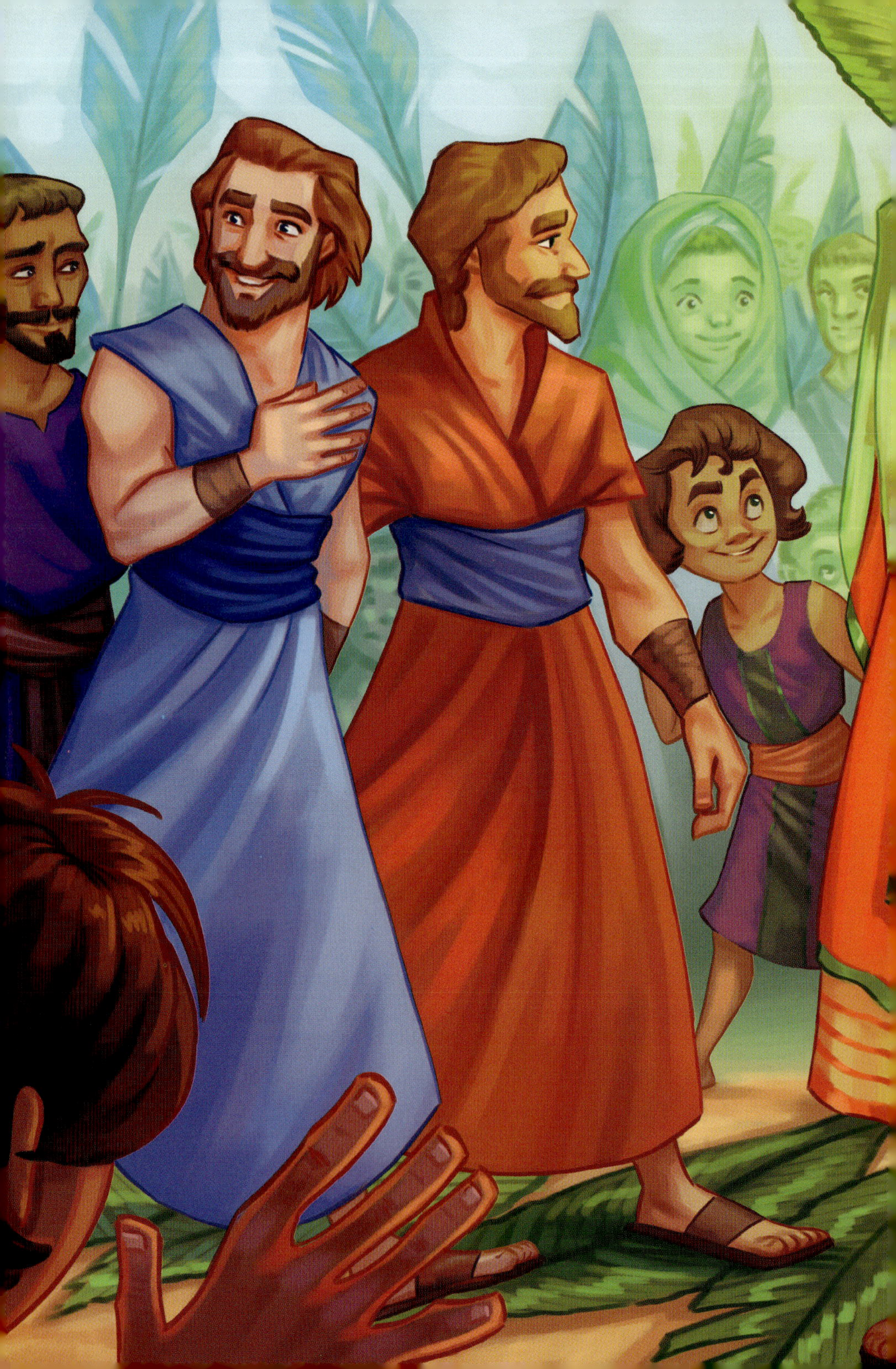

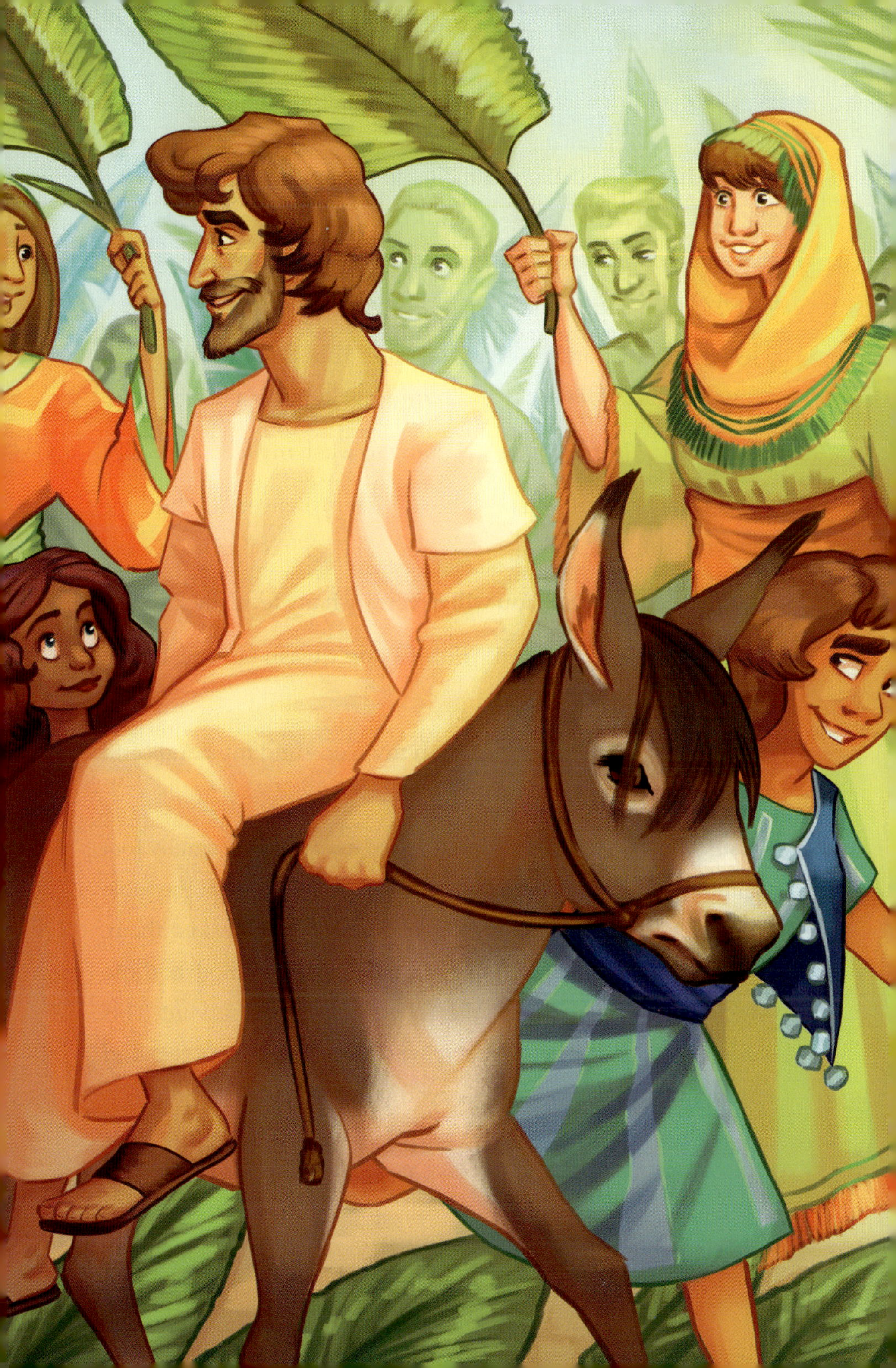

As they gathered around the table to eat, only Jesus fully realized what was coming. It would be the last dinner that they shared together before His death. He wanted to set an example of how to live for His disciples before he left them.

Jesus stood up and took off His outer robe. He then wrapped a towel around His waist and poured water into a basin.

Peter said, "Lord, you're not going to wash my feet, are you?"

"You may not understand now," Jesus answered, "but one day, you will."

Peter stood up. "No, You will never wash my feet," he insisted.

"Okay," Jesus answered. "But if I don't wash your feet, then you aren't a part of Me."

"In that case," Peter said, "wash my feet—and my hands and my head too!"

Jesus, the teacher, the Savior, washed every grimy, smelly foot in that room. He then put His robe back on and sat at the table again. "Do you understand what I just did?" He asked them. "You call Me 'teacher,' and you call me 'Lord.' I am both of those things, yet I have washed your feet as if I were a servant. This is how you should treat others, washing each other's feet and serving each other as I have served you."

When they were eating, Jesus said, "Tonight, one of you will betray Me."

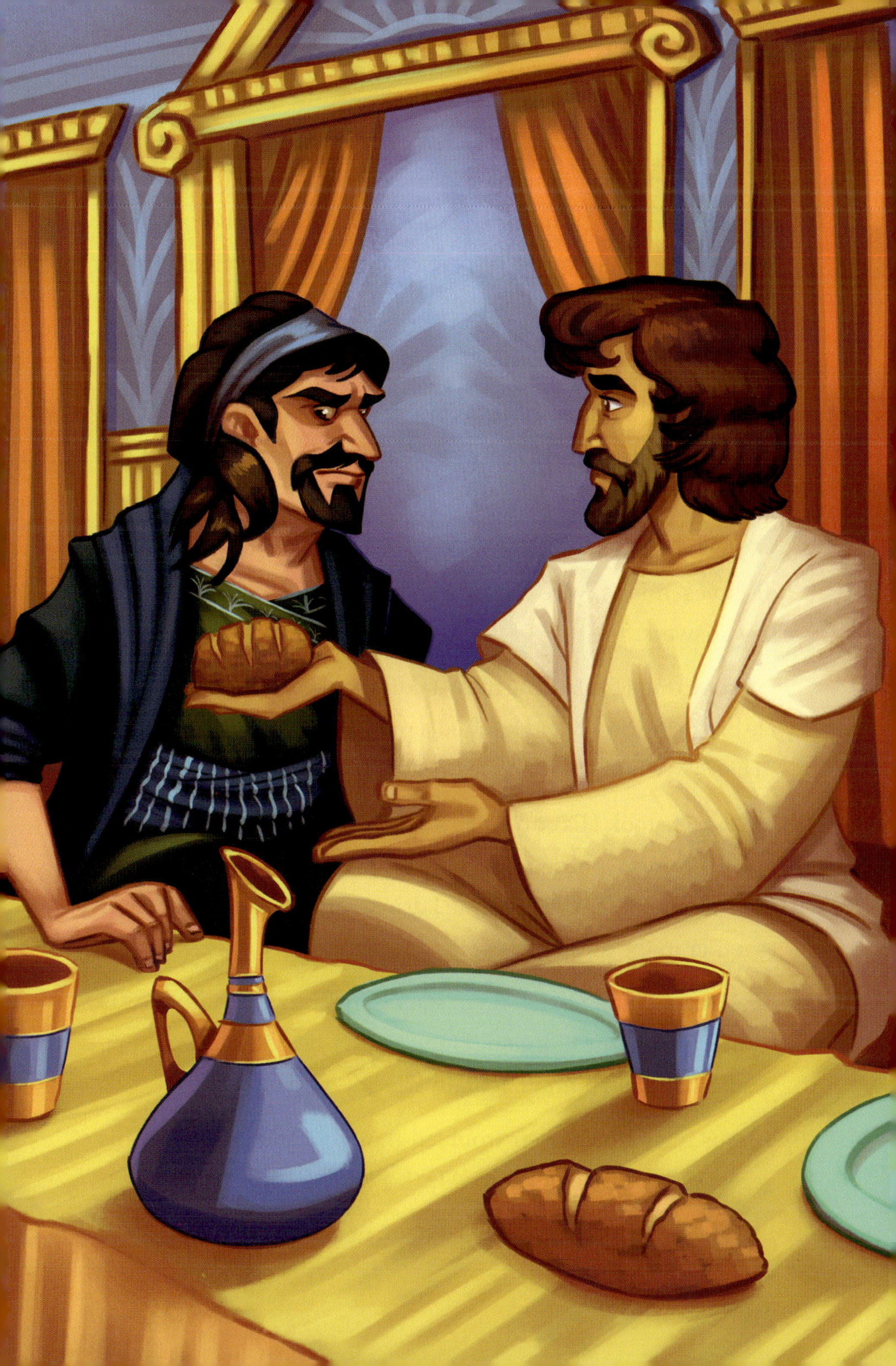

The disciples were shocked. They had walked with Jesus and seen His miracles. Who among them would dare to betray Him? Who among them could turn against the One who had shown them such love?

Judas spoke up, "You don't mean me, do you, Teacher?"

"You said it yourself," Jesus answered. "Go do what you are planning to do, but do it quickly." Judas stood up and left the room.

What could this mean? Why was Judas leaving now? The disciples' minds were buzzing with so many questions and so few answers.

Jesus turned back to the meal, taking some bread in His hands. He broke the bread and handed a piece to each disciple, saying, "This is My body."

Next, He took His cup and said, "This is My blood, the blood of the promise, poured out for everyone for the forgiveness of their sin. It will be the last time I drink with You until we are all together in the kingdom of God."

Jesus was trying to tell them something important, but it was so hard for them to grasp. He wouldn't actually leave them, would he? He wouldn't actually die?

Jesus interrupted their troubled thoughts and said, "On this very night, you will all leave Me."

"Not me!" Peter demanded. "I will never leave You."

THE LAST SUPPER

"Peter, it's true," Jesus answered. "Before the rooster crows in the morning, you will deny Me—not just once, but three different times."

"Never," Peter said, shaking his head. "I would even *die* with You."

The other disciples agreed with Peter, and their last supper with Jesus drew to a close.

With love, Jesus had held their dirty feet in His hands and washed away the grime from where they had walked, making them clean again. He foretold the betrayal and denial of those who loved Him the most on this earth, and yet He still gave the bread and the drink, His body and His blood, for those who would leave Him, for those who couldn't quite understand.

And he took the bread, gave thanks and broke it, and gave it to them, saying, "This is my body given for you; do this in remembrance of me." In the same way, after the supper he took the cup, saying, "This cup is the new covenant in my blood, which is poured out for you."

Luke 22:19-20

JESUS IS BETRAYED

Matthew 26

After their dinner together, Jesus and His disciples went into a garden called Gethsemane.

"Stay here," Jesus told them. "I'm going to go over there and pray."

Jesus took Peter, James, and John with Him and walked further into the garden. His steps slowed to a stop as the weight of all that was about to happen hit Him. The three disciples watched their teacher, concerned.

"My soul is overwhelmed with sadness," Jesus told them. "Please, stay here with Me. Keep watch."

Jesus took a few more steps, then dropped to His knees. With His face on the ground, He began to pray, "If it is possible, Father, take this cup from Me. But even so, let Your will be done, not Mine."

When He finished praying, Jesus went back to His disciples, but they were asleep. "You couldn't even keep watch for an hour?" Jesus said to Peter. "Please, stay here and keep watch.

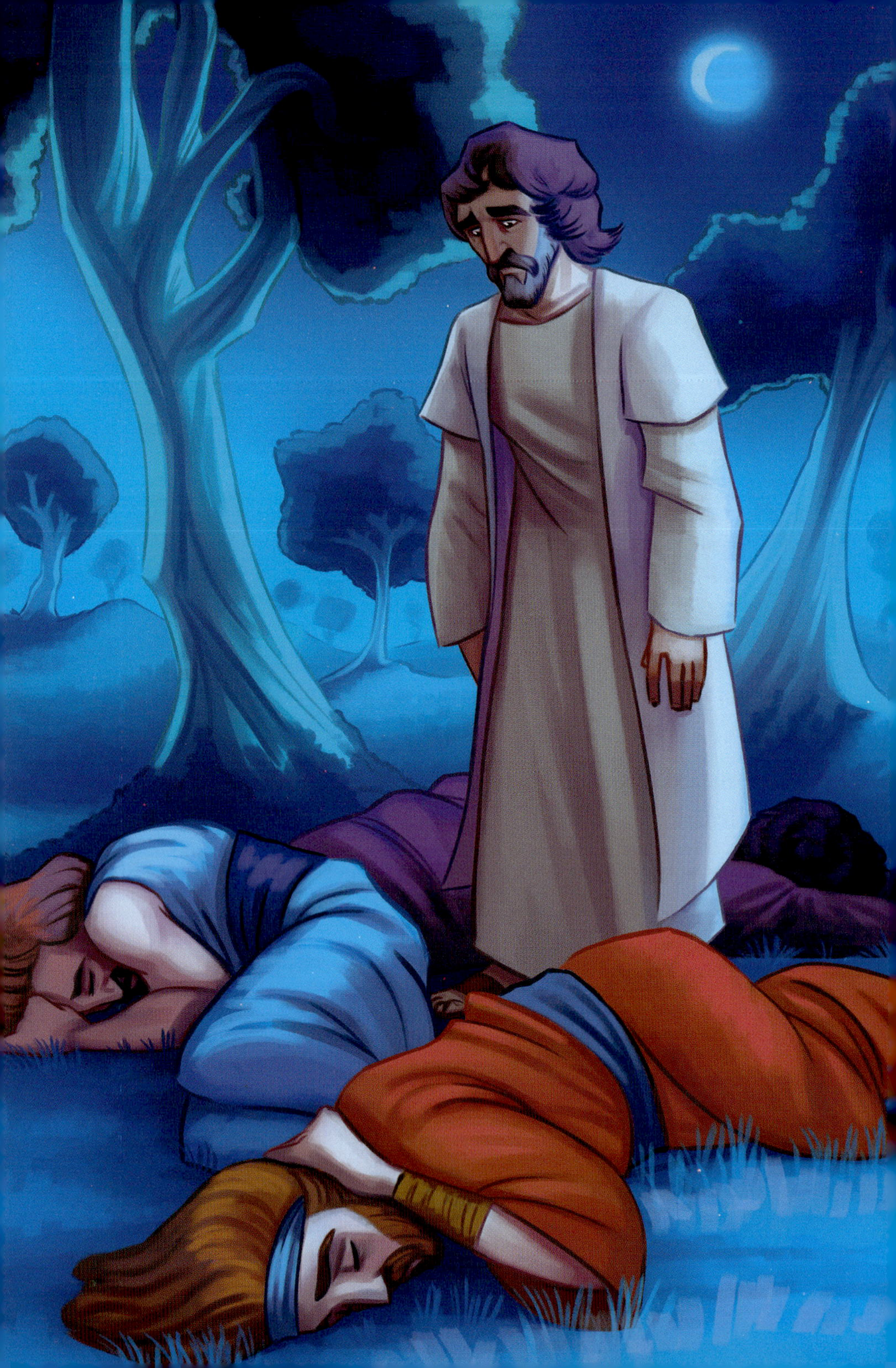

JESUS IS BETRAYED

Pray so that you are not tempted. Your spirit is willing, but your body is weak."

Then Jesus returned to pray again. "Father, if this is the only way, then let it be done to Me. I pray that Your will be done."

When Jesus came back, the disciples were sleeping again. So He left them and went back one more time to pray. When He returned for the third time, He said, "Are you still sleeping? It's time to go. My betrayer is coming."

Before Jesus could even finish His sentence, Judas arrived. Behind Judas was a crowd of men, raising swords and clubs, ready to capture a criminal.

Judas said, "Hello, teacher," and kissed Jesus on the cheek.

"Friend," Jesus replied, "are you betraying the Son of Man with a kiss?"

That kiss was a secret signal. Now everyone knew: *this* man was the One the religious leaders wanted. This was *Jesus*.

Immediately, the men with clubs and swords grabbed Jesus. Peter, trying to defend his teacher, drew his sword and swung it at one of them, the servant of the high priest, cutting off his ear.

"Put the sword away, Peter!" Jesus said. "I could call on my Father right now and have a dozen armies of angels to fight for Me. But if I did, the Scriptures would never be fulfilled."

Jesus reached out and healed the man's ear, saying, "Those who use swords will die by swords."

He then turned to the crowd and asked, "Why did you come out here at night with swords and clubs to capture me? You know that I'm right there in the temple courts every day, but you didn't arrest Me there, did you? This also fulfills what the Scriptures foretold."

The angry crowd led Jesus away, and the disciples scattered. But Peter and another disciple followed at a distance.

The men took Jesus to Caiaphas, the high priest. Many of the other religious leaders were there as well, waiting for them. Peter tried to see and hear what was going on. The men were trying to find evidence against Jesus in order to sentence Him to death. Many people came forward, telling lies about Jesus.

Finally, the high priest said to Him, "Swear an oath to the living God that you will answer truthfully, and tell us: Are You the Messiah? Are You the Son of God?"

"You have said that I am," Jesus answered. "And I'll tell all of you here today—in the future, you will see Me enthroned in heaven, sitting at the right hand of God."

The high priest was outraged. He tore his clothes and shouted, "Who needs witnesses?! You have heard Him yourself!"

Following the priest's example, the crowd grew angry. They hit Jesus. They spit on Him. They made fun of Him. He had likened Himself to God, a crime for which, according to the Jewish law, He deserved to die.

While this was going on, Peter was watching from outside. A girl came up to him and said, "You were one of the ones with Jesus!"

"Who? No! Me? Nonsense," Peter said and walked quickly away.

At the gate, another servant saw him and told everyone around them, "This guy was with Jesus!"

Peter answered, "I swear, I don't even know that man!"

Then the people nearby said, "We can tell by the way you talk. You're from Galilee, just like Jesus! Your accent gives it away!"

"Curse you!" Peter yelled at them. "I told you! I don't know Him!"

At that very moment, a rooster crowed, and Jesus' words rang through Peter's memory: "You will deny Me three times." Peter couldn't believe it. He had denied his teacher, his friend. He ran away from the crowd, hot tears stinging his face.

How had this one night gone so terribly wrong? One minute, they were having their feet washed by this miracle worker, and the next, this man, this Messiah, had been captured, mocked, and beaten. What was happening? How could this be part of the plan?

Going a little farther, he fell with his face to the ground and prayed, "My Father, if it is possible, may this cup be taken from me. Yet not as I will, but as you will."

Matthew 26:39

THE SAVIOR DIES

Matthew 27; Mark 15; Luke 23; John 18-19

As the sun rose that morning, things only appeared to get worse for Jesus. The religious leaders had bound His hands like a criminal and led Him to Pilate, the governor. In front of Pilate's house, the questioning continued.

"Are you the king of the Jews?" Pilate asked Him.

If Jesus said "yes," it would be considered an act of treason, a crime deserving of death.

"You have said that I am," Jesus answered.

The chief priests and elders continued to make their claims against Jesus. Jesus stood there silently, taking it all in, as they made the case for His death. Pilate couldn't believe it. This wasn't the behavior of a typical criminal. There were no arguments, no cries protesting his innocence, no fingers pointing back at His accusers. This man Jesus just listened as a wall of accusations was stacked up against Him. He didn't even try to defend Himself.

"Don't you hear this?" Pilate asked Jesus. "Do you have no defense?"

Jesus didn't say a word. Even though Pilate could tell that these accusations were made up by the religious leaders for selfish reasons, Jesus didn't protest their claims.

"Where are you from?" Pilate asked Jesus, but His silence continued. "Why won't you answer me?" Pilate prodded. "Don't you know that I have the power either to save you or to send you to your death?"

"The only power you have over Me," Jesus offered, "is the power given to you from above."

Pilate had heard enough. He knew that Jesus should go free, but the Jewish leaders kept insisting that Jesus must be punished. Fortunately, it was the Passover Festival and it was tradition that every year, as a part of the festival, the governor would release one prisoner chosen by the crowd. Pilate presented two choices to the crowd: a notorious murderer named Barabbas, or Jesus.

"Now, which of these prisoners would you like me to release?" Pilate asked, taking his seat in front of the crowd.

Pilate watched his plan to free Jesus begin to crumble as the religious leaders persuaded the people, stirring them up to cheer for Barabbas and against Jesus.

"Which one shall I release?" Pilate asked the crowd.

"Barabbas! Barabbas!" they cheered.

"Then what will I do with this One? The king of the Jews?"

THE SAVIOR DIES

"Crucify him! Crucify him!" the crowd shouted.

"For what crime?!" Pilate shouted back.

They only shouted louder, *"Crucify him! Crucify him!"*

Pilate knew that Jesus was innocent. His wife had even sent a message saying, "Leave that innocent man alone. I had a terrible dream because of Him last night!" But Pilate also knew that he was getting nowhere with the crowd. They were determined to see Jesus crucified. If they didn't get their way, the crowd would likely rise up in rebellion against him.

In the end, Pilate gave in. He caved to the power of the crowd and the power of the Jewish leaders.

He called for a bowl of water to be brought for him. In front of everyone, he dipped his hands into the water, rubbed them together, and held them up for everyone to see.

"I wash my hands of this man's blood," Pilate told the crowd. "It is all on you."

The people answered, "His blood is on us! It is on our children!"

It had been decided. Barabbas the murderer was set free, and Jesus, the perfect Son of God, was led away to be flogged and crucified.

After beating Jesus, mocking Him, and stripping Him of His clothes, the soldiers made a crown out of thorns and pushed it

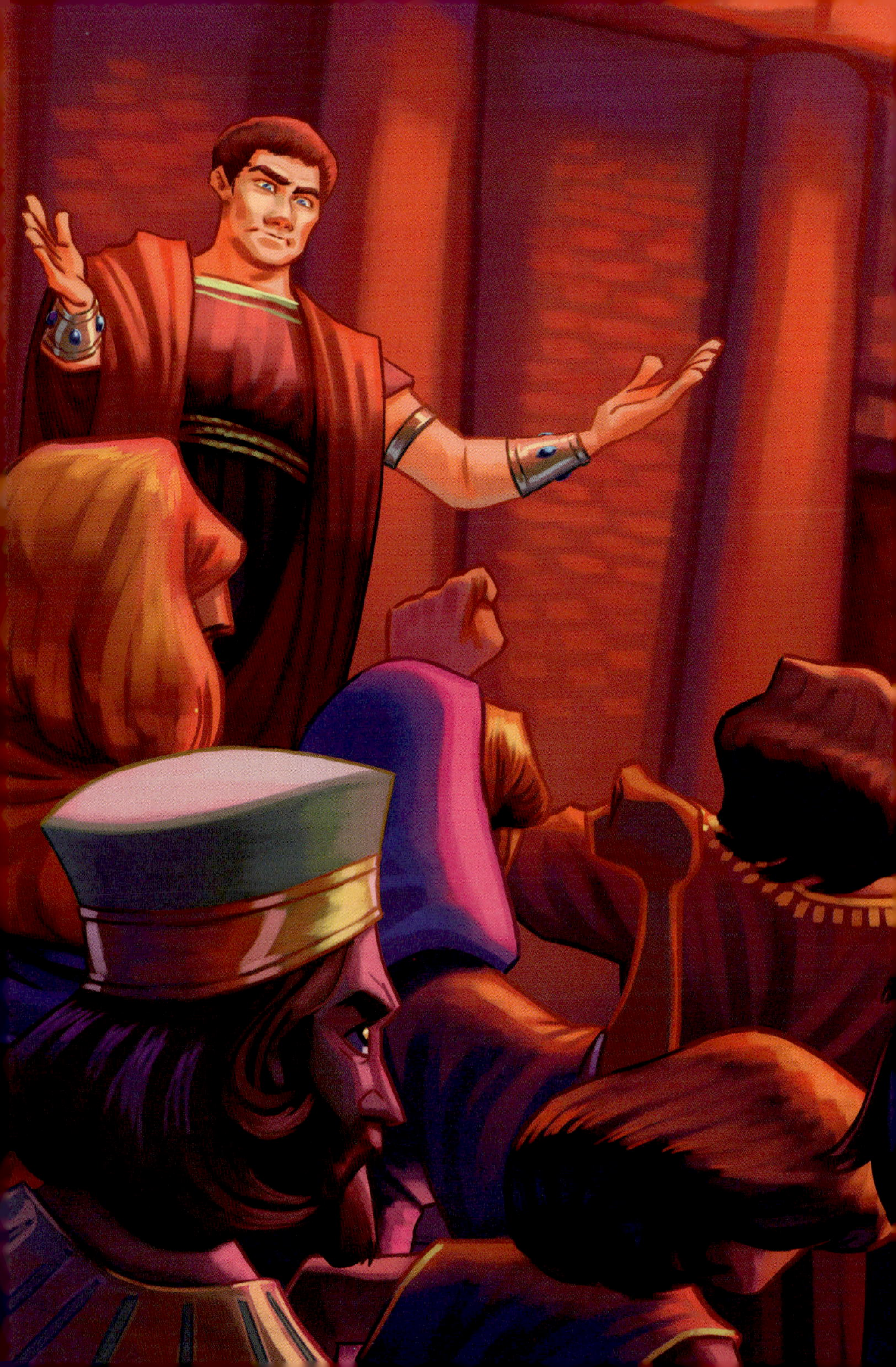

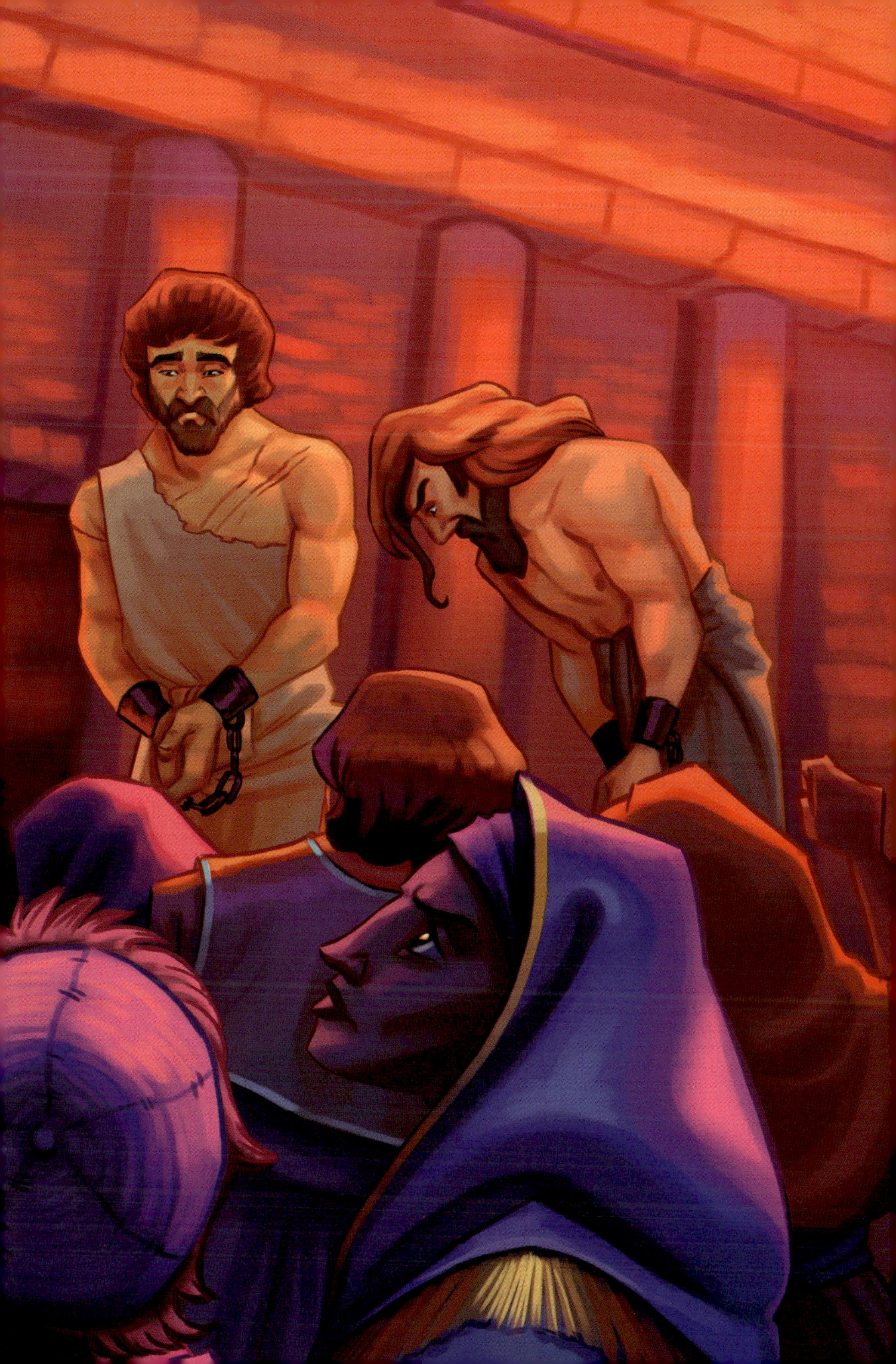

THE SAVIOR DIES

down on Jesus' head. They knelt in front of Him, laughing. "All hail the king of the Jews!" they shouted. Then they led Jesus to the hill where He would be crucified.

Jesus struggled as He walked, trying to keep the heavy cross on His shoulder as it dragged on the ground behind Him. The soldiers pulled a man named Simon from the crowd. "You! Help Him carry this cross!" they ordered.

Together, Jesus and Simon made their way to Golgotha, the hill where criminals were crucified.

Following Pilate's orders, the soldiers nailed Jesus to the cross and hung a sign over His head. The sign read: "Jesus of Nazareth, King of the Jews."

The religious leaders didn't like the sign at all. "It should say that he *claimed* to be the King of the Jews," they argued.

"I've written what I've written," Pilate replied.

The soldiers hoisted the cross into an upright position and Jesus hung there, with a criminal crucified on either side of Him. "So, you're the Messiah?" one of the criminals said. "Why don't You prove it by saving Yourself and taking us with You?"

The other criminal scolded the first and said, "You're not afraid of God, even though you're about to die?! We deserve our punishments, but this man is innocent!" The man then spoke to Jesus. "Please, Jesus, remember me when you get to Your kingdom."

"I will, you can be certain of that," Jesus said to the man. "Today, you will go with Me to paradise."

Jesus' mother Mary and His closest disciples watched in horror as He hung there in the noonday sun. Sweat mixed with blood and ran down His brow as the heat drained the last of His strength from Him. Suddenly, a thick darkness rolled across the land, turning the day to night.

The darkness lasted for hours until, finally, at three in the afternoon, Jesus cried, "Into Your hands, Father, I commit My Spirit."

They were His dying words. Jesus breathed His last breath.

With that last breath, the earth erupted in angry tremors. Rocks split in half. Tombs opened up. The thick curtain in the temple that divided the Holy of Holies, where God's holy ark stood, from the rest of the temple was torn in half from top to bottom. People were running and screaming. They were terrified.

One of the soldiers standing nearby shouted, "He really *was* the Son of God!"

When evening came, a wealthy man from the city of Arimathea went to Pilate and asked for Jesus' body. This man, Joseph, had been a secret follower of Jesus, and he wanted to be sure that Jesus was buried properly. After Pilate granted his request, Joseph wrapped the body carefully in linen and placed Jesus' body in a new tomb. Joseph and some other disciples rolled a huge stone to cover the entrance of the tomb.

It was a dark day for everyone. Not only had a physical darkness covered the land, but a dark cloud of sadness, mourning, and confusion also weighed heavy on Jesus' followers that day. The man they had believed in, Jesus, the Messiah, the Savior, was now gone. Their Lord was lifeless, lying in a tomb.

The One they had been waiting on for centuries, the coming One who had been foretold by the Scriptures, was dead. Sure,

THE SAVIOR DIES

Jesus had taught them about the Scriptures and had worked miracles while He was alive, but He hadn't exactly ruled a kingdom. He hadn't really saved the world, had He?

Together, the disciples and all who had believed in Him mourned the loss of Jesus, the Messiah, their Savior who was gone too soon.

> *Then he said, "Jesus, remember me when you come into your kingdom." Jesus answered him, "Truly I tell you, today you will be with me in paradise."*
> Luke 23:42-43

> *When he had received the drink, Jesus said, "It is finished." With that, he bowed his head and gave up his spirit.*
> John 19:30

HE LIVES!

Matthew 28; Luke 24; John 20

Jesus' followers rested on the Sabbath, obeying the law and following tradition. Bright and early on the first day of the week, Mary and Mary Magdalene, who had been followers of Jesus, went back to His tomb to treat His body with spices, according to their burial customs. When they got to the tomb, the stone that had been covering the entrance was rolled to the side, leaving the tomb open.

The women stepped carefully into the tomb, wondering who could have moved the stone. As their eyes adjusted to the darkness of the cave, they realized that Jesus' body was gone! They looked all around, but it was nowhere to be found!

Suddenly, two men appeared in the tomb with them, clothed in robes shining as bright as lightning. The women were terrified and dropped to the ground, bowing to these strangers.

"Why are you in a tomb looking for someone who is alive?" the men asked. "He isn't here! He has risen from the dead!" The women cautiously looked up toward the men, and they continued, "Don't you remember? He Himself told you that He

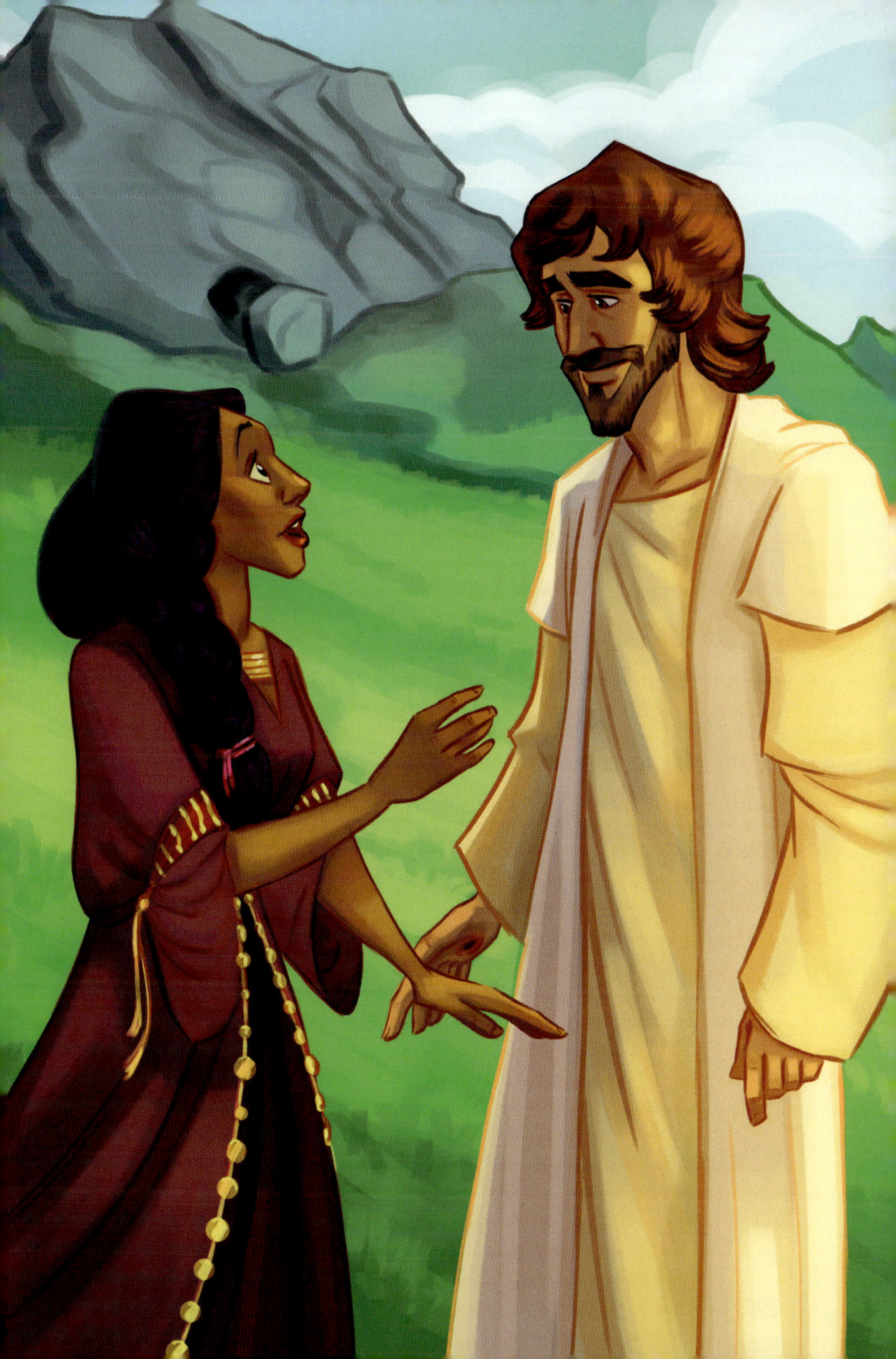

would be crucified and raised to life on the third day."

The women looked at each other, shocked. They *did* remember. He *had* told them that this would happen. Could it be true?

The women dropped everything they had brought with them and ran all the way back to where the disciples were meeting. They burst into the room, breathless.

"He's alive!" one of them shouted. "We went to the tomb and the stone was gone and He wasn't there! Two shiny men came and said, 'He's not here, He's alive! He told you He would die and rise again on the third day!'"

The disciples just stared at the women. Some of them shook their heads in disbelief. Some went back to what they were doing, but not Peter. Peter stood up and ran, along with another disciple, all the way to the tomb. When they got there, they found the tomb just as the women had described—empty. The tomb was empty! The stone was rolled away, and Jesus was gone. Only strips of linen cloth remained where Jesus had been.

After reporting to the disciples that Jesus' body was gone, Mary Magdalene also returned to the tomb, and she began to cry. As her tears fell, she looked into the tomb once more. This time she saw two angels, dressed in white, sitting where Jesus' body had been laid.

"Why are you crying?" the angels asked her.

"Because," she answered, "they have taken Jesus, my Lord, and now I don't know where to find Him."

Still searching, she turned around and saw a man standing there. He asked, "Who are you looking for?"

Mary Magdalene thought that the man must be the gardener. Through her tears and her sorrow, she didn't realize that the very Savior she had been searching for was standing right in front of her.

"Sir," she said, shaking her head, "just tell me where you have put Him, and I will go get Him."

Then Jesus said, "Mary."

"Teacher!" she cried, suddenly realizing who it was and flinging her arms around Him.

"Now go," Jesus told her. "Tell my brothers."

Mary Magdalene ran back again to tell the disciples the incredible news.

The disciples were talking excitedly about the news, the possibility that Jesus had returned from the dead. Could it really be true? As they were talking about everything they had seen and heard, a familiar voice spoke up, stating, "Peace to you all."

They all turned to look at the figure in the room with them. It looked like Jesus. It sounded like Jesus. But, it couldn't be, could it? Was it a vision? A ghost?

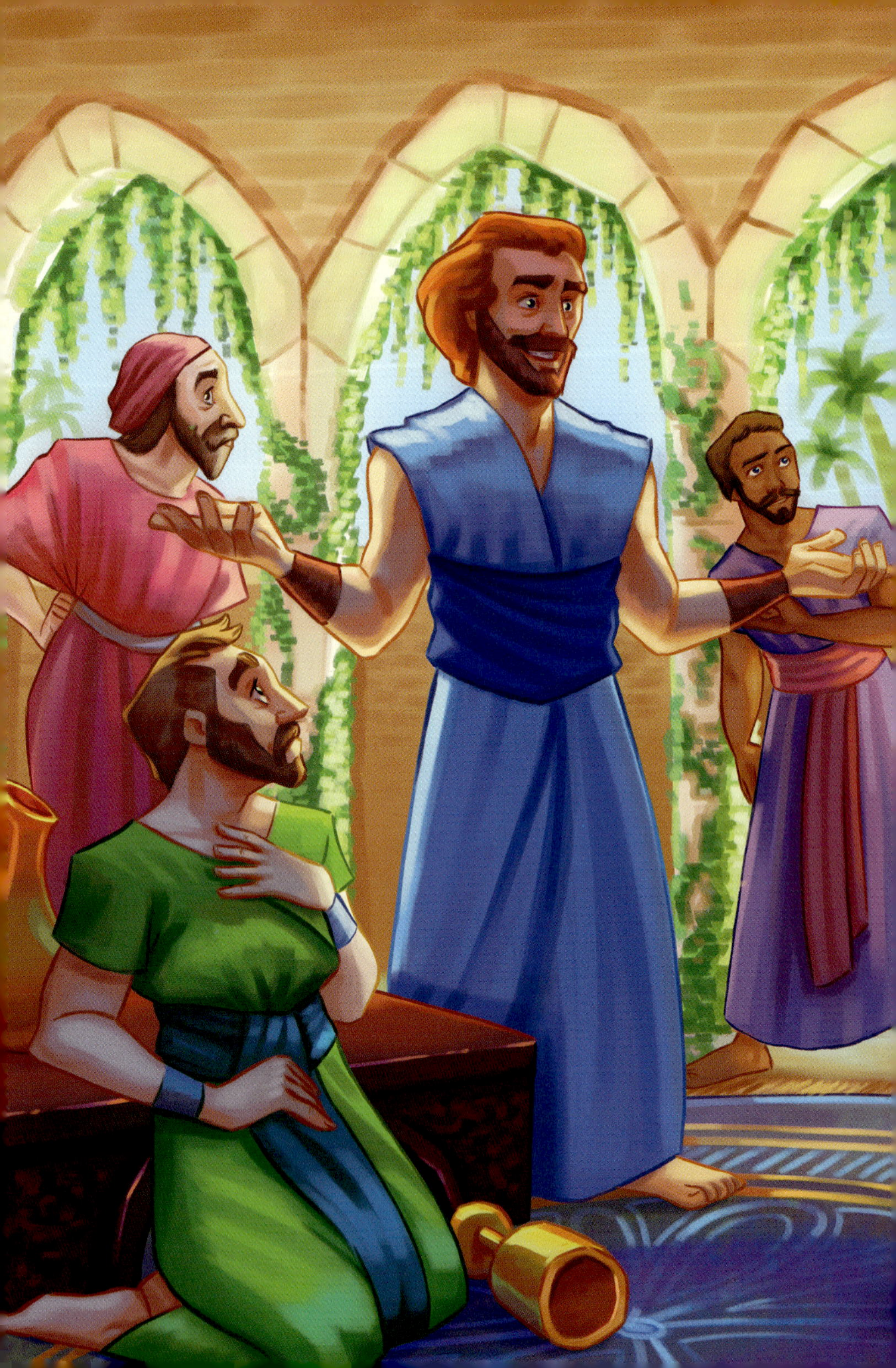

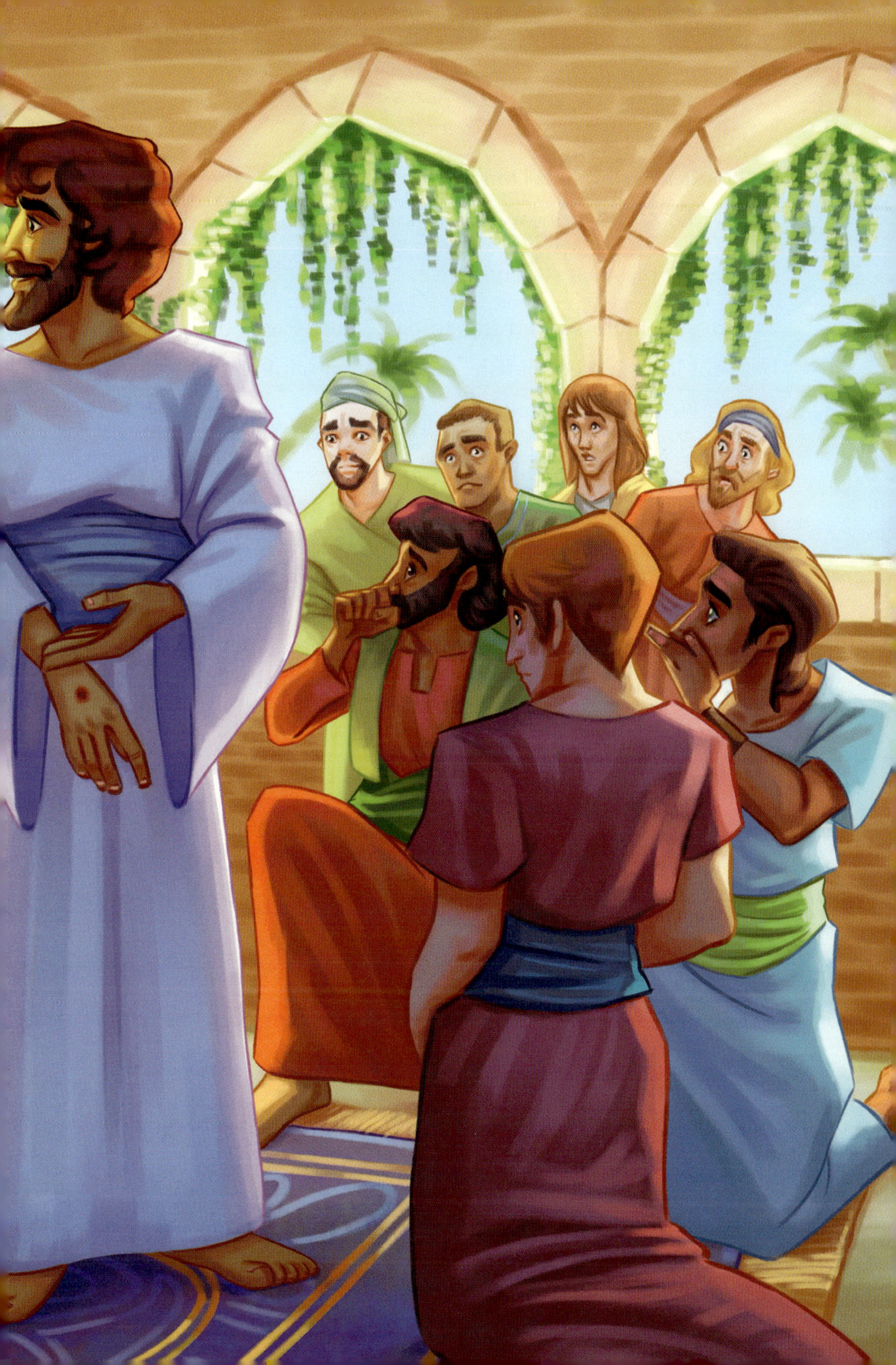

"Don't be troubled. Don't doubt," He said to them. "Here, touch Me! A ghost doesn't have skin and bones like I do!"

The disciples just stared in awe.

"Do you have something to eat?" Jesus asked. Someone brought Jesus a piece of fish, and He ate it while they watched. "See?" He said. "It's really Me."

Slowly, they stepped forward to see if it could be true. They talked to Him, ate with Him, and listened as He spoke to them. They embraced Him and welcomed Him back with joy and tears and complete amazement.

> *The angel said to the women, "Do not be afraid, for I know that you are looking for Jesus, who was crucified. He is not here; he has risen, just as he said. Come and see the place where he lay."*
>
> Matthew 28:5-6

THE GREAT COMMISSION

Luke 24; Acts 1

For forty days, Jesus stayed with His disciples, showing them again and again, in many different ways, that it was really Him, that He was really alive. He spent time with them just as before, teaching them and explaining the Kingdom of God to them.

Once while they were eating, Jesus said to them, "Do not leave Jerusalem yet. Wait here until you receive the gift from my Father that I have told you about. When John was here, he baptized with water, but you will be baptized with the Holy Spirit."

The disciples listened, trying to understand Jesus' words. They obeyed Him and would stay in Jerusalem until they knew it was time to move on.

As Jesus was preparing to leave His disciples, He said, "You are all witnesses to everything that has happened. Go out into the world and make even more disciples. Baptize them in the name of the Father and the Son and the Holy Spirit. Teach them as I have taught you. I will send the Helper to aid you in this mission. Do not be afraid, because I will be with you always, to the very end of time."

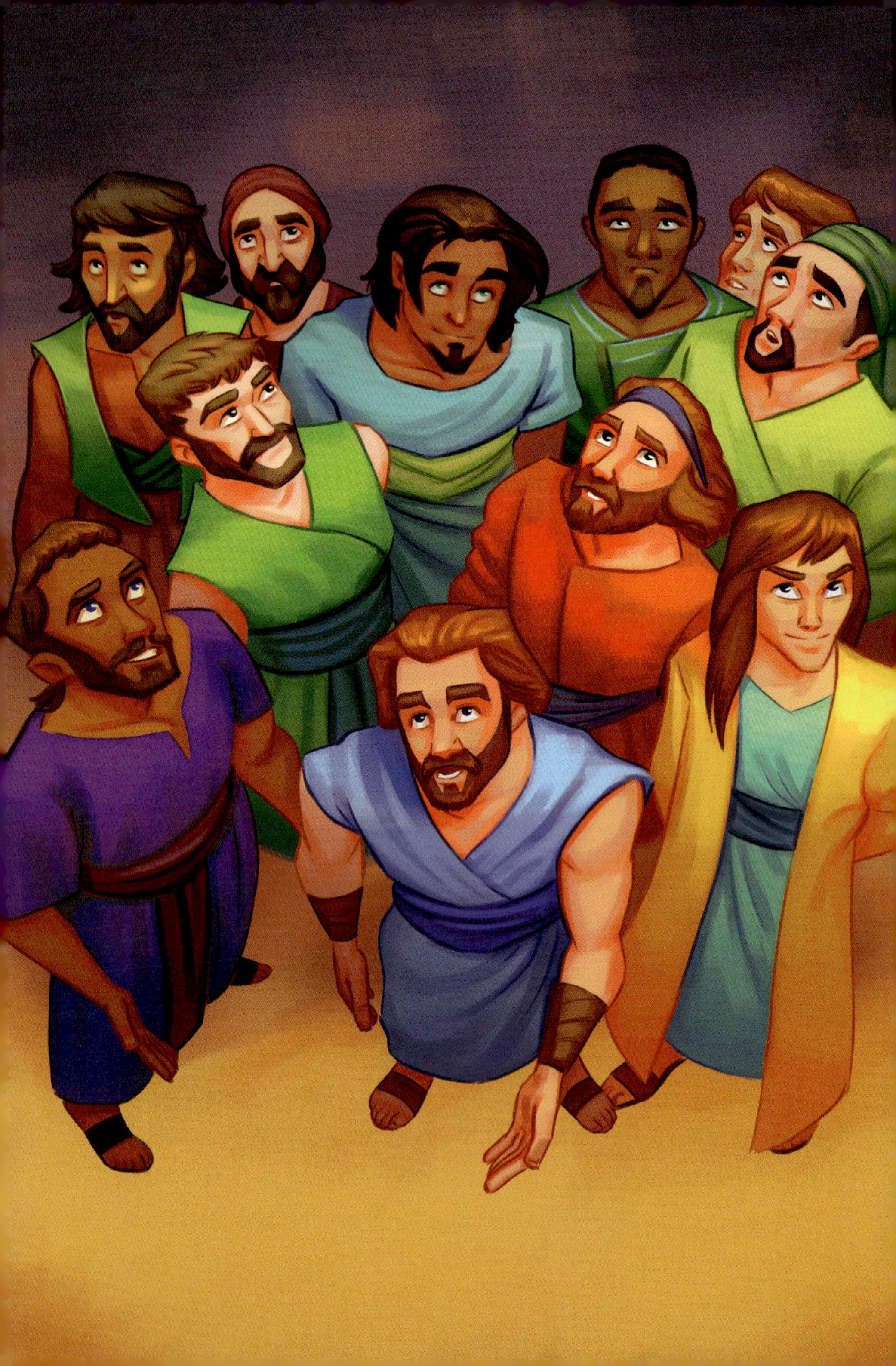

THE GREAT COMMISSION

Jesus knew it was time for Him to go be with His Father. He looked lovingly at His friends, His disciples, and spoke blessings over them. All at once He began to lift off the ground, up into heaven, until He was taken beyond the clouds.

The disciples just stood there in awe, watching and worshipping the One who was the Son of God.

Out of nowhere, two men in white appeared beside the disciples. The men said, "Why are you still standing here, watching the sky? Jesus was taken into heaven. One day He will come back the same way you saw Him go."

For now, however, there was work to be done. The followers of Jesus had an assignment, and it was an urgent one. The people of the world needed to hear about the God who loved them, the Son who died for them, and the salvation that awaited them.

> *Then Jesus came to them and said, "All authority in heaven and on earth has been given to me. Therefore go and make disciples of all nations, baptizing them in the name of the Father and of the Son and of the Holy Spirit, and teaching them to obey everything I have commanded you. And surely I am with you always, to the very end of the age."*
>
> Matthew 28:18-20

THE HELPER IS HERE

Acts 2

Jesus' disciples were all together on the day of Pentecost, a festival—also called the Feast of Weeks—held seven weeks after Passover to celebrate the wheat harvest. They were all in the same house, just beginning their day, when all at once a fierce wind gusted in, filling every room in the house. What looked like a big cloud of flames separated into bits, like little flaming tongues. The tongues of fire hovered around and landed on each of the disciples.

Immediately, they all felt the Holy Spirit flowing through them. They felt God's holy presence and found that they were able to speak other languages that they had never spoken before.

During the festival of Pentecost, Jews from all over the world traveled to Jerusalem in order to celebrate together. Now all these Jews from different countries heard the followers of Jesus speaking different languages—*their own* languages—languages they could understand. They stood and listened in amazement, gathering around the disciples to listen to them praising God in different languages.

"Aren't these people all from Galilee?" one person asked. "How is it that they are speaking the language from our own country, telling us about the wonders of God?"

While some were amazed, others laughed at the disciples. "They've had too much to drink," they said, explaining it away.

Peter stood up in front of the crowd and brought the other disciples with him. "Friends listen to me! Let me explain!" He said, waving his arms to get the crowd to quiet down. "We haven't been drinking. It's only nine o'clock in the morning!" There were a few nods, a few laughs, then Peter continued, "What's happening here is just as the prophet Joel explained. He said that in the last days God will pour out His Spirit on all the people. When He does, the people will prophesy and see dreams and visions. This is all set to happen before the return of the Lord, and everyone who calls on God will be saved."

The crowd had grown quiet and all eyes were on Peter. He said, "My friends, Jesus was given to you, sent to you by God. He worked miracles and signs and wonders through the power of God, and it was God's plan all along to hand Him over to you, who along with the help of some wicked people, put Jesus to death."

Several people shifted uncomfortably, looking down at the floor. They knew what Peter said was true. They had gotten caught up in the moment, believed the lies, and participated in the death of God's holy Son.

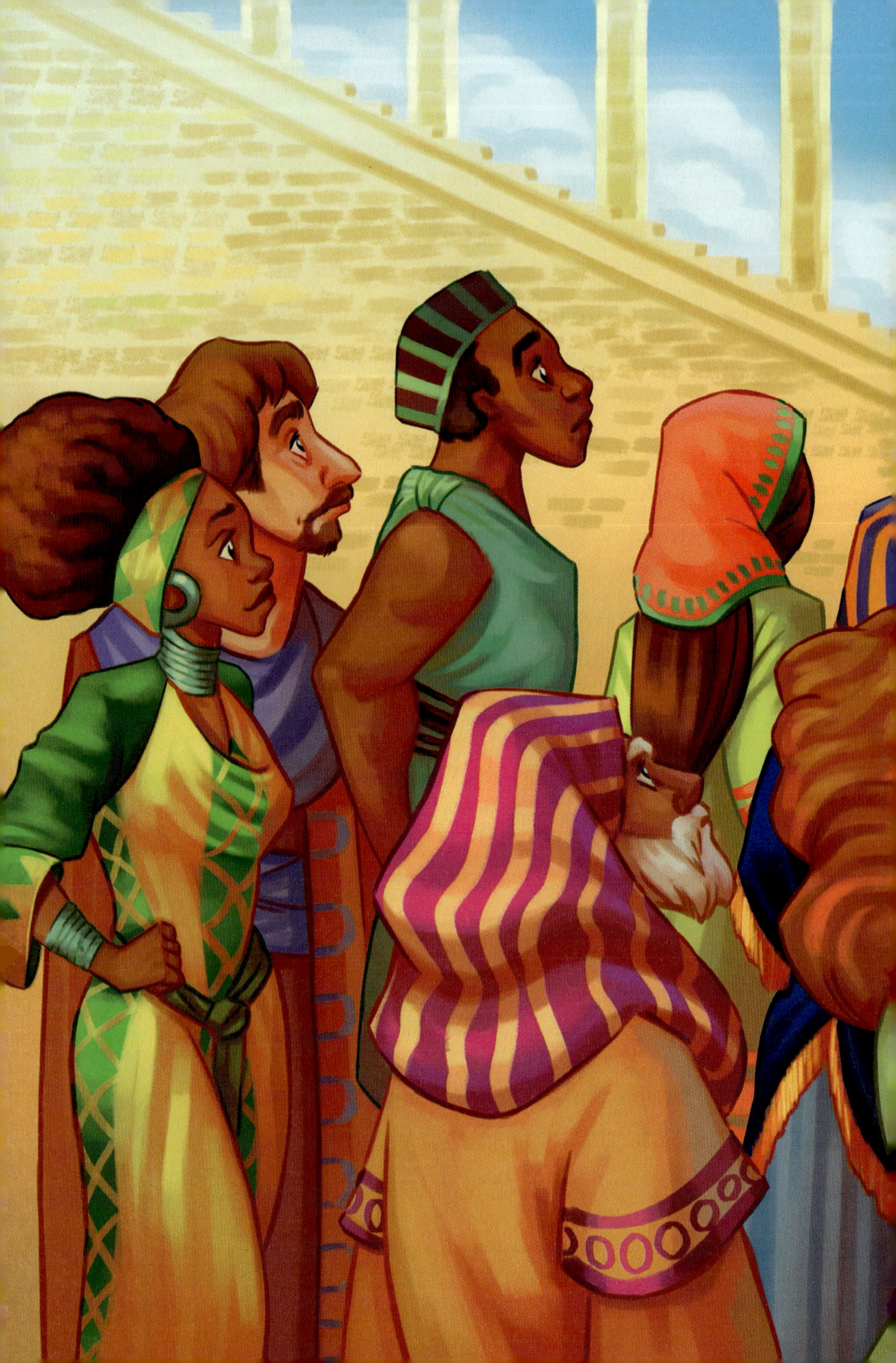

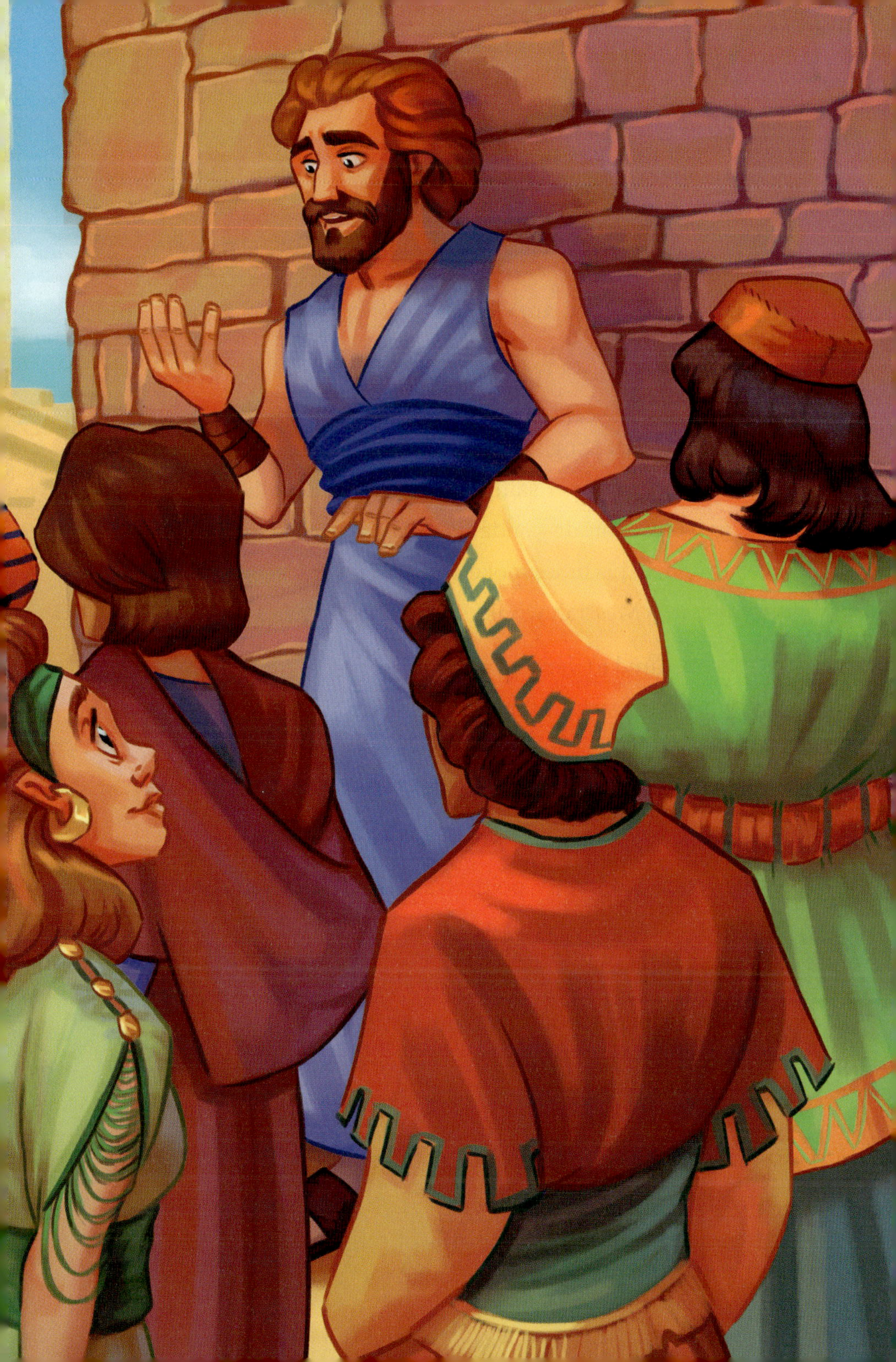

Peter continued, "But it was impossible for death to hold Jesus for very long. God brought Him out of that tomb and raised him to life again, and Jesus was forever set free from death."

Looks of relief and amazement washed over the crowd, and Peter held the rapt attention of this gathering of Jews from all over the world.

"We know that King David died and was buried and is still in his tomb today," Peter said. "But even he knew the promise of God, that one of his descendants would always sit on the throne. Even David, in his time, spoke of the resurrection of the Messiah and how this Messiah would sit at the right hand of God."

Peter gestured to the disciples who stood by his side and said, "All of us have seen it for ourselves. This Messiah that David spoke of—a descendant from the line of David—this Jesus died, but He didn't stay dead. God raised Him up again to sit at His right hand. We saw it all with our very own eyes."

Peter continued, "My point, friends, is this: God sent Jesus, the Messiah, and you crucified Him."

Peter's words, these words from the Holy Spirit, cut right to the heart and soul of those listening. After a moment, they cried out, "What should we do? How do we make this right?"

"Repent," Peter answered. "Turn away from sin and be baptized in the name of Jesus. You will be forgiven for your sins, and you will receive this same Helper you have seen at work today: the Holy Spirit. These gifts of forgiveness and the Holy

Spirit are not just for me and you, but for your children and all children to come, for everyone that God calls to Him."

That day, more than three thousand people chose to follow Jesus, to turn away from their sin, and to be baptized, receiving the Holy Spirit. They were the first fruits of the Great Commission. They would then accept that mission themselves, carrying the Good News with them wherever they went.

The power of the Holy Spirit, through the voice of one man, brought three thousand people into the Kingdom of God, into forgiveness, into the hope of eternal life. Through Peter, who obeyed God and was helped by the Holy Spirit, God made a huge impact for His kingdom, and it was only just the beginning of God's work through these believers.

> Peter replied, "Repent and be baptized, every one of you, in the name of Jesus Christ for the forgiveness of your sins. And you will receive the gift of the Holy Spirit. The promise is for you and your children and for all who are far off—for all whom the Lord our God will call."
>
> *Acts 2:38-39*

TROUBLE FOR THE FIRST CHURCH

Acts 2, 4, 8–9

After Pentecost, the new believers dedicated their lives to learning about Jesus. They spent time with the disciples and other believers, eating together and praying together. The disciples, with the help of the Holy Spirit, performed signs and wonders.

The believers worked together, combining all of their resources. When someone was in need, those who had property would sell it and give their money to the disciples to distribute to those who needed help. It was a time of togetherness and joy, and God continued to add believers to their number every day.

Even though there was great joy among the believers, the outside world wasn't always as welcoming. Some people were eager to listen to the believers, but the religious leaders continued to fight against the message of Jesus. When they heard Peter and John teaching about Jesus, the religious leaders seized them and began to question them.

Even as they were questioned, Peter and John continued to preach the message of Jesus directly to the religious leaders

TROUBLE FOR THE FIRST CHURCH

who had the power to punish them—even sentence them to death! The leaders were astonished by the boldness, courage, and knowledge of these men, who were not trained in the Law at all—just common men with ordinary backgrounds. The religious leaders didn't know what to do with these disciples. They only knew this: they had to stop this message about Jesus from spreading all over the country.

"We have decided to release you," the leaders declared to Peter and John. "But you must not ever speak the name of Jesus from this point on."

"What do you think is right? For us to listen to God or to listen to you?" Peter and John replied. "You can decide, but we can't help ourselves. We must continue telling others about what we have witnessed."

They did just that. Beaten and bruised, threatened and persecuted, the believers continued on their mission to tell the world about the God who loved them so much He sent His Son to die for them.

One of the chief persecutors of the believers was a man named Saul. Saul went from house to house, dragging men and women out of their homes and putting them in prison because they believed in Jesus. He even requested permission from the high priest to go into the synagogues in Damascus to hunt down and imprison any believers he found there.

On his way to Damascus, Saul was surrounded by a bright light that shot down from the sky. He fell to the ground in fear, but the men traveling with Saul didn't move.

"Saul!" a voice called to him. "Saul, why are you persecuting Me?"

"Who—who is speaking, my lord?" Saul replied.

"It's Me, Jesus, the One you keep hunting down and persecuting," Jesus answered.

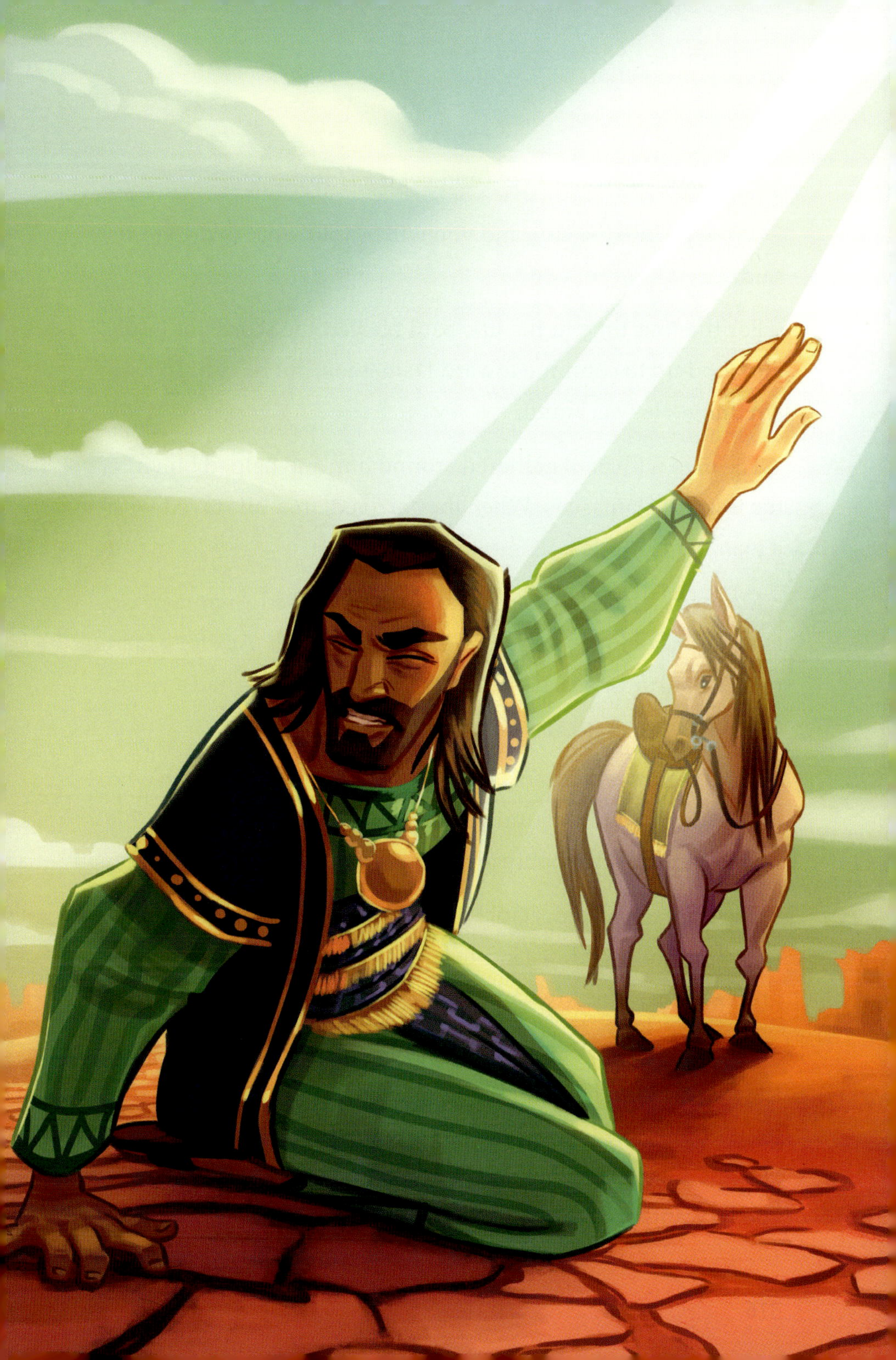

Saul froze. It *couldn't* be—and yet it *had* to be.

"Now go into the city, and you will be told what to do," Jesus said.

For the first time in his life, Saul obeyed the words of Jesus. He stood up to continue toward Damascus, but he couldn't see anything! He was blind!

The men with Saul gathered around him and helped him into the town of Damascus. When they arrived, they all stayed with a man named Judas.

Meanwhile, the Lord spoke to a disciple called Ananias. "Go to the home of Judas on Straight Street," He said. "Ask for a man named Saul of Tarsus. He is praying for help and has had a vision of you coming to pray for him to restore his sight."

"Saul of Tarsus?" Ananias asked. "Isn't that the same man who is arresting and persecuting all of the believers in Jerusalem? If I go to him, he'll probably arrest me—or worse!"

The Lord answered, "Go! I have chosen this man. He is going to spread the word of God to the Gentiles, and he will make great sacrifices for My name."

Ananias obeyed the Lord and went to the house that Saul was staying in. He laid his hands on Saul and said, "Brother, the same Jesus who spoke to you on the road came and spoke to me too. He sent me to come to you. He wants me to help you see again, and he wants you to be filled with the power of the Holy Spirit."

With those words, something like scaly flakes fell from Saul's eyes. He blinked and squinted as the light flowed in and the figures around him took shape again. He could see! Immediately, Saul went with Ananias and was baptized. Afterwards, he stayed with the disciples in Damascus for a while.

This man Saul, now known as Paul, had set out for Damascus with bitterness and destruction in his heart. He was headed for the synagogues to arrest the followers of Jesus. After a meeting with this same Jesus he had hated, Paul changed his ways, changed his heart, and changed his life for eternity.

Paul still went to the synagogues. Instead of persecuting the followers of Jesus there, since he had become a believer himself, he pleaded with his listeners to join them. He told his own story, how he had been saved by God's grace, changed from a foe to a follower, from a persecutor to a believer—a man changed forever by the forgiveness of Christ.

> **When they saw the courage of Peter and John and realized that they were unschooled, ordinary men, they were astonished and they took note that these men had been with Jesus.**
>
> Acts 4:13

PRAISING GOD IN PRISON

Acts 16

Paul continued to spread the word of his conversion from persecutor to believer as he traveled through the region. During his travels, he came across a slave girl who could predict the future because she had an evil spirit living in her. When she would tell someone's future, the person would pay her owners for her messages. She earned a lot of money for her owners.

When the girl crossed paths with Paul and his fellow disciples, she shouted to those around her and said, "Look! Servants of the Highest God! Listen! They are telling you how to be saved!" She could tell who these men truly were before ever hearing them speak a word.

She didn't stop there, either. She followed the disciples around for days, shouting her proclamation over and over, everywhere the they went.

Finally, Paul became so annoyed with her that he turned around and shouted back, "In the name of Jesus, I command you to come out!" Immediately, the evil spirit that gave the slave girl

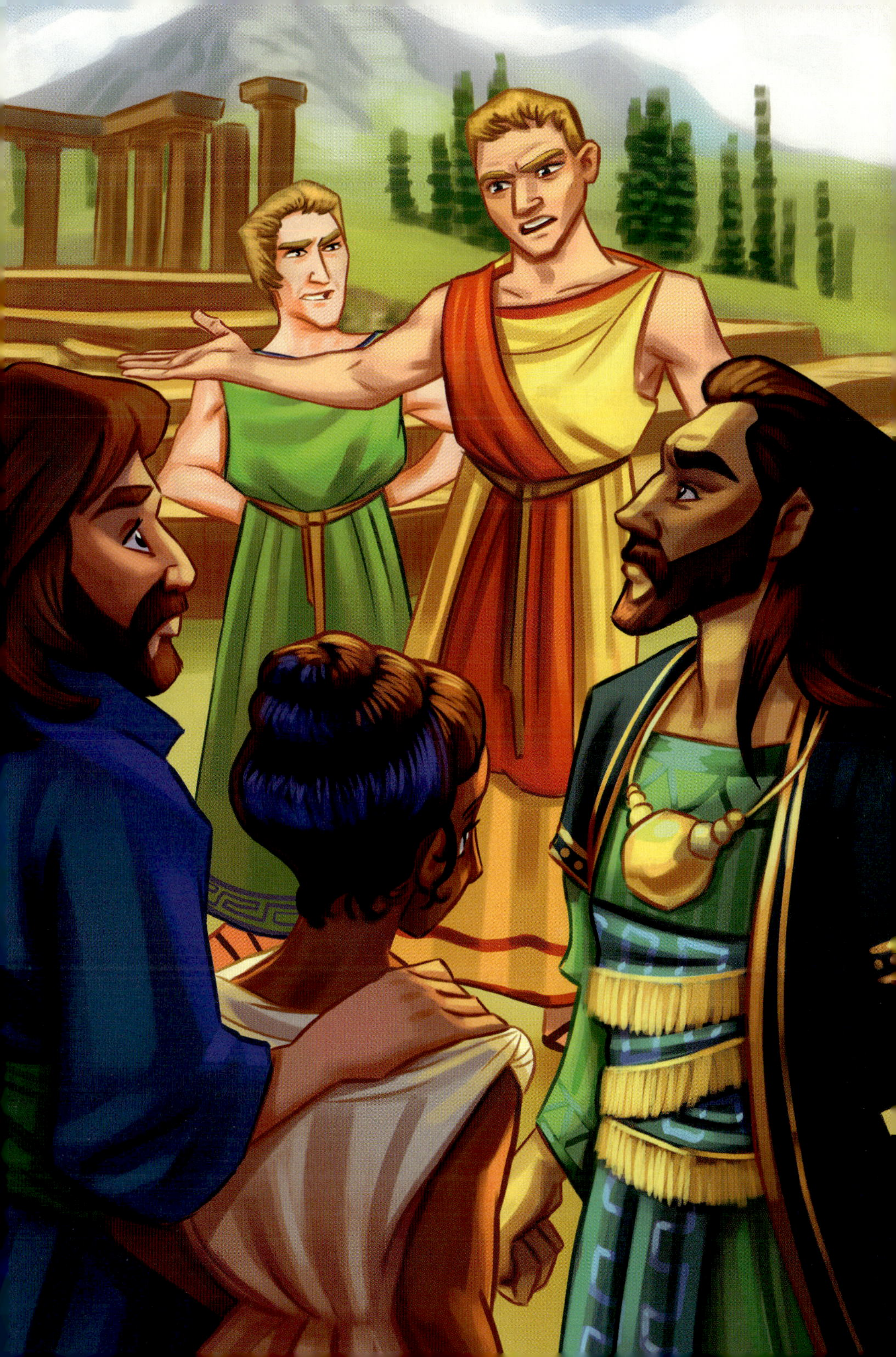

her abilities did just that! Once she was delivered from the evil spirit, the girl lost her ability to foretell the future.

Unfortunately, if she wasn't able to tell the future any more, she wasn't able to make her owners any money. When her owners realized what had happened, they were furious. They went to the disciples, grabbed two of them—Paul and Silas—and dragged them before the magistrates to face judgment.

"These men are causing chaos!" the slave girl's owners told the authorities. "They are breaking the laws of the Romans!"

The crowd joined in and said, "Yeah, we saw them! They were breaking the law! Arrest them!"

Content with those accusations, the authorities ordered Paul and Silas to be beaten and imprisoned. The guards stripped them of their clothes, flogged them, and put them in the innermost cell of the prison, locking their feet into the stocks.

This did not stop Paul and Silas from continuing their mission, however. They prayed and sang songs to God well into the night, with the other prisoners listening. Around midnight, the ground began to rumble, and the walls began to shake—it was an earthquake!

The prison doors burst open. The chains binding the prisoners fell to the ground. All of the commotion shook the jailer from his sleep, and when he looked up and saw that the prison doors were open, he knew that he was in big trouble. Escaped

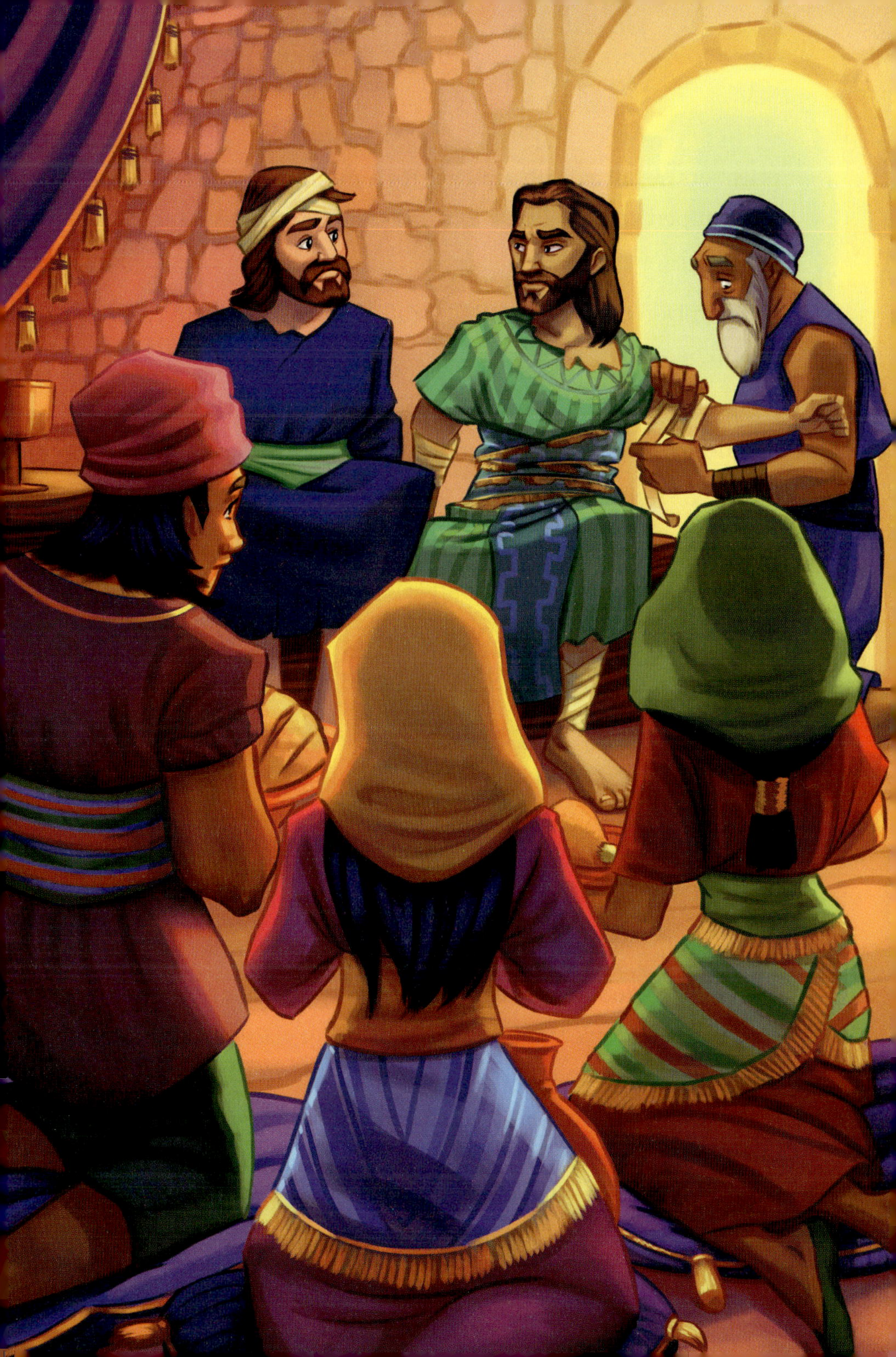

prisoners meant a death sentence for him, since he had allowed it to happen. In despair, he took his sword and braced himself to take his own life.

"Wait! Don't harm yourself!" Paul shouted. "It's okay! We're all still here."

The jailer jumped back. "Lights!" he shouted. He looked around the prison to see the flickering flames of his torch illuminating each prisoner's face.

He needed no further explanation. He ran to Paul and Silas, the men he had heard praying and singing all night. "Please, tell me, gentlemen," he said, "what do I need to do to be saved?"

"Just believe," Paul and Silas answered, smiling at the prison guard. "Believe in Jesus, and you will be saved."

Paul and Silas didn't spend the night in jail after that. They were invited back to the jailer's house, where he cleaned the wounds from their beatings and refreshed them with a hearty meal. Paul and Silas baptized the jailer's entire household, and they all came to experience the great joy of knowing Jesus

Paul understood, perhaps more than anyone, that Jesus calls and converts people from the most unlikely of places. Paul knew that his mission now was to do the same. Wherever they went, whatever the consequences, Jesus' followers told everyone they could of His story and the salvation He freely offers to all who believe.

PRAISING GOD IN PRISON

*The jailer called for lights, rushed in
and fell trembling before Paul and Silas.
He then brought them out and asked,
"Sirs, what must I do to be saved?"
They replied, "Believe in the Lord Jesus, and
you will be saved—you and your household."*

Acts 16:29-31

WHAT IS TO COME

Revelation 1, 21

Many years after Jesus had returned to heaven, the disciple John continued to stay true to the Great Commission, spreading the word of his Savior. But even now that John was an old man, the people in authority still hated the followers of Jesus, arresting and punishing them for sharing the Good News of God's salvation. John's latest punishment was from the Roman emperor Domitian. The Emperor had ordered that John be confined to the island of Patmos, a prison island. Even there in exile, John's mission continued.

Sitting alone on the island one day, John received a visitor of the most holy and spectacular kind. It was Jesus—but not the flesh-and-blood Jesus who walked with the disciples on earth. This was Jesus in his full glory. His face was like the sun, and His voice was like the sound of rushing waters. It was undeniably Jesus, the same Jesus that John had worshipped while He walked the earth, the same Jesus he still worshipped, but now glorified beyond anything John had seen before.

When John saw Jesus, he immediately fell at his master's feet.

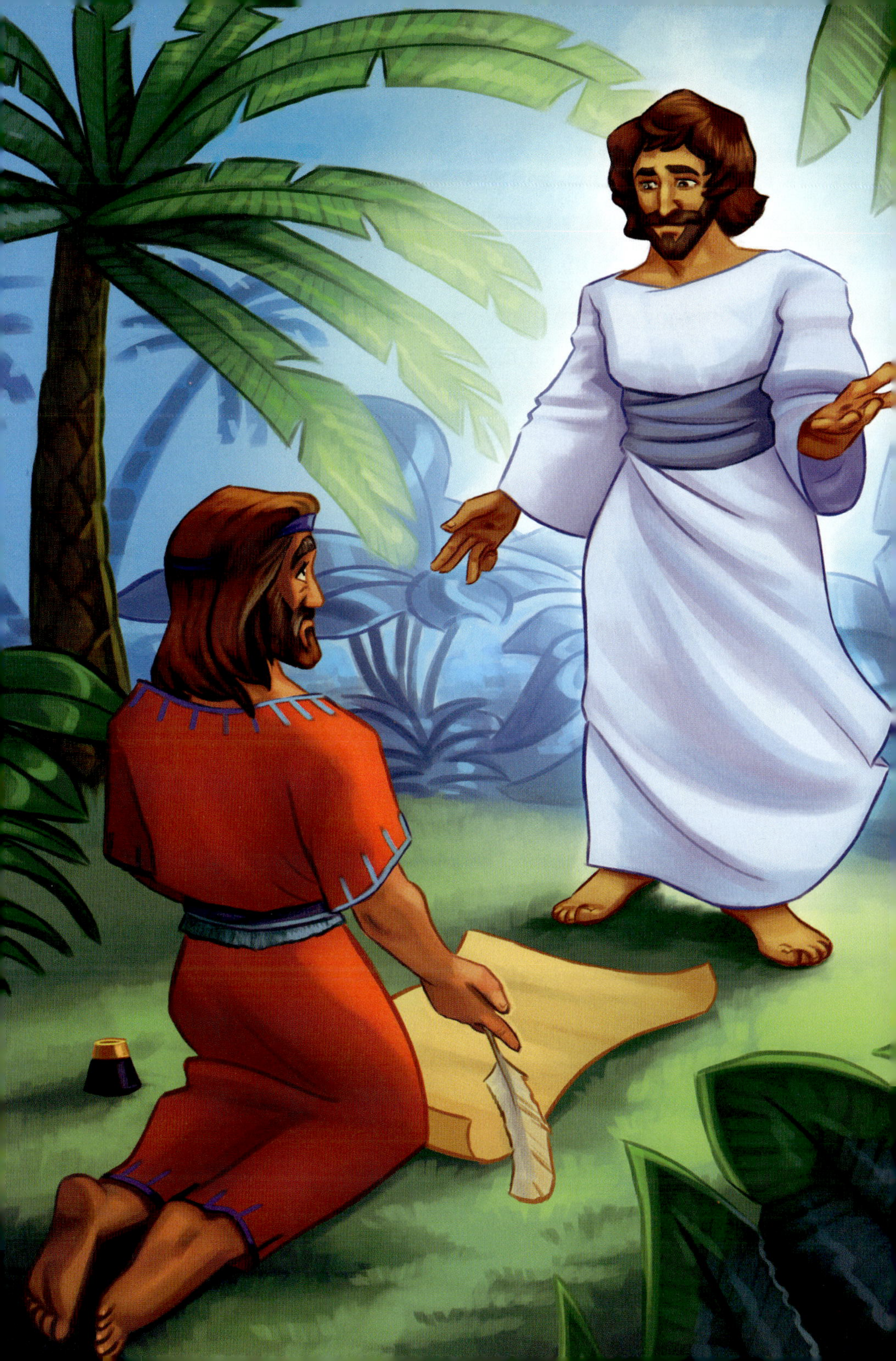

Jesus reached down and put His hand on John, saying, "Don't be afraid. I was dead, but I am now alive forever! Write all of this down, everything you have seen and will see through Me."

Jesus showed John many amazing things. He gave him messages and warnings for the first churches that had been started by the disciples. He encouraged the believers to hold on until His return, and to keep His commands so that they may receive His rewards.

Jesus showed John the condition of the world in the future, the decline and the final judgment for sin. Then Jesus showed him the beauty and glory of heaven. Finally, He took John to see a new heaven and a new earth.

In the new heaven and earth, John saw a place where God will dwell with His people, wiping away every tear from their eyes. There will be no death there—no sadness, no dying, and no pain.

"I am making everything new!" Jesus told John. "I am the beginning and the end of all things, the Alpha and the Omega. I give the water of life, and the victorious will receive all that has been promised, but the evil will be punished."

Then John saw the Holy City, shining like a jewel. Its walls were like glass, adorned with emerald and onyx, rubies and pearls—every precious stone that God had made. Even the streets of the city were made of gold!

WHAT IS TO COME

The city needed no sun or moon or lanterns or lamps, for it was lit purely by the glory of God. The gates would never be shut, and nothing less than holy would ever enter into it. Those who believed in Jesus were welcomed in to live there forever.

As John's vision drew to an end, an angel told him, "You can trust what you have seen. It is all true. The Lord wanted to show you, His servant, what was to come."

Jesus knew that the work He called John to do—the work He calls all believers to do—would not be easy. Jesus had experienced just how difficult it was to preach the Good News of God to an unbelieving world in His time here on earth. He also knew the whole story from beginning to end, what is now and what is to come. He knew how much God loved the world and the people He had made. He knew how much God longed for them to live in harmony with Him, and what He had done to make a way for that to happen—for sinful people to be forgiven and made holy. He promised to be there for His people through everything that is to come, good and bad, until He comes again; when He does, those who believe in Him will live with Him forever in eternity.

And they sang a new song, saying:
"You are worthy to take the scroll
and to open its seals,
because you were slain,
and with your blood you purchased for God
persons from every tribe and
language and people and nation."

Revelation 5:9